ART AND CULTURE OF HIMALAYA

Editor

K.S. Gulia

ISHA BOOKS

DELHI-110009

Art and Culture of Himalaya

Rs. 900

ISBN: 81-8205-418-4

Published in 2007 in India by
Isha Books
B-63, Ist Floor, New Gupta Colony,
Near DDA Market, Delhi-110009
Phone : 9212142040 • E-mail : ishabooks@hotmail.com

Laser Typesetting at : Master Computers, Delhi
Printed at : Salasar Imaging System, Delhi

Contents

Introduction

Two hundred years ago, the entire hill region of north of India, from Jammu to Ladakh, to Himachal to Uttaranchal, Nepal, Sikkim, Bhutan and Arunachal Pradesh was alive with artistic creativity. There is nothing of that vitality in arts and paintings in this region any more. The scene is bizarre, with no new painters emerging, not even those who could do some work to restore the early work done by their ancestors, as is happening in Rajasthan miniature paintings, where the State Government has taken upon itself the onerous duty of bringing that dormant art to life. Industrial house and art connoisseurs have also chipped in.

The appearance of Pahari Painting in the first of the seventeenth century coincides roughly with the coming of what has been called 'ardent Vaishnavism' to the hills. In Kulu, Mandi, Kangra, Nurpur, Chamba, Jammu, missionary activity through Vaishnava saints spread quickly, bring inspiring new subject matter and inevitably affecting the modes of thought and expression in the entire area. The impact on painting was deep and pervasive.

In India, an artist is just one notch above an artisan, depending on the work that he gets. This getting work is what really gave a blow to his art. It is not unlikely that the artist might have risen to the task if other forces had not been simultaneously mitigating against him. It was the combination of circumstances, which led to his failure. What is of interest is that he made a valiant attempt. He took cognizance of a changed situation, produced able and considered responses and tried to move with the times by enlarging the range of his subject matter and adapting to a new technique and style.

In this book, Art and Culture of Himalaya, we are discussing these very situations and circumstances because of which the Pahari paintings became just an ordinary run-of-the-mill drawing without any artistic or business value.

It would be legitimate to divide the art of the Himalayas into two broad but clear categories the hieratic and non-hieratic. In the former category would absolutely fall the sculpture and the painting, which self-consciously served not only religious but clearly defined monastic ends. In the very high Himadri ranges, area like Tibet, or in the upper Himalayas areas like Ladakh, Lahul, Spiti, Nepal and Sikkim, work of great intensity was once being done. Religion was putting art to its particular use, but in a resolute and inspired manner. There were here, as in all hieratic art, attempts to portray closed but self-consistent world, which kept some kind of pace with developments with the faith, alike in the folds of Lamaistic Buddhism and Hinduism. This has been discussed in Chapter One.

Chapter Two is about Himalayan Tribes. The Himalayan cultural matrix that we examine today is a composite culture. The Huns and other Central Asian people who entered India assimilated with the local population, but also left their impression on the indigenous culture in the form of laws, language, literature, dress, art, etc. The inscriptions of all the dynasties such as the Gurjar, Paratiharas, Paramaras, Chahamanas, Chalukas and Gahad Valas of Northern and Central India from the seventh century onward contain an increasing number of non-Sanskrit names of people and places. In fact, in earlier times the Austric, Dravidians, Aryans and Mongolians had a similar impact. An examination of the arts, craft and manner of dressing will reveal the cultural picture of the Himalayas over the centuries.

In Chapter Three : The Rai have given their tradition, thus : Our forefathers came originally from a lake whose waters had dried up. In the centre of Nepal there was a lake which ran dry and the dry basin offered a suitable site for settlements. The first parents of the Rai were Parungo, the father, and Simnima, the mother. They begot three sons, Lapche, Jimdar and Meche. The parents sent the three sons away to live independently and find a country for themselves. The brother Lapche came across a banana tree and tried to hew it down whereupon Jimdar said to him, "If you are the kind of person that is prone to be destructive, we shall no longer stay with you," and with this Jimdar and Meche left him.

Chapter Four discusses Himalayan Polyandry, with specific reference to Jaunsar-Bawar belt. An analysis of family economy should, for the sake of simplicity, be started with a single family. But the case in Jaunsar-Bawar is complicated because of the prevalence of polygynandrous and other forms of polygamous joint family. Monogamy, as a general rule, has not asserted itself. Those of the inhabitants of this belt who have come down to planes and leading a monogamous life do not like this age old practice and look down upon it with distaste. As a result, the social forces have started making dents into the traditional structure of Jaunsar-Bawar society under conditions of polygynandrous or polyandrous joint family. It affects the composition of the already established joint family as far its members are concerned : the increase or reduction in the number of members of the joint family brings about changes in the family economy, making it simpler or more complex as the case may be.

Chapter Five deals with Himalayan Art and other manufacturing and handicraft activities in Himachal. There is not much small-scale industry to talk about in this region. The embroidery work done in Bilaspur is of intricate nature, not like the one that one comes across in the shops at Simla. Metal work is elementary and of very rough nature, there is no finesse about that work. Small brass idols, which resemble Polynesian figures, are found in the temples and are of local make. On investigation one cannot trace the origin of those idols. They might as well have come from some other region. There are not many art manufacturers in Kangra. Nurpur at one time was famous for *pashmina* work, but there is nothing left of that art. The ornaments, sometimes decorated with enamel, showcase those same Polynesian figures. *Kangra ki kalam*, the Kangra artistic touch in everything, from paintings to embroidery to metal work is not seen anywhere any more. No efforts are being made to revive these arts.

Chapter Six deals with Sikkim : Aspects of its Cultural Ecology. The geographical setting has played a major role in demarcation of the boundaries of nations and states and cultural regions with them. The geographical setting has also had its profound impact on historical impulses and human ecology of the residents within a cultural region. The geography of Sikkim lends itself to one major culture region, with three sub-cultural regions within its boundaries. While the Dongkiala and Singalila ranges demarcate the eastern limits of the state, the Chorten Nbyima range in the trans-Himalayan region demarcates the northern boundary. For centuries Sikkim continued to maintain its identity as an independent state under the Chogyals. The isolation of the kingdom helped the prospering of culture and spiritual related aspects within and outside the monasteries. All this has been discussed in this chapter.

Chapter Seven deals with Bhutan : Tradition as a factor in Modernisation. The theoretical construct and modernization assumes model of modernity as an ideal type and it is in relation to it that any individual, nation, society, institution or pattern of life is adjudged as modern or otherwise or as approximating to modernity or behind it. Modernisation, more often than not, is regarded as something analogous to weternization because it is in the countries of the West that development of science and technology has made long strides and the whole life has got revolutionized in the process. As rationality is said to be quintessence of modernization, faith in religion has not only grown feeble but it has also materially changes values of life. This has been discussed in this Chapter.

Chapter Eight discusses Art and Painting in Uttaranchal. It was along the Ramganga valley where Buddhism and Hinduism flourished in the hills of Uttarakhand, Dwarhat, the first important city in the hills tells the story of the region's past. This is where millennia ago, art and painting flourished. Art and painting reflects the socio-economic and cultural life of the people anywhere. The silver mountains, the sparkling streams, vivid green valleys and the cool climate have attracted many into the hills of Uttarakhand for peace, tranquillity and meditation. Maharishi Balmiki and Kalidas had great attachment for these hills. All this laid the ultimate foundation for the literary treasures in Uttarakhand including painting and art. The tradition of folk art has remained totally unaffected in this region due to inaccessibility to and inability of foreign invaders to move into these hills during their rule in India, whereas in the plains they destroyed everything : all types of art, sculpture, painting and performing arts, which they laid their hands on.

In Chapter Nine : The concept of *tirthayatra* (pilgrimage) has for centuries effectively related the frontiers to the farthest flung corners of this vast land. Religious congregations encouraged the building of temples at different locations in Garhwal—on peaks that offer a panoramic view, or at the confluence of rivers in thickly wooded valleys. Some of the holiest Hindu shrines are located in Garhwal. These examples of the Nagar style (classical North Indian temple architecture) bear ample testimony to the talent of local craftsmen and the artistic efflorescence inspired by natural beauty. Badrinath is a principal temple for devotees of Vishnu, and Kedarnath is one of the most important shrines for Shiva worshippers. Hemkund is the site of a prominent gurudwara commemorating the meditation of the tenth Sikh Guru.

In Chapter Ten : The earliest known Pahari paintings dated from as late as the last two or three decades of the seventeenth century. Among them are three manuscripts of the *Rasamanjari*, an erotic fifteenth-century poem by Bhanudatta in which men and women (Nayakas and Nayikas) are classified according to their amorous situations or affective states. This genre, which includes several famous works, provided a great many conventional themes. Sometimes Radha and Krsna appear in the guise of Nayikas and Nayakas. The style of one of these manuscripts, whose colophon indicates that it was made for Raja Kirpal Pal of Basohli (1678-93), is highly distinctive: elongated figures have equally elongated heads to which the eye, drawn with the pupil far advanced to the front, lends an expression of passionate intensity. Angular poses and awkward, jerky gestures intensify the dramatic effect, as in the painting in the Bharat Kala Bhavan, Varanasi, of a woman almost spreadeagled in her reach for a hanging lamp.

In Chapter Eleven : The regional Hindu social setting are the Bhotia. It may be stated that the Bhotia valleys are not ordinary geographical entities, rather these are important structural units of the Bhotia socio-cultural framework. The Bhotia population is primarily seggregrated valleywise; each valley-based group exhibits distinct customary characteristics which, in effect, help to register these valleys as being unique social constituencies in the wider Bhotia cultural scenario. And hence, from an analytical standpoint, the valley qualifies to be the most useful unit for correctly assessing the Bhotia social affairs. However, the cultural variation is rather thin among the groups inhabiting Byans, Choudans and Darma in Kumaon and is mostly restricted to the minor areas e.g. habits, tastes, manners, courtesy rules and the like. These groups may be collectively called the 'Eastern Bhotia' who show remarkable similarity, in many major cultural fields like birth and death rites, marriage, religious and social outlook amongst them. But the Eastern Bhotia offer considerable cultural diversities with the Johari Bhotia which may be the result of the politico-historical happenings of the preceding few centuries apart from factors like isolation and lack of contact between the groups in question. The history of the Bhotia valleys reveals that the cultural similarity of Byans, Choudans and Darma may be due to the fact that though these valleys were ruled by different powers, this did not prevent social intercourse among the people there in the past.

In Chapter Twelve : In Jammu, the Brahmans depend upon agriculture which provides the main source of their income and the calling of religious ministers and priests is confined to a comparatively small number of families. It is strange to see Brahmans holding a position economically inferior to that of the Kshtrayas, most of them being tenants-at-will of the Rajput landlords. They are a peace-loving people and have always borne the hardships of life with a cheerful disposition. They have been greatly benefited by the Land Reforms Act of the present Government. The Dogra Rajputs are not tall men; their average height being five feet four. Of slim build, they have somewhat high shoulders and curiously bowed legs and, though not muscular, are active and untiring. The colour of their complexion is a light shade of brown, rather darker than the husk of the almond. The women because of their less exposure have a brighter tint. They possess well-formed features, composed of a slightly hooked nose, well-shaped mouth and small brown eyes.

In Chapter Thirteen : The outside *jagar* always is performed for the *gram devatas* (e.g., "Haru and his companions") and usually is held in conjunction with a cyclical festival or some major village crisis. The *jagariya* is a professional musician usually a Darji (formerly Das-Dholi *jati* cluster) and he performs on a special drum called a *dhol*. The outside *jagar* can last for several days and in the rare celebration of Baishi lasts up to twenty-two days.

During Baishi a *jagar* would be held every night and sacrifices of goat and possibly buffalo would be offered. Outside *jagars* are relatively infrequent as they are expensive, difficult to organize, and time consuming. They are held only on major festival days or at times of great village crisis (e.g., epidemic or famine).

In Chapter Fourteen : By the 9th century, holes in Nepal have become oval, usually, like the whole stele, with a pearl and flame border. The persistence of spiral armlets and of a fondness for rustication of the bases, together with constant repetition of ancient themes and poses and even details of costume, makes the dating of Nepalese sculpture between the eighth and the thirteenth centuries a daunting task. It is nonetheless a capacity for pastiche that has maintained almost to this day a semblance, at least, of vitality in Nepalese sculpture, rescuing it from the total degeneracy common in India. The heroic panels become more densely peopled, but psychological relationships falter, as a comparison between the latest of the known Vikranta images, from Pharping and probably of the thirteenth century with the image dated 467 makes very clear. The fine ninth-century Visvarupa Visnu at Cangu Narayana is overcrowded, even taking into account the complex iconography of this type, and the organization of the multifarious elements is somewhere simplistic. After the Lichchavi period, Visnu appears most commonly standing in samapada, flanked on one side by Laksmi, on the other by Garuda, who occasionally appears in this position in western India but never in the east. It has been proposed that this icon represents the *para*, or highest, aspect of Visnu. A version exists from as late as 1695. Stone Suryas are very frequent, and caturmukha lingas recur throughout the valley. The oldest for which there are any references, installed in the Pasupatinatha temple at Deo Patan, or its immediate predecessor, was destroyed by the Muslim invaders, but its fourteenth-century replacement is said to be based on the original.

In Chapter Fifteen : Ladakh, the northernmost region in the Indian Himalaya has a special position in the cultural and literary history of the country. Though influenced by other parts of India and Tibet, the people of Ladakh have succeeded in developing their own distinctive culture. Ladakhis are simple and more or less traditional in their religious practices and they stick to the old cultural values. The distinctive Ladakhi way of life is upheld not only in the far-flung villages of the region but also in the comparatively modernized city of Leh. In his book Magic Ladakh, Major M. L. A. Gompertz wrote 'Ladakh is very much a self-supporting country, and produces everything, or nearly everything it wants except tea, which is the staple drink of the country'.

1

Lost Vision: Art in the Himalayan Region Today

Himalayan Art

Till two to three hundred years ago, the entire Himalayan region was thriving with creative activity. The tiniest principalities in the region from Kashmir to Arunachal Pradesh were flush with artisans, working on handicrafts, spinning and weaving classy fabrics, murals, bronzes and doing beautiful paintings. Those works of art were integrated and of chaste vision. This had been happening for more than thousand years. Not even the onslaught from the Sultanate since the beginning of the eleventh century going up to the eighteen could make any dent in that creativity. When one comes upon such works today, one starts wondering if the predecessors of these people who, in the present time, do not know anything about those arts did these. One who looks at what is being done now feels depressed at the contrast in creativity of the two periods. There is none of that faith any more with which a world-view was once presented in its art, little of the warmth and the richness of human elements it once possessed. In the late seventies one is greeted by an arid spectacle of mechanical repetitiveness in the arts, a living on the past, as it were. And no one is troubled by this. It appears as if art does not really matter to anyone any more.

Broad Generalisation

Because of this contrast, one is forced to look into the causes of the loss of this creativity in the region. The vast geographical extent of the areas in which Himalayan art once flourished, and the time-span which is covered by it, are such that it is possible to approach the subject here only in terms of very broad generalizations. And yet even these may be of some use: the many valuable studies of the art of the Himalaya by many very distinguished scholars, centre round specific areas and deal with 'their own' problems of art-history; possibly an overview, however quick, would be of value.

Categories of Himalayan Art

The Himalayan arts follows a certain style bound by religious conventions, i.e. it was hieratic. Not that this was the only art form, which was followed. There was the other kind, the non-religious, the personal, of limited range. In the former category would easily fall sculpture and painting which self-consciously served not only religious but clearly defined monastic ends. In the very high Himadri ranges, areas like Tibet, or in the upper Himalayan areas like Ladakh, Lahul, Spiti, Nepal and Sikkim, work of great intensity was once being done. Religion was putting art to its own use, but in a resolute and inspired manner. There were here, as in all hieratic art, attempts to portray a closed but self-consistent world which kept some kind of pace with developments within the faith, alike in the folds of Lamaistic Buddhism and Hinduism.

The icon is what is most typical of this art; whether it is a *Prajnaparamita* or a *Tara*, a *Bhairava* or a *Yamantaka*, the images have a sense of immediacy about them. They represent with singular force what the artist saw within himself and what a devotee, monk or layman, wanted to look at. For centuries together, in sculpture or murals, miniatures or ritual objects, it was religion which served almost exclusively as subject matter.[1] There were some influences that came in from outside, impulses that were registered with varying degrees of understanding, such as the art of the Chinese or the Mongols, the styles of Western Asia or India, and there was a certain amount of interaction between different expressions. Artists travelled both into and out of the area.

We find Pala artists going to Nepal, Nepalese artists going to Tibet, Kashmiri artists working at Alchi, monks on the move all the time. But what remained *dhruva*, unchanging, was the nature of the vision even as it was being expanded and deepened. The repertoire of the artist was occasionally enlarged; his skill was marginally affected; his technique underwent some change; but his world-view remained clear in its essence. The painter and the sculptor drew sustenance from given subjects with their given iconography; the patrons earned merit from commissioning works on the same themes; heaven was important, and so was hell. The demons were very real, the powers of god truly beneficent.

Nature of Work

This situation was there for a thousand years. There was no let up in this activity over all this period. However, many a time critics point to the continuity of the static nature of the works turned out over all this period. But at least two other points can be made: one, about the enormous quantity and the high level of work done in the region, and the other about the affinity between the art and the culture in which it was produced. Today, much of this is changed. In a sense, the quantity of work being turned out is still impressive: apart from the renovation of old murals in places like Likir, Tikste, and Hemis in Ladakh, the *thangkas* that refugee Tibetan artists produce today in Sikkim or in Dharamsala,[3] or the countless 'bronzes' being cast in workshops in Nepal or Delhi (and sold for the most part to tourists) are to be seen everywhere.

Ossified Vision

Not all of it is inconsiderable in terms of quality; in fact, some of it has been taken somewhat seriously by collectors and museum curators alike. But what is really lacking in it is the sap, that vitality which coursed through the earlier work. For most of it is the product of an ossified vision; the repetitiveness palls; the artist no longer seems to reflect the urges of the society which in itself has changed, for he is at a considerable distance from it, certainly psychological, quite often physical. His *samadhi* has become *shithila* (slack), so to speak: art is no longer a matter of spirit, but of money. One has come a long way from the times in which the art of these regions, with all its hieratic insistence, was alive, and created areas of dazzling beauty.

Non-hieratic

The other category of art that prevailed alongside the hieratic art was non-hieratic art. In this art form, the issues were entirely different and they developed at an entirely, rather structurally different plane. One could take, as most typical of this kind of art, painting in the Pahari region, for it is one of the most intensively researched of Indian art expressions.[4] Here, as an illustration of the many changes which came about in non-hieratic art, one is able to sense a perceptible and quicker degree of responsiveness to changes of various kinds; political, religious, social and economic. To the layman, mostly because he sees the glossy volumes that are reasonably priced and aim at a given public, most of this art might appear to be predominantly 'religious' in its subject. Much is omitted from this popular coffee-table book view: the portraits, the satirical themes, the references to historical events, the caricatures,[5] the recording of pilgrimages.[6]

Religio-Poetic Themes

But even if, in terms of quantity, it is demonstrated that religious-poetic themes take a precedence, the approach of the artist remains, for the most part, non-hieratic. He was interested in producing intensely moving human images, mythological figures cast in every human situation. Inter-penetrated with illustrations of religious works, the *Ramayana*, the *Mahabharata*, the *Bhagavata Purana*, the *Markandeya Purana*, the *Sivamahima Stotra*, are themes which lean upon works of poetic literature that were avidly read in the hills. The archetypal figures in these works may have been religious or mythological, Krishna and Radha, Rama or Siva, but the appeal really is that of the poetry that inheres in the subject.

Lyrical Depiction

The great sets that we know of: the *Rasamanjari* of Bhanudatta, the *Gita Govinda*, the *Sat Sai* of Bihari, the *Rasikapriya* of Keshava Dasa, the *Sundara Sringara* of Sundara Dasa, the *Naisadhacarita* of Sriharsa, are all works in which legendary and religious figures occur repeatedly, but the main concern is a lyrical depiction of such themes and the archetypal figures are used to enrich the content, to evoke associations which broaden the impact of the verses.

But even if one confines oneself to a study of these religious and poetic works from this area, it is possible to assert that the character of the art in general is by no means static or unchanging in quality. The active period within which Pahari painting flourished is about 250 years. In this period, short as it is compared to the millennium or so of which we speak in relationship to the hieratic category of art in the Himalaya, there are not only numerous expressions of it; within each there are significant changes which are clearly visible, not merely subtle and imperceptible.

Channels of Communication with Plains

If one lives in an area where there is no interaction with the outside world beyond one's own enclosed environs, cultural changes do not take place. The society stays cocooned, inward looking. The Pahari areas were, for one thing, not as isolated and cut off from the rest of the world as is sometimes believed. Impulses from the major centres of culture in the plains of northern India were received with surprising swiftness through different channels. Not only do we know of frequent incursions into the hills by adventurers, we also know of the hills serving as a refuge to princes and generals fleeing from pursuing armies. There were also more peaceful channels of communication between the hills and the plains, like for instance, the great Indian institution of pilgrimages. The regularity with which rulers of the hill states, their families, and the people in general, went out to the plains for earning merit by bathing at Hardwar or Kurukshetra, or securing *darshana* at Gaya or Jagannath Puri, was singular.

Influence of Travel

A painting in the hand of the great Pahari painter Nainsukh, showing an idol at Allahabad,[8] a temple with the three Jagannath images in the tiny Pahari principality of Jasrota,[9] a charming drawing showing pilgrims bathing in the nearly dry bed of the river at Gaya,[10] are among the more obvious results of this travel. The large number of entries by Pahari visitors one finds in the records of the *pandas* (priests) at centres of pilgrimage in the plains indicates the extent of such traffic.[11] At the same time there were people from the plains visiting the great hill shrines of Jwalamukhi or Kangra Bhavan. These must have acted as equally effective channels through which influences travelled. The long series of *pattas* (records) and letters that are still maintained by the *pandas* of these temples are a fair indication of this. It is only geographically that the Pahari areas were removed from the plains. The quiet flow of men and ideas went on even while there was bloodshed between rulers and armies marched up and down the Punjab.

External Influence

Another channel of communication occurred during the seventeen and eighteenth centuries. In his reign, Emperor Akbar had been able to take control of Kashmir and some parts of Himachal. Jehangir further consolidated the Mughal position in the hills. The movement of people from the plains to the hills and other way round opened new vistas. New idea flowed in. This is when the rulers of the Pahari areas were frequently commissioned by their overlords, the Mughals, to take charge of campaign in different parts of India. Man Singh of Guler serving in the Northwest Provinces,[12] Raja Basu of Nurpur going out to Rajasthan,[13] or Ajmer Chand of Bilaspur moving down to the Deccan under Imperial orders,[14] are typical cases.

When we find Mughal costumes appearing in the hills very soon after they had been adopted at Agra or Delhi or Lahore, or Mughal and Rajasthani architecture affecting building styles all over the hills or when a great work like Bihari's *Sat Sai* comes to the hills within a decade of its having been composed in the plains,[15] it is symptomatic of the situation. Understandably, the initial impact was felt in the outer hills, but it travelled fairly quickly, in ever-widening ripples, further into the interior. What was registered in the states of Nurpur or Bilaspur or Basohli often reached states which were contiguous very quickly, and became evident all over the hills the next day at an unprecedented speed. In terms of stylistic development, in the field of Pahari painting it may be possible to see three major waves of influence from the plains.

Ardent *Vaishnavism*

The appearance of Pahari painting in the first-half of the seventeenth century coincides roughly with the coming of what has been called 'ardent *Vaishnavism*' to the hills.

In Kulu, Mandi, Kangra, Nurpur, Chamba, Jammu, missionary activity through Vaishnava saints spread quickly, bringing inspiring new subject-matter, and inevitably affecting the modes of thought and expression in the entire area. The impact on painting was deep and pervasive.

Mughal Influence on Style

Since the beginning of the seventeen-century, the impact of Islamic thought was being felt in the Pahari art. But it was not that much; it stayed limited. In the eighteen century, the Mughal influence took complete control of the thought and vision of the Pahari artists. The painters of the Pahari area seem to have responded to Mughal works most warmly. This may have been due to Mughal paintings in large numbers reaching the hills, and not due to refugee artists from the Mughal court going into the hills, as is sometimes believed.[16] Whatever the circumstances, the shift towards a fluent, naturalistic style from the earlier, highly mannered and intense style linked with the name of *Basohli* can be assigned to the period that we are speaking of.

The change is by no means sudden, the artist explores various possibilities, makes adjustments, engages in experiment, and takes from Mughal painting what agrees with his own temperament to incorporate it into his own style.[17] Change is effected most intelligently, brought about apparently as a result of a warm understanding between patron and painter. The process can be seen in the work of gifted artists like Manak of Guler, or his younger brother Nainsukh who worked for Balwant Singh of Jasrota. By the middle of the eighteenth century, the style had become significantly different from what it was in the seventeenth century. Responses to the new situation had been slow but extremely cultivated.

Impact of Sikh Kingdom

As the nineteenth century dawned, Pahari art saw another major change in concept and execution, first as a result of the political and economic decline of the hill states and the corresponding rise of the Sikh kingdom in the Punjab, and then, from the middle of the century onwards, due to European impact when the area passed under British supremacy. The first part of this change had more than merely political consequences. The artist had now the clear option either to look for patrons other than rulers in the Pahari area, or to move in search of patronage towards the new centres where money and power now resided.

A series of remarkable documents that have fortunately survived[18] tell us about the decision made by at least one major family of Pahari painters. They decided to move to serve the new masters at Lahore. Among the people they were attached to were not only the Maharaja himself but nobles closely related to the Maharaja, like the Sandhanwalia Sardars. This group of documents clearly shows painters moving to the plains and becoming attached to new patrons, while retaining their little *jagirs* in the hills where their small houses and plots of land were. These *muafis* had sustained them and their families over generations, and these they were allowed to enjoy through royal orders given to the local Sikh Governors of the hills areas.

Change in Political Situation

In 1847, the Sikh empire fell to the British. When they took over the rule, they saw a mushroom of Pahari painters doing portraits of the masters who had engaged them. The British were not interested in the art or themes of the Pahari painters, and the painters had to fend for themselves yet again. They turned to royalty for patronage once more, because royal houses had survived in some of the cis-Satluj states like Patiala, Kapurthala, Nabha and Jind. We have remarkable evidence of this kind of migration in the movements of an artist like Devi Ditta of Basohli who moved first from the hills to Lahore, and then from Lahore to Patiala after the fall of the Sikh kingdom.[19] A painter needed both appreciation and financial support, and it was natural for him to attach himself to the entourage of a prince or great noble.

Mobility and Adaptation

As a result of this ostracism by the British, the Pahari painters moved away from Lahore. Some stayed back, could not find any patrons and as a result suffered. Those who moved continued their work, though in an entirely different field. They had preferred to move to the Jammu area where the Dogras had founded a kingdom of their own under Maharaja Gulab Singh and his successors.[20] Many of them moved to the plains, as we have seen, in order to be able to survive. Some of them apparently took to doing mural work for the *mahants* (abbots) of the various religious establishments that lay at the foothills, places like Pindori, Damthal and Ram Tatwali.[21] Artists became absorbed in the struggle for a livelihood in which art itself just managed to survive. The frequent changes in his situation vis-à-vis new patrons made several demands upon the painter. Among them was continuous adjustment to a new range of subjects: the Sikhs for instance were avidly interested in portraits, for these reflected their newly-won glory; their splendour was for them a substitute for dynastic pride.

Sikh Influence

The painter was even earlier wholly capable of good portraiture, which he had done at different periods, and in different styles in the Pahari area: some remarkable work in portraiture belongs to the seventeenth and the eighteenth centuries.[22] But portraiture received new emphasis in the plains, for the Sikh patrons were far less interested in conventional mythological-lyrical themes. Thus, the painter, drawing on reserves of skill, concentrated on the task of producing these splendid portraits, some of which are brilliant by any standard. The decline in other works of standard subject-matter was almost made up for by the quality of portraiture at this time.

The Local Raphael

During this period it is not only the formal portraits of the Maharaja and his entourage that impress; the informal, half-finished studies show nearly as much observation and penetration.[23] Whatever notice was taken by the British of Indian art is marked by a sense of superiority. Ridicule of 'the local Raphaels' is common.[24] They did not understand the conventions of this art, and fortified with political power, made fun whenever they could of these clumsy products of the natives. Worse still, the small *jagirs* which painters had enjoyed as part of traditional payments made to them, were confiscated. The land was returned to them for cultivation but on payment of the usual land revenue.

The British Influence

But, for a short while, the British also decided to make some use of the painter's skill. This was for the production of whole series of drawings or coloured sketches showing 'the curiosities of the east', the trades and professions, and the innumerable types of ascetics and holy men, that generally go under the name of 'Company Painting' in India.[25]

But this interest was really the product of curiosity and these sets, which were often mass produced for the British civil servants could, strangely from the Indian point of view, be bought and sold in the open market. Much of the work was uninspired and only a small part of it was aesthetically valid. Truly speaking, the Pahari painter whether working in the hills or in the plains of the Punjab, did not feel comfortable with this distortion of his talent.

Patron's Taste

When the British became the masters, the people subservient to them, the patrons of the painters, changed their tastes also. Their frame of reference changed, their vision changed began to favour the more realistic kind of work that had come in with the British.[26] The grandiose oil painting, reflecting all the glory and some of the 'savage splendour' of an eastern potentate's court, was dramatic in its appeal and far more impressive than the tiny miniatures which could neither be displayed to advantage in a darbar hall nor portray photographically the ruler with this debased taste.

Copying the Europeans

In the middle of the twentieth century, some sketchbooks were found in far-flung areas in the Himalayas, mostly in Himachal Pradesh. These were found in some family junks. These belonged to some painters who in the nineteenth century had worked during the Sikh and Dogra period, in Punjab and Jammu. The sketch books are revealing.

The painter had been partronised by the Court or by those who were very high up in hierarchy. The painter and artist had always been working with these people. When the fortune of the patrons declined, or when he was asked to change his style by the new patrons, he did not know who to fall back on. He had never worked for the common man, so could not go to him for work. And the commonman was not interested. The painter did not have a second line of defence.

The patrons put them to the task of copying elegant designs from European fashion magazines, producing in their own technique the effect of oils and etching, and performing tricks of a similar kind. Some of the painters did make an effort.[27] The move in the direction of realism produced, occasionally, very telling work. But the experiment as a whole did not succeed. The emulation of European painting was beyond their capacity, at least in the short time given them to adjust. The technique was vastly different, the scale of work much larger, the entire outlook radically changed.

Adapting New Technique

It is not unlikely that the artist might have risen to the task if other forces had not been simultaneously militating against him. It was the combination of circumstances which led to his failure. What is of interest to us is that he made a valiant attempt. He took cognizance of a changed situation, produced able and considered responses, and tried to move with the times by enlarging the range of his subject matter and adapting to a new technique and style. A point which emerges with some clarity from what has been said is the firmness of relationship between patronage and painting in the Pahari area. As soon as patronage shifted, the artist moved; when the level of discernment in the patron declines, art declines. And whatever else this may prove, this firm link between patronage and painting worked both to the painter's advantage and disadvantage. It became a source of strength for him at one time, and, at another, the cause of his decline.

Flaw in the System

The common man was very rarely a patron of the art produced in the Pahari area. The ordinary man and woman possessed a feeling for nature, a keen sense of beauty in general, but these manifested themselves in other ways, not in their appreciation of 'high' art, or pride in its ownership. Art was confined to a small circle, restricted within a narrow area.

Court Painters

The patron visualizes, he sets the frame of reference. The artist and the painter give shape to that vision. Ritualistic paintings had always been done by inferior artists; symbolic drawings on the occasion of marriages in ordinary households or sketches for goldsmiths and embroiderers had always existed. But sophisticated art had never really been brought to the people by court painters. By the twentieth century, the painters from traditional families had very little work. In order to survive, to begin with many of them tried to make use of their inherited skill and worked as draughtsmen or cartographers in government departments.

This had a Deteriorating Effect

This also could not go on for very long. Their skill rapidly declined, and such jobs were in any case comparatively scarce. Within a generation we hear of members of the old painters' families joining the police, the railways and even taking clerical jobs. When I located the artist Chandu Lal of Rajol,[28] he was working as a petty silversmith in his tiny hut using worn instruments and barely making enough to keep his considerable family alive. One of his sons was a mechanic in a road transport company.

Quality of Art

For good or ill, in the matter of formation of taste, the general populace in the Pahari area took its cue from above. The taste displayed by a ruler and his family communicated itself to the nobility; then to the lower officials, and through them to the people in general. Occasionally this also resulted in bad taste percolating to the lowest level, but fortunately most of the time the taste that was handed down to the people from above was refined and mellow. In any case, the sense of direction in matters of art and taste was not developed by the people themselves but was 'received' by them.

The situation has changed very considerably today in other respects but somehow the general public still depends for its values in the matter of taste upon those that are 'above'. The old Sanskrit adage, '*yatha Raja, tatha praja*' (like king, like subject), is wholly applicable also in the matter of art. There are no Rajas any more, but the *praja* still looks for guidance in taste, and much is left to be desired. Not only is there a general lack of sensitivity, a want of purposeful direction, but there is also bad taste, and patronage without any discrimination.

No More Good Taste

The patron visualizes, he sets the frame of reference. The artist and the painter give shape to that vision. The vulgarity that one sees becoming increasingly a part of public life in the Pahari area today, especially in the small urban centres, the woeful dulling of sensibilities, is at least in part a general reflection of the fact that good taste is no longer established for people. Such a need for guidance places far greater responsibility upon informed art lovers than is elsewhere the case. In fact, the problem is especially acute in the Himalayan regions where the old kind of art has not yet been replaced either by a new aesthetics which has come in from outside, or by a new response to the changed condition from within the soil itself. In the Pahari regions as we know them today, thus, there is no visible native impulse in the arts. In the vacuum created by the decay and disappearance of the old art, and in the confusion created by indiscriminate patronage, the whole area seems to be succumbing to philistinism, encouraged by a new-found love of money, the forces of unthinking urbanization, and the industry called tourism which seems bent on sacrificing everything at its own altar.

References

1. This would appear to be a general statement to which exceptions can be cited. But it does represent the truth about this art in substantial measure.
2. In the Himalaya, as in Tibet, it is no longer feasible after about the eleventh century A.D. to assign a work of art to a period, school or artist on the basis merely of distinguishing their manners and styles. Nor did geographical vicinity determine the style because the monastic studies entirely depended on models sometimes procured from distant centres of Buddhist learning and copied for hundreds of years. Thus, Madan Jeet Singh in *Himalayan Art*, (Greenwich, 1968).
3. There are, in fact, regular workshops where these *thangkas* are being produced and sometimes sold as antiques by dealers to unsuspecting buyers. It is also possible to pick

up for petty sums woodcuts based on old *mandalas* designs, copied exactly from very old works.

4. Prominent scholars are W.G. Archer, Khandalavala, and M.S. Randhawa. There are several others of course who have also taken serious notice of Pahari painting in recent years.
5. Some of the most delightful of these caricatures make fun of Vaishnava saints and their activities. S.S. Gupta reproduced some of these in his 'Catalogue of Paintings in the Central Museum, Lahore', and in *Modern Review*, Calcutta, 1922.
6. Several drawings showing pilgrimages or journeys are found in public and private collections. The artists attempt to show both the pleasure of these visits and the difficulties inherent in them.
7. It is unnecessary to refer to this body of work in any detail, because it is much too well-known. Almost always, it is a poetic smile or conceit that the painter draws attention to.
8. This painting showing the idol of Beni Madho is in the Bharat Kala Bhavan at Banaras.
9. Sree Karuna Goswamy, 'A Pahari Painting of Jagannath Temple', *Chhavi*, B.K.B. Golden Jubilee.
10. This very attractive large drawing was once in the collection of the art dealer, Mohan Lal Bharany of Amritsar.
11. For more information on this, see B.N. Goswamy, 'The records kept by priests at centres of pilgrimage, etc.', *The Indian Social and Economic History Review*, Vol. III, No. 2.
12. The *Diliparanjani*, manuscript history of Guler, makes prominent mention of this commission to Raja Man Singh.
13. The Emperor Jahangir, in his *Tuzuk* (Indian Reprint, 1968) Vol. I, p. 200, makes mention of Raja Basu campaigning against the Rana of Udaipur.
14. M.A. Macauliffe, *The Sikh Religion* (Indian Reprint, S. Chand, 1963), Vol. V, p. 165, draws attention to this visit of the Raja to the Deccan.
15. This copy of the *Sat Sai* was at one time in the collection of Sh. Bhu Dev Shastri of Sujanpur Tira in the Kangra Hills.

16. The date often given for this 'migration' is 1739, the year of Nadir Shah's sack of Delhi. But I have tried to show in my "Pahari Painting: The Family as the Basis of style", *Marg*, Sept. 1968, that this assumption is questionable.
17. See my *Pahari Painting* for an analysis of the style of Manak at this point of time.
18. This group of documents, mostly in Persian, has been unpublished by me under the title *Painters at the Sikh Court*, from the University of Heidelberg (Wiesbaden, 1975).
19. See, for further details, my *Pahari Painting* on this family and its style.
20. Names of Kangra artists like Ruldu and Kanchanu are mentioned at Jammu. There is a drawing with small portrait heads of these artists in the Chandigarh Museum, mentioning them as being *mulazims* of the Maharaja of Jammu.
21. Attention to this aspect of patronage of painting by the *mahants* has been drawn by Karuna Goswamy in her doctoral dissertation, 'Vaishnavism in the Punjab Hill and Pahari Painting' (1968) and, more recently, by Usha Bhatia in her dissertation, 'Painting in the Hindu monastic establishments in the Punjab plains' (1977).
22. Some very distinguished portraiture was done at Basohli, Mankot and Mandi in the seventeenth century and the Guler, Jasrota and Kangra in the eighteenth.
23. In fact, some of the informal studies have even greater power than the formal portraiture. Many of them came from family collections of Pahari painters and are now scattered.
24. G.T. Vigne and von Ujfalvy, who both travelled in the hills in the nineteenth century, make caustic comments of this kind. These are then echoed also in the causal notice that is taken of the work of the Indian painters by the British in the Punjab Hills.
25. For a distinguished study of this subject, see M. Archer, *Company Drawings in the India Office Library*, London, HMSO, 1972.
26. This is one of the saddest chapters in the history of Indian taste. Nearly all Rajas in the nineteenth century preferred these theatrical works to the works done in the earlier tradition by old artists.

27. A collection of drawings belonging to an old family of artists settled at Patiala, or the remainder of the collections with the Rajol family of artists gives clear indication of the rulers expecting them to do this kind of work.
28. Chandu Lal belongs to the distinguished family of Pahari painters that was headed by Pt. Seu, and is thus a direct descendant of the great Nainsukh. The copies that he makes today based on works by his ancestors contain only faint echoes of the brilliant work of the eighteenth century.

Selected Bibliography

Archer, W.G. 1973. *Indian Paintings from the Punjab Hills*. London: Sotheby, Parke, Bernet.

Francke, A.H. 1914, 1926. *Antiquities of Indian Tibet*, 2 vols., Calcutta.

Goswamy, B.N. 1961. 'The Social Background of Kangra Valley Painting' (Dissertation, Punjab University).

Goswamy, B.N. 1975. *Painters at the Sikh Court*. Wiesbaden: Franz Steiner Verlag.

Hackin, J. 1931. *La Sculpture Indienne et Tibetaine au Musee Guimet*. Paris.

Khandalavala, Karl. 1958. *Pahari Miniature Painting*. Bombay: New Book Company.

Madanjeet Singh. 1968. *Himalayan Art*. New York: Graphic Society.

Moorcroft, W. and G. Trebeck, 1841. *Travels in the Himalayan Provinces of Hindustan and the Punjab*. Ind. Reprint. New Delhi: Sagar, 1971.

Monod, O. 1954-55. *Peintures Tibetaines*, Paris.

2

The Himalayan Tribes

Cultural Picture of the Himalayas

The Himalayas have been a cauldron of cultures. Over three millennia, people of different races have been entering India through the Himalayas. The Himalayan cultural matrix that we examine today is a composite culture. The Huns and other Central Asian people who entered India assimilated with the local population, but left their impression on the indigenous culture in the form of laws, language, literature, dress, art, etc. "The inscriptions of all the dynasties such as the Gurjar, Paratiharas, Paramaras, Chahamanas, Chalukas and Gahad Valas of Northern and Central India from the seventh century onward contain an increasing number of non-Sanskrit names of people and places."[1] In fact, in earlier times the Austric, Dravidians, Aryans and Mongolians had a similar impact. An examination of the arts, craft and manner of dressing will reveal the cultural picture of the Himalayas.

Costume

What one wears is very clear mark of his status in his tribe or his society. The style of dressing and costumes reveal the culture of a tribe. In many cases, they also reveal the status of a person in tribal society. The tribes of the Himalayan belt are fond of dressing colourfully. The manner of dressing and costume in each area is briefly described here.

A Baluch

A Baluch likes to grow a beard but he generally keeps his hair short. A Baluch likes to grow a beard but he generally keeps his hair short. His head dress is a white turban with or without a cylindrically shaped skull cup called Kwah, adjusted in the centre, just over the crown of the head. The shirt is a long cotton robe with loose full sleeves, gathered often at the waist with a sash. The pyjamas are loose. The shepherds sport home spun wool. They use caps with folded rims. The sash serves as a receptacle for tobacco pouches, swords or stilettoes.

A Baluch lady parts her hair at the centre and arranges it in a plait. Some arrange their hair in numerous plaits on both sides, especially tribal or shepherd women. In general, Baluch women sport a *burka* (veil) from the crown to the feet. The body garment is a loose shirt of diverse colours in silk which reaches the ankles. In the case of rich ladies, the garment is richly embroidered with mirror pieces and coloured threads forming geometric designs. The women also sport a *salwar* (a loose type of trousers). The ears, nose and head are profusely decked with silver or gold ornaments. The nostrils generally have silver or gold rings on both sides. Silver necklaces and bracelets are also sported. In the cities, the males now wear trousers, shirts and coats.

A Pathan

A Pathan's turban is his distinct mark. He is very proud of his turban and the way he wears it. He also sports a beard; he may also like a Baluch keep his hair short. On ceremonial occasions, he sports a conical skull cap, the *kurla*. A loose shirt, knee-high, is the upper garment and a salwar is the lower garment. A sash is very often used at the waist. The ladies, upper garment is a loose shirt (*kameez*), extending to the knee, or thigh embroidered or plain. The lower garment is a salwar which is tied at the waist with a *nara* (thread). Over the salwar kameez a veil covers the woman from head to toe.

The Pavindah women inhabiting the highlands of Khorasa dress in black-blue veils; Marwat women generally use red and blue salwars and black veils; Bannu women use black veils and red salwars. Some women tattoo their faces especially the Pavinda. All women part their hair and plait it. "Plaiting of hair is also distinctive to each tribe and reveals the women's marital status. The ladies bathe in the rivers and streams in a state of nudity, regardless of passers-by."[2] A Pathan woman is very fond of jewellery and is profusely decked in gold and silver ornaments. Necklaces with silver and copper coins of high workmanship are worn. Some deck their foreheads with ornamental strings or head bands.

The Dard

The hair a Dard male is a distincition, which he has not done away with in all the centuries he has been in the Himalayas. He keeps long hair reaching below the ears touching the shoulder. Sometimes a piece of cloth is tied round the head which serves as a turban. The Bushgalis among the Dards shave their heads expect for a circular patch about three inches in diameter on the crown. On this patch, the hair is allowed to grow long and many even reach upto the waist. They do not wear any turban or head dress. The Bushgali woman parts her hair and then plaits it into numerous stands which are coiled under the head dress.

All Dard women wear a loose type tunic and a pair of trousers. The tunic may have some geometric designs embroidered with hand. The ladies also sport gaiters. The males wear a loose long tunic extending below the knees, gathered at the waist with a sash. The lower garment is a pyjama. The robes may be of coarse cotton, but the Dards of Sirikol, Wakhan, Zeba, Chitral, Yassin, Hunza, Nagar and Yaghestan use woollen garments in winter. The women wear necklaces made of silver beads and medallions. They also sport a triangular silver ornament called 'Pesharvez' which is a sort of necklace. This is often studded with stones in many colours.

The Gujjar

A Gujjar sports a beard. To give a reddish brown colour to it, he dyes it with *mehndi*. They keep their hair trimmed. They wear a turban. Some Gujjars, on ceremonial occasions, may use the *kurla*, a conical skull cap. The upper garment is a loose tunic or shirt with a pair of trousers. Some Gujjars use salwars like the Pathans. Over the shirt is worn a jacket which may be well embroidered. The ladies part their hair and arrange it in plaits. They wear a *dupatta* on the head. This also serves as a veil. They generally wear salwar-kameez. The kameez may have cross-stitch embroidered designs.

The Phulkari designs of Punjab are also popular among the women and these are often found on their dupattas. Over the salwar-kameez, a shawl may be worn to keep the body warm. A Gujjar woman is fond of jewellery. Necklaces, bracelets and other ornaments profusely adorn their bodies. The ear-rings are bunches of silver medallions, with studded stones in some cases. Similarly, silver necklaces studded with red, green and blue stones are also worn. The nose-ring is a flat, round, gold or silver ornament. Young ladies prefer small nose-rings. Gujjar women are very proficient in cross-stitch embroidery.

The Gaddi

In earlier times, the Gaddi used to keep moustaches. But now many of the male are clean-shaved. His headgear is a turban of white cloth or a cap. He wears a shirt, pyjama and *chola* (cloak). The chola is a long tunic extending to the thighs, generally of homespun wool, gathered at the waist with a *dora* (long woollen rope of black colour). If the chola is not worn then shirt is sported. The shepherds among them wear a coat made of homespun wool. The dora serves as a receptacle for a tobacco pouch and ignitor (kuthalu and saz), small hukka and drat (stiletto).

The Gaddi woman parts her hair and makes a single or double plaits. Her head dress is a long dupatta. The body garment is a very distinct skirt called *Gaddini ka Ghagra* which completely envelops her from shoulders to toes. Its sleeves are loose and full and it is gathered at the waist by a dora, which is about a 20 feet long woollen rope. *Choli* is the upper garment. It is made from cotton or muslin. A ghagra needs about eight metres of cloth, which may be woollen, cotton or muslin. In Gadderan, the ladies generally wear woollen ghagras in winter. The Gaddi lady is profusely decked with ornaments. On the head they wear a flat silver plate with a ring of silver medallions. The ears have large gold or silver ear-rings, nose-rings are found on both nostrils. The necklaces are single-stringed or multi-stringed. A necklace with triangular silver plates and many strings and medallion is worn. This is called *Chander Har* (silver garland) and is the most popular ornament. Some use waist bands of silver. Rings are worn on at two or three fingers. Bangles and anklets are popular.

The Jhecha

The same is the case with Jhecha male. He prefers trimmed hair, clean shaved face with or without moustache. His headgear is the kulbi cap or topi. In fact, the topi was the original head dress and is not in use any more. The kulbi has a colourful flap with a lining or border. Jhechas and the natives of Kulu are very particular about their head-dress: a person is not supposed to got a temple or meet the village chief and relatives without sporting it. While touching the feet of an elder one must have a cap on. The dress of the Jhechas in olden times was a *chola* (tunic, knee-long having several pleats and open at the front) adjusted at the waist with a sash. The lower garment usually was a pair of trousers. However, shepherds preferred a loin cloth (*khesari*). Below the chola, a gentleman used a shirt. Nowadays, the general dress is a coat, shirt, pyjama and a sash at the waist. A dora at the waist supports a tobacco pouch ignitor (saz), darat (sword), hukka, etc.

Jhechas and Kulu native dress similarly, except that the Jhechas use mostly garments made of homespun wool. The Jhecha woman parts her hair and makes it into a single plait. A cotton or silk tassel *(jutu)* is attached to this and dangles to the waist. The head-dress of a lady now is the *thipu*. This is a piece of cloth about a metre in length and breadth, triangular in shape. The thipu is black or red and it is made of silk, muslin or synthetic cloth. Young women nowadays use a dupatta or *chunri* instead of the thipu. A married lady cannot move about without a head-dress. A widow wears a white thipu. In general, salwar-kameez are worn with the salwar sometimes termed as *pidhi pyjama* (tight fitting pyjama).

In olden times, the women used gaiters *(pahuchas)* as the lower garment. These extended from just below the knee to the ankle, encasing the calves. The thigh and above were bare but hidden from the gaze as the body was covered by a shawl called *pattu*. A pattu is a piece of woollen cloth with chequered block *(dabeedar pattu)*. Ornaments hold great fascination for the women: the ears are entirely punctured with silver ear-rings *(balus)*, globular gold ear-rings *(gokharu)* or gold and silver medallions *(kante)*. Both nostrils have large flat gold nose rings *(phulis)*. The neck is decked with a *chhata* (a necklace) and the Chander Har.

The fingers have gold or silver rings with precious stones. The churi, maridari, kanganu and bahi are all silver bracelets. Anklets are not used by Jhecha women. As a matter of fact, the use of cosmetics by Jhecha Kulu women is rare. Application of powder on the face is considered a disgrace. Harcourt has commented: "Many of the Kulu women are strikingly handsome, and their very light complexion, rosy lips, brown hair and sparking eyes would be noticeable features in any country in the world."[3]

The Nepalese

The famous Bhatgawle Topali is the one from which a Nepali can be spotted from a distance. It is boat-shaped. They also wear a cap made out of muslin with coloured designs. Nepalis have different tastes when it comes to hairstyles. They have different tastes when it comes to hairstyles. Some keep it trimmed, others let it run to their neck or even shoulders. The face is clean shaven. The men's upper garment is called *Laor Labeda.* It extends upto the thighs and is fastended a across the chest with strings and at the waist with a sash. The lower garment, called *surnwa,* is a pyjama which is close fitting at the legs but becomes incrcasingly loose as it goes up to the waist.

Nepali ladies part their hair and arrange it into one or two plaits or gather it into a bun. Their head-dress is a dupatta, the upper garment a choli and the lower garment a skirt. Nepali women also wear saris but this is not their traditional dress. They are also fond of ornaments which are similar to those sported by Pahari women.

The Bhotia

Bhotias can be found from Ladakh to Arunachal Pradesh, so all across the length of Himalayas, the personal styles of the males and females differ. The hairstyle of Bhotia males differs: some shave their head like the Lamas: in the interiors, some Bhotias like the Ladakhis, Zanskaris, Pitials, Sherpas, Monpas of Thinglu, a few Mombas and Khambas keep their hair long and parted at the centre and arranged in one or two plaits which are sometimes coiled round the head. Other Bhotias prefer to keep their hair long upto their ear, necks or even shoulders without plaits. But mostly the males prefer trimmed hair. The Bhotia head-dress also varies. There is the Tibetan felt hat which is dome-shaped.

The Lahauls

The Lahauli-cap which is maroon in colour with a flap as a border having a silver lining *(magzi)*, the Bushahri cap, which is worn by the Kinnauras is made of a brown or white woollen cloth having a flap, the skull cap used by the Ladakhis, Changpas and Sherpas, the Gardam made of Yak hair with finger like projections which is worn by the Monpas. The ladies generally grow their hair long. It is parted at the centre and made into one or two plaits. Sometimes beads and tassels are attached to the plaits which dangle down the back or are coiled round the head.

In Ladakh and Spiti the head-dress of a lady is most elaborate, with precious stones, massive in size. It is called *Perak*. The Pangwal woman uses a cap which is adjusted with the plaits. Kinnauri women wear the Bushahri cap. In Ladakh, Lahaul, Spiti, Kinnaur and the U.P. Hills, Bhotia ladies very often use scarves as their head dress. The Monpa and Sherdukpen ladies wear a skull cap made of cloth. Its brims are embroidered with golden thread. The ladies' garments also differ from area to area. The Tibetan grown is a common dress throughout Ladakh, Garhwal Hills, Nepal, Sikkim, Bhutan and Arunachal. It is a big skirt covering the entire body from the shoulders to the toes, with oversized sleeves which are folded to fit the arm. The Pangwal lady wears a *cholu* (tunic) with a *churidar* (light housers).

The Lahauli women also wears a colourful cholu of silk, cotton, synthetic material or wool. It is worn over a pajami and kameez tied at the waist with a sash. Kinnaur women wear a Pattu like Kulu women but follow a different style in wearing it. Memba and Khasba women from Garhwal, Sikkim, Bhutan and Arunachal Pradesh wear a Tibetan skirt with an apron over it: women who are married wear a checked piece of cloth to denote their marital status.

Sherdukpen women sport a Pattu. Over this may be worn an embroidered jacket with sleeves. Tattooing is not practiced, but the women paint their lips and their cheeks with cream made from pine resin mixed with charcoal. A Bhotia lady sports beads, precious stones, heavy gold ear-rings, silver or gold pendants, necklaces of coins, silver or gold bracelets, a few of which are studded with turquoise and other precious stones. Some Sherpa women wear very big and heavy silver ear-rings.

The Lepcha

The Lepcha has no particular headgear; a round cap of knitted thread, wool or synthetic yarn is worn. He either keeps his hair trimmed or lets it run long so that it reaches the neck. The upper garment is tied across the chest with strings. It extends to the hips. The lower body garment is a pair of trousers. The ladies keep their hair long parted at the centre and arranged in a plait. Their head-dress is a scarf. The upper garment is a loose full sleeved shirt-like garment. This is worn with a skirt. The ornaments are necklaces of precious or ordinary beads as found among the other tribes of the bamboo cultural area. The Lepchas do not use very artistic silver or gold ornaments. These are mostly plain silver.

Other Tribes of Arunachal Pradesh

Arunchal is also a state where composite cultural intermix. There is an area in Arunachal Pradesh, which is called bamboo culture area; anther one is pastoral culture area. The tribes of the bamboo cultural area of Arunachal Pradesh have variety of costumes. These are described below. The Aka men keep their long hair tied in a knot in the middle of the head. On ceremonial occasions they wear a bamboo cap called Musgara. A piece of a cloth of Assamese silk or cotton called Tonga is wrapped round the body and pinned at the shoulders. At the waist there is a sash. A jacket with or without sleeves is worn over the Tonga. A sword may be supported by a sash at the waist.

The women part their hair. Their ear-rings are vase-shaped. Necklaces of coloured beads and silver coins are worn. Rich women wear beautifully designed head bands of silver. The ladies paint their lips with lipstick or Lingchang made from pine resin. Tattooing is very common. The Nishi man gathers his hair into a knot at the forehead called the *podum*. Through this tangled knot is passed a brass bobbin about 12" long. The headgear is prominent and made from cane. The upper garment is a piece of cotton or silk. The lower garment is a loin cloth which is generally hidden by the folds of the upper garment. The Nishis also sport cane rings round their waist, arms and legs. Bead necklace may also be worn.

The woman part their hair and plait it. They cover their body with a long piece of striped or plain cloth. Some ladies also use belts of metal plates as waste bands. There ears are adorned with large silver or brass rings. Multi-coloured beaded necklaces and brass chains are common. The Apa-Tani gentleman also gathers his hair in a podum. A brass skewer of 10 to 12" is passed horizontally through the knot. The headgear is also a cane helmet. Some males adorn their ears with large rings. At the waist they wear a special type of cane belt which is coloured red. A series of rings are arranged in the belt in such a way that there overlapping forms a sort of a appendage which hangs from the waist. This is unique to the Apa-Tanis and has been termed a "Bushy Tail" by Dalton. Dao is a weapon which every male carries. Apa-Tani women also gather their hair into a knot. They have no specific head-dress.

The Tagin

The Tagin gentleman's hair may run to his shoulders. The headgear, called Botung, is a cane helmet. A piece of bear skin is attached to the front of the helmet. Helmets made of deer or mithun hide are also in use.

The ladies part their hair and arrange it into plaits. The head-dress is a round cap which just covers the centre of the skull. It is made of Tibetan wool and generally red or maroon in colour. The neck is adored with bead necklaces, especially of blue colour. On the upper portion of the body, the ladies wear a loose garment of cotton or silk and cover themselves from the shoulder down to the calves with the help of a Tibetan blanket. Generally, both sexes among the Adis do not keep their hair long. The men cut it above their ears. The headgear is a cane helmet. Some such helmets have yellow colour yak hair attached to it.

The Adi

The Adi women have no particular head-dress, but often use the fold of their garment to cover their head. Their ear-rings are heavy. Their necks are lavishly adorned with bead strings or necklaces. The upper garment is full sleeved blouse, which may reach up to the waist or hips. The lower garment is a skirt supported at the waist with a band made of metal.

The hairstyle distinguishes the Idu Mishmis men from Digaru Mishmis (Taraons) and Miju Mishmis (Kamans). The Idus cut their hair short up front but long at the back. Because of this hairstyle they are called 'Chulikatas' by the Assamese. But the Digaru and Miju males cut their hair and keep them short and above the ears. The headgear also varies. The Idus wear cane hats, the Digmas and Kanam sport turbans. The cane helmet (Apoto) of the Idu-Mishmi is a massive thing. It has a conical dome and a flat brim. The male's upper garment is sleeveless cloak. The lower garment is a loincloth. The men also adorn their ears with ear-rings of metal or bamboo plugs.

Idu-Mishmis

Idu-Mishmi ladies cut their hair like men. Their necks are profusely adorned with coloured bead strings. Metal necklaces having silver coins are very common.

Young Khampti men cut their hair short, while older males gather it into a knot. The headgear is a white or multi-coloured silk turban. A loose shirt with a collar is the upper garment. Over this worn a tight fitting cotton jacket. The lower garment is coloured lungi called Phano. The women part their hair and plait it. Some also raise it into large rolls which are decorated with bands. The women sport a blouse, with a silk or cotton shawl type of garment worn over it. A striped or plain piece of cloth is used as a skirt. The women wear bead necklaces.

The Singpho men cut their hair but the older among them sport it long and tie it into a knot. The headgear is called Bumbam. It is a turban of white cotton cloth, but a silken turban (Tatak Bumbam) is worn by some on ceremonial occasions. The upper garment of Singpho males is a loose shirt with or without a collar. The lower garment is a chequered lungi. The women part their hair and plait it. Some gather it at the crown in a tangled knot. A few women sport a scarf. Bead strings are in common use. The upper garment is the blouse with sleeves. From the waist down a dress called the Bukang is worn.

The Tangsas keep their hair short. The headgear is a turban. A shirt type garment is worn and waist down is wrapped in a lungi. Some males sport ear-rings adorned with coloured beads. The ladies part their hair and tie it into a bun at the back or gather it at the nape into a knot. The ladies' upper garment is sleeved or sleeveless and below this is worn a skirt called Khallung. The neck is covered with bead necklaces. Necklaces made with silver coins are also in common use. The ear-rings are in made of transparent crystal. Silver and gold rings are common use.

The Noctes keep their hair short or long as they please. The headgear is a conical cane helmet which is adorned with wild boar tusks. Sometimes, it is also adorned with dyed goat's hair or hornbill feathers. The dress of a Nocte gentleman is scanty and in the Naga fashion. Ear-rings adorned with bead strings may be worn. On ceremonial occasions, a long scarf with horizontal bands is thrown over the shoulders.

The women in general keep long hair, parted at the centre and tied into a bun at the nape. Tattooing is practised. It is done after puberty. The ladies wear blouse and knee-long skirt. They use a variety of necklaces of beads, precious stones, metal strings, etc. Jinthap, a necklace, is a very costly ornament made from beads, precious stones, ivory, conch shells, bones or buffalo horns. Another ornament called Tanphiyang is a multi-coloured bead necklace worn down the back necklaces made of silver coins are also commonly used. Ear-rings of metal in different shapes and bangles are popular.

The Wancho males keep their hair long which is gathered into a bun or encased in a tube with leaf covering. The headgear (Longso Khohom) is a conical cane helmet with wild boar tusks and hornbill feathers. The hornbill plumes have significance. Only the chief can use three to four plumes while the commoners use only one. Sometimes tassels of hair of forefathers are fixed to the headgear. Tattooing of face, neck, arms and chest is seen in the case of many old gentlemen, but present-day Wanchos do not tattoo their bodies. The loincloth is the lower garment.

Daos and spears are carried on festive occasions. The ladies generally have long hair. Some Wangpen ladies crop their hair. The head-dress is a round cap with a rim decorated with the tiny beads patterned into geometric blocks. Ear-rings of metal are preferred. The neck is lavishly adorned with massive bead strings. There was a time when women did not wear any upper garment but now they use blouses. The lower garment is a piece of cloth tied at the waist with a band. The women are fond of tattooing their faces, thighs and calves like Nocte ladies.

Sema Nagas

The Sema Nagas wear tufts of cotton wool (akin-bupha). The women wear a short petticoat with coloured bands and cowries sewn on. Lhota Naga males sport cotton wool tufts which are wing shaped. Their head-dress is made from the skin of Himalayan bear or that of the male gibbon.

Hornbill feathers are fixed to it. The ladies wear cornelian and other cheaper beads. Bracelets and necklaces profusely adorn the body. Ao Naga women are entitled to sport a hornbill feather on the head for a mithun sacrifice conducted by their husbands or fathers.

Both males and females among the Angami Naga wear a spiked head-dress. Angami ladies do not sport cowries. Pistu-Kwe is the distinctive cloth worn by Angami priests. The ladies wear a special bugle-shaped bracelet on their upper arm. The Tangkhuls of Manipur wear a big loose brass collar. Both males and females among the Nagas go in for tattooing. The head-hunters sport a monkey skull or a replica of a human skull made of brass. This is supposed to provide them spiritual strength.

The Khasi Male

The Khasi male keeps his hair trimmed and his face clean shaved. The head-dress is a turban of white or coloured cloth. On ceremonial occasions the head-dress is decked with plumes. The upper garment is a long tunic extending to the knees with loose sleeves tied at the waist with a sash. The lower garment is a pyjama or a loincloth. Over the upper garments is worn a jacket without sleeves which is fastened at the waist with a sash. Necklaces of precious stones and beads are worn. The gents also use ear-rings of gold or silver. The Khasi lady parts her hair and makes a single plait to which is attached a cotton or silken tassel. The head-dress of a Khasi lady is a cap with embroidered brims. This is worn on ceremonial occasions. Some ladies also use coloured scarves. The upper garment is like a shirt with slightly loose sleeves.

Manipuri

Manipuri males mostly prefer to keep their hair trimmed, though some let it grow to their shoulders. The head-dress is a white turban. The upper garment is a shirt and lower garment a dhoti of white muslin. The hair growth in Manipuri women is luxuriant. They keep this parted at the centre and combed backward. The upper garment is a choli and a skirt type of dress called Fanek is wrapped round the waist. This reaches the ankles.

Kuki

The Kuki male keeps his hair long and trimmed as is his wont. It is very rare to find him sporting a beard. Being Mongoloid, he has very scanty facial hair. The male generally sports a cloth around the waist and covers the body with a coarse sheet. A ceremonial dress is more colourful. A geometrically designed scarf type of cloth is thrown round one of the shoulders and ends allowed to hang from the side. The head-dress is made of cotton or silk to which plumes are attached. The Kuki women wear a choli and a skirt.

Garo

The Garo male prefers trimmed hair to long hair. His principal garment is the Gando which is a piece of cloth having blue and red stripes decorated with conch shells. The head-dress is a turban usually white or blue in colour. The women keep their hair long, part it and make a single plait. Their head-dress is the Salchok-Mandong or Tilum. It comprises a comb sticking out of a piece of cloth decorated with beads. The upper garment of a lady is called Marang Jasku. This is wrapped round the body by passing it under the right arm and attaching it to the left shoulder. This covers the body to the knees. Underneath is worn a petticoat. The ladies sport a Riking which is a type of shawl of blue or white cotton. They also wear ear-rings, necklaces and bracelets. The males also wear brass ear-rings and necklaces.

Himalayan Crafts

Crafts are never far away from the minds and thoughts of village people. They may not be painters and fine artists, but they are artists of some other type in their own right. They have their own way of looking at nature, its bounties, and its beauties. In both the pastoral and bamboo cultural areas one witnesses a variety of crafts forms. The pastoral cultural area shows a bucolic influence in the crafts designs. The bamboo cultural area crafts are based chiefly on bamboo material with the designs being primitive and the South-East Asian type. In the Himalayan villages, one finds people engaged in spinning, weaving, wood-carving, basket making, rope making and stitching. Most of these tasks are assigned to the women. Some of the crafts of the area are described here.

Kashmiri Shawls

You spread a Kashmiri shawl before you, or you wear it, you have beauty right there. It overpowers you. The Kashmiri shawl is famous the world over. It is known for the hand made floral motifs. The main peculiarity of this shawl is that the designs are created after the shawl is woven and not during the process of weaving, unlike in the case of Kulu shawls. A shawl could be made of Asali Tus, the wool of wild goat, or Pashmina, a special wool collected from the Pashmina goats of Gia-Miru (Ladakh), in Lahaul and Spiti. The shawl is also made from sheep wool. Different elements in the shawl are: Hashia, the border on each side; Zanzir, a chain running above and below the principal part of the Pala; Dhour, a running ornament; Kunj-Buta, a corner ornament with floral motifs.

A buta has three parts: pai, root or pediment of leaves; Shikam, body; Sir, the head. The design is created with the darn-stitch method. Welch describes the style where the white area of the shawl is worked in twill tapestry weave, the narrow bands filled with undulating stem-bearing leaves.[4] The Kashmiri carpet is equally as famous as the Kashmiri shawl. The designs are created by the weft thread. The general design patterns are geometric or floral motifs. Kashmiri carpets reflect the Persian and Central Asian influence in design but in overall detail they are a combination of Persian, Central Asian, and Indian styles with a special local touch.

Kashmiri Embroidery

Kashmir is nature's gift to India. The artisans and craftsmen of Kashmir see its beauty every day. They bring it down from their imagination on to their crafts, their items of every day use and the clothes they embroider. Kashmiri embroidery is very famous for its floral motifs and adorns saris, gowns, house coats, curtains, bed sheets etc. Kashmiri papier-mache products are also popular. Articles like small boxes, plates, jars, handles, drawing room decorative pieces, etc. are made. The designs on such articles are painted with lacquer in a variety of colours. High-class papier-mache products are painted with gold water and rare pigments. Kashmiri carved wood products are also well-known. Walnut wood is especially used for this purpose. Beds, almirahs, jewel boxes, tables, chairs, trays, book ends, cigar boxes, lamp stands, etc. reflect the Kashmiri mastery over the craft. In Kashmiri houses, the ornate ceilings are a testimony to the skill of the wood carvers.

Kulu Shawl

Kulu shawl is different from the Kashmiri shawl. This is a hand woven woollen product made on a local handloom (Rachh) or an improvised loom *(khaddi)*. The peculiarity of the Kulu shawl is that the design is created during the weaving. Generally, the warp *(tana)* thread is more twisted and made tight with the help of spindles or machines but the weft *(bana)* thread is kept light and loose so that it imparts softness and smoothness to the shawl. A well designed Kulu shawl presents a riot of colours with intricate patterns of diamonds, geometric blocks, stars, etc. The design element is restricted to the extreme ends and the portion in between is generally kept plain or stars etc. may be interspersed. Both extremities are symmetrical. "Nature has inspired them to weave her colours and forms into abstract geometrical symbols to establish these draperies with glowing vivid colours. The green of the young fields, the reds and pinks of the wild flowers and orchard fruits, the deep blue of the Himalayan skies, and the yellow of the mustard in full bloom, are mirrored in the alluring intricate designs of square, triangle, diamond shapes, chevrons and crosses that have made these shawls famous for their fine quality, softness and craftsmanship."[5]

Its Variations

Variations on the Kulu shawl are also found. Pattu is a big shawl used by the local ladies. Doharhu is a long and thick woollen covering used like a blanket. Loi is a white shawl of wool or Pashmina used mainly by men. As per the design, a Kulu shawl is categorised as "Ekfulawali", "Dofulawali" or "Trifulawali." 'Tara Gudiwali' is a shawl with stars *(tara)* and Gudis (anthromorphic designs). Kushtiwali is a shawl border. Chitri is one with alternate black and white blocks. Davedar Chardu is a shawl with chequered blocks of black and white, red and white, red and black.

Chamba Rumal

One can't remember when Chamba Rumal was created and by whom. It is thought to be as ancient as Nature itself. This is a very big kerchief or a wall hanging on which are found themes from the *Ramayana* and *Mahabharata*. The piece is square with the size being about 11/2' to 4'. The designs are "embroidered" with coloured silk threads in double satin stitch. It is believed that the style is of Chinese origin. In the four corners, there are floral designs, enclosing a central Mandala. The motifs and idioms are borrowed from contemporary painting, in fact the paintings have been transcribed into rumals." 'Some rumals depict the Dashavtaras: Matsya (fish), Kurma (tortoise), Varaha (boar), Narasimha (man-lion)' Vamana (dwarf), Parasurama, Ramachandra, Krishna, Buddha and Kalki (shown riding a white horse). Others depict the Astha-Nayikas. Some secular scenes are also depicted like court life, hunting scenes, etc. The colours used for Brahma, Vishnu and Siva are red, blue and white. Red is also used to depict passion. White depicts life, fertility and the sun; yellow is used to depict costumes, etc., green is used to depict foliage and nature.

Bhotia Carpets

Where did the carpet weaving come to India from? The origin of carpet is not known. However, the carpets are produced in the Bhotia cultural area (Ladakh, Lahaul, Spiti, Nepal, Sikkim, Bhutan and Arunachal Pradesh). Their design has Central Asian, Mongolian, Tibetan and Chinese influences. The border is generally ornamented with Swastika design in various forms. Red, maroon, green, yellow and blue yarn is used. The craftsman follows a flock system. "The knotting is done by looping the thread around the wrap and the rod which is used for looping is placed horizontally and at right angles to the warp. When a motif or a colour block is to be introduced, the ground colour is cut and a new thread inserted by twisting into a single warp thread by lopping. Then a three ply twisted wool is drawn across twice to be used as weft."

Terms for the Design

Some of the terms for the design are as follows: Duk (dragon design), Pema Gyaja (lotus and bird design), Pema Thana Tsi-Tsi Gmpo (lotus and bats design), Gyaja Thang Medok (bird and flower design), Nehtsho Thang Medok (parrot and flower designs), Ganachari (Wall of China design), Yong-tong (Swastika design). Textile designs in general have distinguishing characters for each tribe. Monpa and Sherdukpen designs on jackets, shawls, and bags are almost identical. Monpa jackets are beautifully designed. There are different bands with colourful starts, zoomorphs and anthomorphs and (especially human figures shown ridding horse or yaks).

Sherdukpens follow the Swastika motif in their textile designs. This design is very old and popular in the Western Himalayas, in Ladakh, Lahaul, Spiti, Kinnaur, Nepal, Sikkim and Bhutan.

Though carpet weaving has been prevalent all along the Himalayas, it was very common amongst Monpas, so much so that a cluster of villages used to work on this craft. Now, carpet manufacturing centres have been established at Bom-de-la, Tawang and Tanzingong. The border of the Monpa carpet has the Swastika motif, the central design consists of a dragon. Designs with geometric patterns and floral motifs are also used.

The Nishis are not expert in weaving like the Apa-tanis but they produce textiles for their own use with simple stripes and lines. The Hill Miris are unknown to the craft of weaving but now some women have learnt this art. Simple cotton cloth is produced sans designs. In this cultural area the Apa-tanis are the expert weavers. Noctes and Wancho textile designs ape those of the Nagas. The Wanchos adorn their bags with anthromorphic figures along with other geometric designs.

References

1. Sankalia, H.D., *Aspects of Indian History and Archaeology*, B.R. Publications, Delhi, 1997, p.180.
2. Pennel, T.L., *Among the Wild Tribes of the Afghan Frontier*, George Bell & Sons, London, 1990, pp. 199-200.
3. Harcourt, A.F.P., *The Himalayan Districts of Kooloo, Lahul and Spiti*, N.H. Allen & Co., London, 1871, p. 143.
4. Welch, Stuart Cary, *India: Art and Culture*, 1985, p. 264.
5. Bhavani, Enakshi, *Flok and Tribal Designs of India*, Taraporewala Sons & Co., Bombay, 1974, p. 18.
6. Aryan Subhashini, *Himachal Embroidery*, Rekha Prakashan, New Delhi, p. 14.
7. Chattopadhyay, Kamladevi, *Handicrafts of India*, Indian Council of Cultural Relations, New Delhi, 1975, p. 67.

Bibliography

Ahluwalia, H.P.S., *Hermit Kingdom Ladakh*, Vikas Publishing House, Delhi, 1980.

Allen, B.C., *Assam District Gazetteers*, Vols. IX, X, Darang, Allahabad, 1905.

Barnes, G.F., *Land Revenue Settlement Report of Kangra District*, 1889, Punjab Civil and Military Gazette Press, Lahore.

Barnes, G.F., Harakanta Barua, *Assam Bhuranji*, Gauhati, 1939.

Barua, Tapan Kumar, *The Singphos and their Religion*, Director of Information and Public Relations, Govt. of Arunachal Pradesh, Shillong, 1997.

Berreman, Gerald D., *Hindus of Himalayas*, Oxford University Press, Bombay, 1963.

Bhattacharjee, Tarun, *Idus of Mathun and Dri Valley*, Directorate of Research, Govt. of Arunachal Pradesh, Shillong, 1983.

Bhavani, Enakshi, *Flok and Tribal Designs of India*, Taraporewala and Sons, Bombay, 1974.

Bhuyan, S.K., *Tung Khangia Bhuranji*, 1939.

Bidulph, J., *Tribes of the Hindo Kosh*, Office of the Supdt. of Govt. Printing, Calcutta,1880.

Campbell, George, *Ethnology of India*.

Casewit, Curtis, W., *The Mountain World*, The Ridge Press, New York, 1976.

Chakravarty, L.N., *Glimpses of the Early History of Arunachal*, Research Deptt., Arunachal Pradesh Administration, Shillong, 1973.

Chatterjee, S.K., *Kirata-Jana Kirti*.

——*The Cultural Heritage of India*, Vol. I, the Ramakrishna Mission Institute of Culture, Calcutta, 1973.

Chattopadhyay, Kamladevi, *Handicrafts of India*, Indian Council of Cultural Relations, New Delhi, 1975.

Chattopadhyay, Kamladass, *Tribalism in India*, Vikas Publishing House, New Delhi, 1975.

Chaudhary, J.N., *Arunachal Panorama*, Directorate of Research, Arunachal Pradesh, Shillong, 1982.

Chaudhry, P.C., *The History of Civilization of the People of Assam*, Spectrum Publication, Delhi, 1987.

Chetwode, Penelope, *Kulu: The End of the Habitable World*, Allied Publishers, New Delhi, 1984.

Christina, Noble, *Over the High Passes: A year in the Himalayas with the Migratory Gaddi Shepherds*, Fontana Collins, Glasgow, 1988.

Copeland, E.B., *Rice*, London, 1924.

Crooke, William, *Races of Northern India*, Cosmos Publication, Delhi, 1973.

Cunningham, Alexander, *Ancient Geography of India* (Ed. S.M. Shastri) Chakravorthy Chatterjee and Co., Calcutta, 1924.

Dalton, E.T., *Descriptive Ethnology of Bengal*, Office of the Supdt. of Govt. Printing, Calcutta, 1872.

Dasgupta, Kalyan Kumar, *A Tribal History of Ancient India* (A Numismatic Approach), Nabharat Publishers, Calcutta, 1979.

Dey, Nandolal, *Civilization in Ancient India*, Kanti Publications, New Delhi, 1986.

Dobzhansky, Theodosus, *Genetics and the Origin of Species*, Oxford and IBH Publishing Co., New Delhi, 1968.

Dun, E.W., *Gazetteer of Manipur*, Vivek Publishing Co., Delhi, 1981.

Dutta, Parul, *The Tangsas*, North-East Frontier Agency, Shillong, 1969.

——*The Noctes*, Directorate of Research, Govt. of Arunachal Pradesh, Shillong, 1978.

Eskine, *Babar's Memoirs.*

Ferishta, *History of Rise of Muhammadan Power in India*, Briggs, Reprint 1908-09.

Fleet, J.F., *The Topographical List of the Brihat Samhita*, Ed. K.K. Dasgupta, Somshi Sarat Bose Road, Calcutta, 1973.

——, *Corpus Inscriptum Indicarum*, Vol. III, No. I.

Foning, A.R., *Lepcha My Vanishing Tribe*, Sterling Publications, Delhi, 1987.

Forester, G., *Travels*, London, 1798.

Francke, A.H., A History of Western Tibet, London, 1907.

——*Antiquities of Indian Tibet*, Vol. II, Calcutta, 1926.

Freud, S., *Totem and Taboo*, Pelican, 1938.

Firth, Raymond, *Essays on Social Organisation and Values*, University of London, Athlone Press, 1964.

Gait, Edward, *History of Assam*, Thaker and Spink Co., Calcutta and Simla, 1926.

Gaugin, T., *History of Zomi*, Zomi Press, Churchandpur, 1984.

Geoffrey, Gorer, *Himalayan Village: An Account of the Lepchas of Sikkim*, Thames Nelson and Sons Ltd., London, 1967.

Goetz, Hermann, The Early Wooden Temples of Chamba, E.F. Baill, Leiden, Netherlands, 1955.

Goldzier, *Muhammedanic studies, Islam in India.*

Goyal, D.R., *Afghanistan Behind the Smoke-Screen*, Mamta Publishers, Delhi, 1984.

3

The Tribes of Nepal

The Kirat-Rai

The Kirati also called Kiranti or Kichak are the oldest inhabitants of Nepal. These names were originally used for the *Khambu* or *Rai*, who are also called *Jimdar*. The name Rai is of recent origin. As the Gurkhas conquered the land, they gave the more important people among the Khambu and Yakha the title of Rai or "Chief," to the Limbu the title "Subha," which also means "Chief."

The Rai have given their tradition, thus : Our forefathers came originally from a lake whose waters had dried up. In the centre of Nepal there was a lake which ran dry and the dry basin offered a suitable site for settlements. The first parents of the Rai were Parungo, the father, and Simnima, the mother. They begot three sons, Lapche, Jimdar and Meche. The parents sent the three sons away to live independently and find a country for themselves. The brother Lapche came across a banana tree and tried to hew it down whereupon Jimdar said to him, "If you are the kind of person that is prone to be destructive, we shall no longer stay with you," and with this Jimdar and Meche left him.

Later Jimdar Meche separated and each went his own way. And so in course of time the three tribes, Lapche, Jimdar and Meche originated. The Rai say, "We were the first farmers of Nepal and were there before the Newar and Hindus. Gradually our people grew stronger and formed 'ten,' i.e. numerous, tribes." Among these are the Limbu or Subha, the Khaling, Thulung, Shuotang, Bahing, Nedsa, Tara, Yakha, Lohorung, Dsamling, Bonta, Thami, Amtzoge—to mention some of them. The main point of difference amongst these tribes is the peculiar dialect spoken by each one of them.

Fr. M. Wery gave the following tribe-names of the Rais : Ambole, Alcoke, Antapa, Athpare, Baigya, Baiyang, Bantawa, Chamling, Dungmali, Khaling, Kulung, Lohorung, Nehali, Rumtali, Sangpang, Thulung, Yakha and some others.

These tribals honour Bume as the deity of the farmers and consider her to be more than a mere female potentiality. At the completion of the sowing of corn the housewife must. offer her a hen in sacrifice. This offering, however, is forbidden to the men. Dances are arranged in honour of this deity. A leader goes forward and demonstrates how it is to be performed, and the others imitate him. All the prayers and chants arc recited in their own respective languages. The Rai Matampa from the tribe of Dsamling, who came from Nepal and has now settled in Maria-Basti near Pedong, Kalimpong. While, his brother Sosbir, made the following statement : As their Supreme God, the Rai honour Paruhong. At the outset Paruhong killed all the demons so that he could create the world without let or hindrance. He created water first. Then he made the earth come forth from the water. He created mankind to inhabit the earth, and animals at a later stage. The first man was Mina which means "man", who is also called Hodza, and the first Woman, Simnima, which means "woman." The Supreme God gave man dry rice, maize and millet and taught him how to cultivate these grains in order to procure his food.

In order to make the fields fertile the female deity, Bume, came forth from the Supreme God. She must be specially honoured by an offering of hens which the housewife offers, as mentioned above. The master of the house carries out the dances which are held in her honour at the time of full moon. The god Paruhong has also arranged marriage with its concomitant ceremonies. In the above two stories narrated by the two brothers it is remarkable that the one names the first man Parungo, the other names the first man Mina or Hodza, while he names the Supreme God 'Paruhong' which sounds similar to Parungo. When his attention was drawn to this fact, Sosbir reiterated his statement that Mina was the first man, Paruhong the highest creator, and Bume a kind of female power that emanates from the creator.

It is also noteworthy that the three sons of the first man are called Lapche, Jimdar and Meche, which are the names of the three oldest tribes of the country.

A Rai of Gid biyong listed the following tribes of the Rai: Nedsali, Dsamling, Sangpang, Hoduali, Yakdung, Waling, Hangkun, Dzogkang, Mululang, Isara, Kulung, Thulung, Bungtheng, Khaling, Sotangmang dewa, Dzamrase, Bangdale, Songdale, Damgule. He stated that the language, Bontawa, was spoken by the following tribes: Waling, Hoduali, Dzogkang, Isara, Khaptna, Mululang, Sogtan, Sawali, Luhun, Yakdung, Dilumpa, Dilpali, Newahang, Rupabung. The other tribes had different dialects.

Another tradition gives the following tribal names : Athpahare, Dsamling, Dsaurasia, Bangtawa, Kulung, Lohorung, Thulung, Nawahang, Sangpang, Nehali. As there are many sub-tribes the choice of names often differs. Yet another Rai named the following tribes as the Tibetan Rai—

Khaling, Thulung, Rachali, Palali, Songdal, Bangdal, Damdzan. Some of the Rai who settled in the neighbourhood of the Hindus have their myths and traditions strongly influenced by Hinduism. For three days after death, food has to be prepared for the dead. The wife, brother and other relations of the dead may not eat salt during these three days. When three days have elapsed, the oldest people come and say, "The dead shall not return to molest the living any more." After that the mourners can eat any food they choose.

In the mythological period it is said : In ancient times Nepal was covered by a large lake encompassed by high mountains. A deity opened a crevice so that the waters of the lake could run out. A large valley then appeared. As the earth grew dry the first settlers could live there. They came from the north. The very first settlers were the Kirati, who came there in the 15000th year of the Dwapar Ingar and ruled the land for ten thousand years. After the Kirati the gods dwelt in the land. Dharmadatta Raja ruled for 1000 years. After him the land was without a king for another 1000 years. Bisalnagara lasted during 2000 years. When Buddha visited the land it was ruled over by a Kirati Raja. Thus, the most diverse sources indicate that the Kirati or Rai were the oldest inhabitants of the land.

The Rai are also the most numerous of the tribes of Nepal. As a general rule they are characterised by strong Mongolian features. The Mongolian eyes are specially noticeable among the children. Occasionally, among the older people, you can also find a fairly wide open eye without the typical Mongolian fold. The long faces of the Rai prove that they have undergone some intermixture.

The Limbu

The original home of the Limbu is the district of Jangrup. This is the name of the river which divides the districts of the Limbu and the Rai. The Limbu and the Rai are supposed to be the two constituents of the Kirati. Today the river Arun is the dividing line. The Limbu occupied the land as far as Sikkim where they were known as the Tzong pa by the Tibetans. In this area they called themselves Yaktampa or Ektampu. In Nepal, the Limbu district is called Dumriche, which is adjacent to the frontiers of Nepal, Sikkim and Tibet. In the ancient times the Limbu had no kings ; they were subordinate only to individual group-leaders until the king of Nepal brought them under his jurisdiction. The Limbu can be classified under two main heads : the Tzotore kewa, who speak a slightly differing language, and the Junga who in turn are divided into many sub-tribes : Satda, Pago, Nugo, Mejangbo, Hellug, Lingden, Tchigtzaba, Samba, Nembang, Hanggam, Songbangbe, Lochsom, Kamdachba, Soodung, Kambang, Sendang, Pedaphe, Nakkim, Seren. The Limbu are also called "Subha." Fr. M. Wery has also mentioned the following tribe-names : Athrai, Bakkim, Carkhola, Charbiya, Chemjong, Hurpa, Kambang, Libang, Lingden, Locksom, Mademba Mahbo, Nalibo, Phenduwa, Samba, Sanwa, Sering, Sonpangpe, Takeling, Tamiling, Thegim, Yongya, Yangrup, Yungwa.

The Limbus name their Supreme God as Niwa-Buma. This God appears under various forms : as an old man or as a young lad, as a dignified woman or as a pretty young girl. He is the creator of all things. At first he created the world, and then man. He formed the first man out of gold, but before creation was complete, as "the man was just beginning to speak," i.e. just before a soul was infused into it, a monster appeared in the form of a horse and destroyed the golden man. The monster had been moved to envy because God had made man so well. God was indignant with the horse and punished it for having destroyed the perfect masterpiece of his creative genius. Hitherto the horse had been able to walk upright on his hind legs ; henceforth, as a punishment, it was compelled to walk on all fours and serve as a beast of burden. God set to work again and created another man from ashes and the offal of poultry. This man was the first Limbu. God created the woman in exactly the same manner. Nothing more is known about the names of these two prototypes of the race.

Earlier, God created first the earth and then the water. As the world was quite new everything ran smoothly and the first inhabitants of earth had a peaceful and comfortable life. Without undue anxiety and effort they were able to procure their livelihood. God gave them seeds to sow : maki, maize ; ihena, millet ; ya, dry-rice (not water-rice). God also created animals and gave them to man. They were pag, the pig ; garongbi, a small-sized cattle which did not live on grass but on excrements ; the sheep, bera ; (the Tibetan sheep, banglug did not as yet exist), the goat, mendag ; the hen, wa ; the dog and the fish. The water-buffallo was non-existent in the very early times and the horse was the enemy of man. When God walked on the earth, springs bubbled up wherever his feet touched the ground. When the Limbu offer sacrifices to the deity they observe the following ritual: Three pairs of banana leaves are placed in a row on a clean spot of ground. A banana leaf plate is laid on the pair in the centre and bamboo vessels are put on the pairs on either side. Millet and fermented Kesung are poured into the vessels and they are filled with water. (May be millet beer had its origin in this manner.)

After the completion of these initial preparations the one who offers the sacrifice invites God with the words : "Come ! I offer you pig, rice and beer." At this invocation God comes down to earth. The man then kills the pig by piercing it with a lance from behind the shoulder blade, penetrating the heart and passing right through the body. The body is cut up and a little piece is taken from each part. These pieces serve as the proper sacrificial offerings. Meanwhile the rice has been cooked. The preliminary preparations being complete, some of the blood is poured on the leaves in the centre, where the plate will be placed. The one who performs the sacrifice fills the banana leaf plate with the cooked rice and the selected pieces of meat and deposits it on the leaves in the centre. He then offers the sacrifice to the deity saying, "Come hither, Lord, for we have prepared the meat, the rice, and the beer. Accept them, and do not be angry with us." The remainder of the meat is consumed by the people in a kind of sacrificial meal. But if pig is not available, a sheep, duck, fish or waterbuffalo, in that sequence, may be offered. These sacrifices may be offered every year, but only by someone who is called "Pedangma" in the Limbu language. There are very few people who understand the rites, which are traditionally handed down in certain families. The Pedangma of the Limbu differs from the others who perform the sacrifice in that he does not tremble; -by this is meant the trembling that comes over them when they are possessed by a spirit. The man who performs the sacrifice plays a cylindrical drum with a hide stretched over each end. It is about three yards in length and one foot in diameter. This drum, called Gemunga, is hung in front of the body and is beaten with the bare hands. Several drums are used at wedding ceremonies, while the dancing goes on. Today, however, only the men dance. In the olden times women danced too; but today they have forgotten the art. The hour-glass-shaped Shaman drum is unknown to them.

They also honour the goddess Buribodju, who was created by God and endowed with magical power by him. The younger brother of the Mandal from Lingse related the following tale : The Limbu or Subha belong to the Jimdar. Because of this common ancestry the two groups may have their meals in common. Their language and religion are different. The Limbu worship the goddess Buribodju, or to call her by her Limbu name Yumasam. The one who performs the sacrifice offers her every year, or every three years, a pig, a buffalo, a goat or a duck. This yearly sacrifice is called "Noagi". It must take place at night in an uncultivated place near the settlement. Everyone may take part in the sacrifice. The victims are beheaded with a knife. The sacrifice is performed at the commencement of the harvest of the rice-crop. The goddess Yumasam lives in heaven. These are some religious ceremonies of this people.

The Limbus have flat faces, Mongolian eye fold and yellow complexions. The Mongoloid characteristics are stronger in their case than in the case of the Lepcha. Anthropologically they correspond with the Rai.

The Magar or Mangar

The Magar or Mangar is another Nepali tribe. According to their tradition, they came from Bokim, a land behind Nepal somewhere in Tibet. The history of their settlement is in keeping with this tradition. Larger colonies of the Magar live in Kangpachen in the north-east near the Tibetan frontier. Their language is still preserved there today and this seems to indicate that they had once been powerful and influential. The conflicts between the Tibetans and the Magar are mentioned in the local legends. All this implies that at one time the Magar settled mainly in the northeast. Currently, they live in districts west of Kathmandu even as far as the rivers Bheri and Karnali. They are in possession of strips of land which are more suitable for cultivation right up to the high mountains.

The Magar are outstanding as farmers and are known as the Pakali Magar. They also collect berries, roots, herbs, and everything edible from the woods. They comprise several subtribes : the Thapa, Pitakote, Gjapsake, Burbadsam, Drundzangi, Lungeli, etc. Others mentioned six sub-tribes : Thapa, Rana, Ale, Pun, Burathoki, Gharti. Only the first three are pure Magar. The Pun and the Gharti speak different languages. They live also in the higher isolated valleys. Their long hair gives them an unkempt appearance and they are of a coarser build.

The sub-tribe of Magars is called the Kaniwale Magar. They work as smiths, miners, besides quarrying out ores and minerals. They are looked upon as the lowest class. The Gharti are shepherds.

Two Magar dialects are chiefly to be distinguished. As the Magars lived near the Indian plains, and were more exposed to Hindu influence they absorbed a great deal of Hinduism into their religion, customs and habits and departed from many of their own. It is extremely likely that the old traditions may have survived among a few isolated tribes high up in the mountains, but as yet it has not been possible for us to let into contact with them. Racially, Mongoloid features are less in evidence among the Magars. The open eye and well-formed nose are of frequent occurrence. Their language falls into the Tibeto-Burman group.

The Gurung

The Gurung claim to have come from Po hiung, a land that lies beyond Nepal somewhere in Tibet. There once lived a Gurung who had two wives, the chief of whom had four sons, Ghale, Ghotani, Lama, and Lamchane. These four brothers with their tribes comprised the ruling class and they were the ancestors of the Char-jat Gurung class. By his second wife the Gurung had twelve sons, while some aver that he had sixteen sons. They with their descendants were called the Solah-jat Gurung, and were slaves of the superior class. Intermarriage between these two classes was forbidden. The youngest of the twelve brothers approached the king of Nepal with a letter complaining about the behaviour of his step-brothers and their oppressive methods. On hearing this complaint the king invited the four brothers to his court and enquired of them as to whether the complaint was just and whether intermarriages were really forbidden. They admitted the truth of the complaint, whereupon the king commanded that intermarriage among all should be permitted.

Now if a girl of the Char-jat Gurung marries a boy of the Solah-jat Gurung, the latter must pay a varying sum and vice-versa when a girl of the Solah-jat Gurung marries; a boy of the other tribe, the latter must pay a varying sum. However, under Hindu influence this legend was modified to run as follows : The king of Nepal was desirous of having as his wife the daughter of Ghale, the Gurung ruler. Among his daughter's attendants Ghale had a girl of outstanding beauty. Under pretence of being his daughter he sent this girl to the king. This ruse, however, was detected. The angry king demanded the real daughter whom Ghale could no longer refuse. They were marred and she bore the king the sons Ghotani, Lama and Lamchane. Their descendants had the same standing as Ghale and his successors and constituted the ruling class. The descendants of the girl who had been sent previously to the king mere the Solah-jat Gurung and were the slaves of the ruling class.

This indicates the attempt made by the Gurung to prove that they came from a higher Hindu caste. The racial differences among them certainly came from mixing with other peoples. These mixed peoples formed a tribe of their own. As the Gurung increased in numbers and were faced with food shortage, they emigrated. Among the emigrants was Gabring of the Solah-jat. He was a priest and had to perform the ceremonies like birth, marriages and funerals. However, he did not go to Char-jat Gurung families. These, therefore, let a Lama come from the Tsin Land (China). Because the Lama was "hired" in this way, they called him the Puon dchu Lama. He was supposed to instruct a few scholars and then return to his own country. The presence of a foreign Lama gave rise to quarrels between the two Gurung classes—the Solah-jat Gurung having grown envious of the fact that the others now had a Lama of their own. To put an end to the quarrel both the Lamas decided on the following plan : the first one to reach the peak of the Himalayas at sunset would be the leader. When the night was still young, Gabring awoke and rode to the mountains on his Shaman drum. The Puon dchu magician slept the whole night through, got ready just before sunrise and with the aid of his magic powers reached the mountain top immediately. As he arrived there he saw Gabring riding on his drum. Thereupon Puon dchu destroyed the drum of his rival by demolishing the drum stick and the skin from one side of the drum. Gabring fell to earth. Puon dchu then burnt the magic books of his rival. But Gabring instantly swallowed the ashes of the books. And so it is that these Lamas only know the prayers by heart, and do not know how to read or write. Their drums have the skin stretched across one side only, and they do not use a drumstick. The Lamas from Tsin on the other hand can read and write and they have the complete drum. Competitions among magicians of different sects and riding on magic drums are familiar Tibetan themes.

The Hindu version of the story runs as follows : Ghale, the Char-jat Gurung Lama, used to wear a cord like the Brahmins. He was journeying once in the company of his slave who was a Gabring of the Solah-jat Gurung. After journeying for a long while they were both tired and lay down to sleep. Vishnu appeared to the Gabring during his sleep and said, "Pour alcohol into your master's mouth and steal his holy cord." Gabring did as he had been bidden to do. When Ghale woke up he noticed the fumes of alcohol on his lips and that his holy cord had disappeared. "I have been robbed of my caste. I am ruined," he moaned, and fled into the wilderness to make atonement. These two stories show that there were two opposing elements among the Gurung. Like the Lamaist magicians, the Ghale Lama can also ward off hail, prevent storms, exorcise those possessed by demons, and perform many other feats of magic.

In former times they offered a bull in sacrifice at funerals. This could certainly not be the water-buffalo.

Owing to Hindu influence the slaughter of bulls no longer takes place ; an image of a bull with horns of gold, silver or wood is put up instead. The Gurung mainly settled down on the slopes of the mountains near the snow line, on a basis parallel to the Mangar. Thus, they live in more isolated districts and have preserved their individuality better than the Mangar. Cattle breeding plays an important part in their lives. On the average, the Gurung have Mongoloid features. Now and then some of them are with open eyes without the Mongolian fold, with well formed noses and brownish complexions. This type strongly resembles the Tibetan nomads. Their language also belongs to the Tibeto-Burman group.

The Tharu

An antithesis of the Gurung are the Tharus. They live south of the Mangar in the low hills and the Terai in the malaria-infested jungles at the foot of the mountains. From a legend of their descent they try to claim relationships with the Indians. They say that when the Rajputs were threathened by the Moslems, the Rajput women fled into the jungles. After the destruction of the Rajput army, the women, robbed of their husbands, married servants. That is why the Tharu women are held in such high esteem. There are other legends concerning their descent which are contradictory to one another. The confused traditions pertaining to their descent show that the Tharu are a mixed people.

The biggest colony is in the Naini valley, where the Bhoksa, probably an old section of the Tharu, also settled. They are also found in Bihar and Orissa. These Tharu, it is true, deny that they came from Nepal ; and this, in all probability, is because Nepal is less important than India. The Tharu are excellent farmers, but they are also good fishermen and brave hunters. Even the women take part in fishing and hunting. The women hold a dominant position in domestic life. They are a very diligent and hardworking people. The Tharus are at home in their malaria-infested jungles and for the most part have become immune to malaria.

Beyond the natural boundaries of their land, they are feared by the neighbouring people because of their magical prowess. The Tharu have thus preserved their old religion intact, and their arts of magic are more highly developed than the other Himalayan tribes. The Tharu have well-formed Mongoloid features slit eyes, brown or brownish yellow complexions in general, moderate sized noses, and a little hair on the body. In physical appearance the Tharu resemble the Mangar and other Nepalese, but not the Indians. There is a non-Mongoloid element to be found among them, which comes from their mixing with the Khasa, who are their neighbours in the north and northeast. The form of their head is dolichocephalic. The Tharu may be classed with the Mongoloids. The blood-group research carried out among them by D.N. Majumdar bears this out.[1]

The Tharus, near relations, the Bhoksa, belong to the same race. The main point of difference between them and the Tharu is that they were much more strongly influenced by Hinduism and gave up their primitive religion. The Tharu, are also said to be the distant relations of the Newar. The Tharu bear evidence to the fact that the Mongoloid elements descended to the Indian plains. There they may also have absorbed Austroasiatic and Dravida admixtures. Among these people the inner angle of the eye is covered by the upper eyelid and forms the Mongolian fold. The upper lid droops and the whole eye is slit-shaped. The cheek bones are strong ; the face and the nose are broad. The "Nomadic Dom" especially are widely scattered and thus have acquired elements of different races. The same is also true of the mountain Dom in the forests of the Himalayas.

The Newar

The Newar tribals live in the district of Kathmandu, in the centre of Nepal. The following tale is their version of their origin : In the centre of Nepal there lay a great lake encompassed by high mountains. Every day a goddess came to bathe in the lake. Her name was not known but she wrote her name on the leaf of a tree. The god, Bim-sin, came there one day and saw the virgin goddess bathing. He also found the leaf with her name on it, and called out to her to come to him. She refused to do so and demanded the leaf back. "I will return the leaf to you," said the god Bim-sin, "if you come and look at me." She did so and thus became pregnant. The god then returned to her the leaf with her name on it. Ten months later she bore a son and named him Pirtinaran. The boy grew up and one day asked his mother, "Who is my father?" She replied, "He is the god Bim-sin." The mother then asked the god what he intended to do for her son. The god replied, "I shall give him this land." So saying, he opened a gorge in the mountains and let the lake run out. He gave the land thus freed to his son so that he could rule there. This boy was the first Newar.

According to this tradition the Newar were the first inhabitants of the Kathmandu valley.

There are other legends in support of this interpretation. They relate further that the Newar came into this valley from the east of Mahachina, which is supposed to be China.

Other traditions hold that the Nayer came to Nepal as soldiers under Nanda-Deva from South India. These diverse traditions indicate the racial intermixture of the Newar which includes many components. The same differences are evident in the religious structure. The religious groups of the Newar come under the following classification :

(1) The *Shivmargi*, who are sub-divided on basis akin to the Hindus (a) the Brahmin, (b) the Kshatriya, (c) the Vaisya who include the Joshi (astrologers), Achar (priests of local deities), the Kau (smiths), Nou (barbers), Tati (spinners), Bhati (undertakers), Katha (wound-dressers). The latter were formerly Buddhists and have only recently been admitted into the third caste of the Newar.

(2) *Buddhamargi*—They are the followers of Buddha and fall into the following classifications : (a) Bandya or Banra, the descendants of married monks, (b) the Uda, dealers and merchants, (c) the lower castes of the peasants and artisans. In addition to these are the untouchables, the butchers, musicians, tailors, woodcutters, charcoal burners, sweepers, fishermen and those employed in the leather industry. This classification of the Newar gives us an insight into the historical development of Nepal and the various influences of Buddhism and Hinduism. It is true, indeed, that the Newar have lost some of their characteristics through these influences. But they were the most cultured people of Nepal prior to the invasion of the Indian Aryans. Their language could also be written. The Newar have exercised a great influence on the cultural structure of Nepal.

They were very able farmers. In very early times they had not learnt the use of the plough and tilled the soil with their hoes, Kodali. They did not employ the services of oxen until they began to use the plough in preference to their hoes. They were also capable at handicrafts and were successful merchants. Anthropologically the Newar stand out strongly. As a general rule they have wide, open eyes without the Mongolian fold. The nose is well formed, but wider than the characteristic Aryan nose. The complexion is yellowish. Some anthropologists are of the opinion that the complete absence of, or the very slight evidence of Mongoloid elements in the Newar, is due to their strong intermixture with the Indians. It must be admitted that the cultural influence of the Indians over the Newar is stronger than their racial influence over them. There is greater evidence in this case of the old non-Mongoloid substratum which is prior even to the Aryan. The same is true in the case of other people. The language of the Newar falls within the Tibeto-Burman group.

The Sunwar

The Sunwar tribals have settled in the north-east, from the district of the Rai to that of the Newar. Kisi and Busi, two places rather centrally situated, are said to be the most important settlements. Djoi and Kimti were near the Tibetan frontier. Tradition relates that the Sunwar came to Nepal from the very distant land of Churdji bangchi after the Newar but before the Brahmins. The three brothers, Jetha, Maila and Kancha, are said to be their forbears. The descendants of the eldest formed ten tribes, while those of the two younger brothers formed one tribe each. These twelve tribes were called the "bara-tharai" and they live in the mountains north of the valley. They constitute the highest caste. In addition to these there were ten Sunwar tribes, the "das-tharai" who were born of mixed marriages of the Sunwar with other peoples. They form a socially lower strata.

Thus, we are able to understand other traditions which relate that the Sunwar came from Kashmir, or the Ganges, or other districts. The Sunwar are small and of slender build. They are somewhat smaller in size than the average Nepalese. The cheek bones are fairly prominent and the eye and nose are typically Mongoloid. Their language belongs to the Tibeto-Burman group. The Sunwar claim that they were originally hunters. Their main occupation was dress and basket making. They lived in symbiosis with the Gurung and the Mangar.

The Dhamang

The Dhamang tribals, also called Murmi or Lama, came from a place which was about a fifteen days' journey inside Tibet. This homeland of theirs is called Chivali. Another legend says that they came from Mudimirge in Gipod. There are many tribes among the Dhamang: Lo, Gole, Lingdan, Djabag, Bakrin, Bomdzan, Hingkar, Ting, Geching, Jondzan, Mugdan, Togor, Blon, Glan, Weiba, Galdan, Didung, Goangdan, Hiangdan, Hiangba, Dong, Dumdzan, Niagi, Nisu, Djimba, Rumba, Bol, Lamagor, Ngarba. All these tribes fall into two categories—the bara, the twelve, and the atharra, the eighteen Dhamang tribes.

The Dhamang claim their descent from the three brothers—Tshenggu, Lung and Tulgu. Their mother was a cow who died after the birth of the three sons. Her parting words to her children were, "Eat my flesh, and you will be like God." The brothers did as they were told and divided her body among themselves. The youngest brother took the entrails and went to the river to have them washed. The two elder brothers divided the flesh into three parts, cooked it and each of them buried his share. When the youngest brother returned they deliberately deceived him saying, "We have already eaten our share of meat. You must now eat yours." The youngest brother complied with their request, but no sooner had he done so then they heaped insult on him and said, "You have eaten the flesh of the cow, and hence you are guilty of the murder of our mother." They then uncovered their hidden shares and tried to drive him away. This act roused the fury of the youngest brother who took up the entrails he had with him and struck his brothers with them. When the eldest was struck he turned into a Brahmin ; the second into a Thakur. The youngest became an Avatta, a Lama, and the father of the Dhamang. Their mother, the cow, is known by the name of Kun-tu-zang-mu. It is apparent that the Tibetan Kun-tu-bzang appears in this name. Kun-tu-bzang-po is the principal god of the Bon po. The first heavenly Bodhisattva and the Adibuddha are also called by this name. Kun-tu-bzang-mo was the wife of Shakta.

In the Dhamang story she appears in the form of a cow. We know of other Tibetan myths in which god appears in the form of a bull. Hindu influence has caused the following changes in the myth of their descent. Once there lived three brothers Brahma, Vishnu and Mahashur. One day they went out hunting for game. After spending many hours without sighting any game, they were suddenly confronted with a wild bull, the gauri-gai. Vishnu shot the animal. The three brothers then commenced carving up the meat with a view of eating it. Mahashur took the entrails to be washed in the river. In the meantime the other two brothers cooked the meat and divided it into three parts. Only then did they realise that it was the flesh of a cow and that they could not eat it. The two brothers concealed their portions of the flesh. When the third brother returned they deceitfully said to him "We have eaten our share of the meat. Now you must eat yours."

After he had done so they brought out their hidden portions, and rebuked him severely for having eaten the flesh of a cow. This vicious behaviour on the part of the two brothers so infuriated the youngest that he lashed out angrily at his brothers with the entrails he had in his hand until they hung in strips about their shoulders. These strips were the prototype of the holy cord. Mahashura, thus degraded, became the ancestor of the Dhamang who eat the flesh of the cow. Similar legends are current among several Indian tribes: hunters shot a bullock which they mistook for a deer. As a punishment they must eat its flesh and lose their caste. And so it was, as we see, but a step from the original Dhamang myth to the Hindu version of the same.

They call their principal god Bim-sin. We have already come across a Newar god bearing the same name. This principal god had in addition five brothers who took over duties from him. The god who undertook the creation of the world is called Naua-daia. Bim-sin killed all the devils in the world. Stones are supposed to be the bones of the devils. The devils are called Dai-te. In the beginning all men were equal and there were no class distinctions. These distinctions were arranged later by a deity. The Dhamang are also called Dhamang-Bhodja, because they are supposed to originate from a mixture of Tibetans with Nepalese. This is another indication of the mixture that exists among these people. Their language points to the existence of close connections with Tibet. Their bodily structure shows Mongoloid features. They are scattered over the whole of East Nepal, but they are also numerous in the mountains which surround the Nepalese valley, particularly in the northern mountains.

The Sharpa

The Sharpa have the strongest Tibetan features. The name Sharpa means "Eastern people" in the Tibetan language. The Sharpas in Nepal are said to be the people who have come there from the east of Tibet. They lived originally in the frontier districts in the Tsing-hai-Se-chwan provinces of China. This is in Eastern Tibet where they are called Shar-pa, Eastern people. They are divided into ten tribes; Salaka, Pinasa, Lama, Gotarma, Dachchindo, Dagdoch, Khambadje, Djawa, Gardza. The Lamas of this tribe belong to the Ning-ma and bKa-gyud-pa sects. They live high up in the north-east of Nepal and are the nearest inhabitants to Mount Everest.

The porters for the Everest expeditions are selected from these people, because they are outstanding as mountain climbers and are remarkable for their endurance. The best mountaineer among them is Tensing, the Everest hero. The race as a whole has totally Tibetan features. There are nomadic types among them with open eyes, strongly formed noses, and bronze-tinted skins. Others among them have more strongly marked Mongoloid features with slit eyes and prominent check bones.

Some Minor Tribes

The Thakale are settled in the northern sector of Central Nepal in the Muktinath district. In appearance they resemble to the Gurung. Their language also bears an affinity to Tibetan, and therefore they are Mongoloids. The Rohani, the Binge and the Kolme also live in the neighbourhood and they resemble the Thakale in appearance. Further south-east, the Thami live along the banks of the rivers Sunkosi and Tamburkosi, and they number a few thousands. They claim relationships with the Kiranti, who however, do not admit this relationship on the grounds of the strong intermixture evident among the Thami. Their features, which are similar to the Kiranti, are Mongoloid.

The nomadic Kusunda tribes and, a little further west, the Chepang live in Central Nepal. They dwell in caves and under the trees and it is only in very recent times that they have learnt the techniques of house-building. They are small in stature and have a dark coloured skin. These factors have led some to believe that they are related to the Indian Oroan and Kol, and that they are the remains of an Austroasiatic people. The land lying between the rivers Kauriala and Kali, to the west of Nepal, has a different set of inhabitants. The Hindu elements become more strongly marked as one advances further to the west. The Mongoloid characteristics disappear entirely, in spite of the fact that the Nepalese from East and Central Nepal are scattered all over the land. These inhabitants have dark skins, longish faces, straight noses and open eyes. They bear a close resemblance to the Kumaoni and speak the same language. They are, therefore, Indo-Aryans. This is no longer a sphere of strong Mongoloid influence.

Many other tribes are settled in the Terai. We have already mentioned the Tharu. Other inhabitants of the jungles at the foot of the mountains are the Meche, Dhimal and the Koch or Rajbansi. We have already made the acquaintance of the ancestor of the Meche, who, as we said, was the youngest brother of Lapche and Rai. The Meche live in the woods between the rivers Brahmaputra and the Kosi. As is the case with the whole Terai region, their district is also severely infected with malaria, and is, therefore, avoided by other people. This odd circumstance serves them as a natural protection and enables them the better to preserve their own individuality. Their language is still preserved. They are wont to burn out large tracts of forest and build little farms which they cultivate by the most primitive forms of agriculture, akin to the methods prevalent in the Southern Himalayas. A government order controls this activity for the preservation of forests.

The Meche, like all other jungle inhabitants, are enthusiastic hunters. They have Mongoloid features but we shall deal with this at greater length later on. The facts mentioned above are also true of the Dhimal who have likewise preserved their language. The Koch live in the jungle of Siliguri right up to Jalpaiguri and have spread even to Koch Behar and Goalpara in Assam. They have dark complexions and for this reason are reckoned by some to be an old Indian stratum (Austroasiatic) with traces of Mongoloid influences. They have through strong Hindu influence lost their original language. The Koch link us with Assam and we shall deal with them at a later stage.

The Indo-Aryan element passed on by the Gurkha conquerors is noticeable throughout the whole country. The castes are mostly Brahmin, Kshatriya, the Thakuri, Kami (smiths), Damai (tailors), Sarki (shoemakers), Khawash or Bhujel (slaves). The impress of Hinduism has been due rather to cultural than to racial penetration. The *lingua franca* of the country is now Khaskura, the language of the Khas. This is an Indo-Aryan dialect and is more akin to the Kumaoni in the west than to the Aryan of the Indian plains. Khaskura, also called Parbatiya, Gorkhali, Nepali, is that Indian Aryan dialect which has penetrated farthest to the east in the Southern Himalayan mountains and is also the language of commerce in Indian Sikkim.

Bibliography

D.N. Majumdar, The Fortunes of the Primitive Tribes, Universal Publishers, Lucknow, 1944.

Dr. Matthias Hermanns, The Indo-Tibettans, KL Fernandes, Bombay, 1954.

4

Himalayan Polyandry

Culture: Family Economy

Polygynandrous and other forms of polygamous practices are prevalent in the Himalayas. Therefore it is very essential that for the study of the family economy of the region, these practices are taken into consideration. Monogamy, as a general rule, has not asserted itself though the social forces have already made dents into the traditional structure of Jaunsar-Bawar society under conditions of polygynandrous or polyandrous joint family. Marriage, birth, or death do not bring about a new family unit into existence.

Joint Family Composition

It affects the composition of the already established joint family as far as its members are concerned. The increase or reduction in the number of members of the joint family brings about changes in the family economy, making it simpler or more complex, as the case may be. The people of Jaunsar-Bawar are agricultural as well as pastoral. They practice terrace-cultivation, the produce from which varies both from field to field and from year to year, and hence is difficult to assess. The people have to live a semi-pastoral life on the forest-clad hills during certain parts of the year, when there is an acute shortage of fodder and grazing fields for the cattle and sheep in the village or near *chhanis*

Average Size of the Family

To study the family economy in Jaunsar-Bawar, and idea about the average size of the family in different castes and villages is necessary. Tables 4.1, 4.2 and 4.3 show the composition of the population at Lakhamandal, Lohari and Baila, as well as the size of the family. Lakhamandal is a Brahmin village, while Lohari and Baila are villages where the Rajputs are numerically predominant over the other castes.

Village Lakhamandal (*Table 4.1*): The total population consists of 202 members, and there are 43 families in the village. The average Brahmin family in the village is composed of 5.9 members. The maximum number of families, namely 27, fall in the group composed of 1 to 5 members. The families composed of 6-10 members number 14, and include 8, 2, 4 families of Brahmins, Jagdis and Koltas respectively. The average family in this village consists of 4.7 members.

Village Lohari (*Table 4.2*) : Lohari is again a Rajput village. There are in all four castes–Rajput, Nath, Bajgi and Kolta–in the village. The Rajputs are divided into 32 families, of which 8, 20, 4 fall in the group of 1-5, 6-10, 11-15 members per family respectively. Twelve out of the 21 Kolta families have 1-5 members, while the rest are larger. Bajgis and Naths consist of two families each, all of which belong to the group of 1-5 members per family.

Village Baila (*Table 4.3*): Baila is predominantly a Rajput village, for they compose 48 per cent of the total number of families–29 families out of 60. The next group is of the Koltas who have 13 families. But from the point of view of the population the Rajputs are still more important, because, although they claim only 48 per cent of the total number of families, they form 59 per cent of the total population. The Kolta families are 21.7 per cent of the total, while they constitute only 16.2 per cent of the total population. There are 29 families in the village under the group of families composed of 1-5 members.

The next highest number of families, 23, are composed of 6-10 members. There is one Rajput family of more than 16 members. The majority of Rajput families have 6-10 members. This group of families constituted 38.3 per cent of the total Rajput families in the village. As far as the Koltas are concerned, the majority of the families, 9 in number, have a size of 1-5 members. The average family of the village, however, consists of 6.5 members.

Pressure on Land

At Lakhamandal the people have nearly five members per family while at Baila the average works out at 6.5 members per family. Cultivation is the most important means of satisfying the needs for staple food crops, including wheat, rice, pulse, and vegetables. The fats and vegetable oils consumed by the villages are also produced in the fields.

The family economy and the organizational control vary considerably according to caste. The land owned by Rajputs in Lohari averages about 7 acres per family. Out of 20 families of Koltas only 11 possess land, and that too at less than 1 acre per family. Out of the 11 Kolta families who possess land, only one Kishiaru owns 3.47 acres, and Tolu 1.11 acres, the rest possess less than 1 acre of land. Out of 30 Rajput families 13 have their own Koltas. The average holding for Bajgis and Naths also works out at less than 1 acre per family.

Table 4.4 reveals that 10 out of 21, that is, 47.6 per cent of Kolta families own no land. They are 17.5 per cent of the total number of families (57) in the village. There are

Table 4.1

Size of Family at Lakhamandal (December 1957)

No. of Family Members	Brahmin		*Rajput*	*Jagdi*	*Badi*	*Bajgi*	*Kolta*		*Others†*	*Total*	
	*fr.**	%*	*fr.*	*fr.*	*fr.*	*fr.*	*fr*	%	*fr.*	*fr.*	%
1-5	11	52.4	2	-	1	1	11	73.3	1	27	62.8
6-10	8	38.1	-	2	-	-	4	26.7	-	14	32.6
11-15	2	9.5	-	-	-	-	-	-	-	.2	4.6
Total	**21**	**100.0**	**2**	**2**	**1**	**1**	**15**	**100.0**	**1**	**43**	**100.0**

*fr. = frequency or number of families; % = percentage

† including the family of a Sindhi shop keeper

Total number of families in the village = 43. Total population = 202

Average number of persons per family = 4.7

Table 4.2
Size of Family at Lohari (December 1957)

No. of Family Members	Rajput		Nath		Bajgi		Kolta		Total	
	fr.	%	*fr.*	%	*fr.*	%	*fr.*	%	*fr.*	%
1-5	8	25.0	2	-	2	-	12	57.1	24	42.1
6-10	20	62.8	-	-	-	-	9	42.9	29	51.9
11-15	4	12.3	-	-	-	-	-	-	4	7.9
Total	**32**	**100.0**	**2**	**-**	**2**	**-**	**21**	**100.0**	**57**	**100.0**

Total number of families in the village = 57, Total population = 369
Average number of persons per family = 6.5

Table 4.3
Size of Family at Baila (December 1957)

No. of Family Members	*Rajput*		*Brahmin*	*Badi*	*Sunar*	*Bajgi*	*Kolta*		*Total*	
	fr.	%	*fr.*	*fr.*	*fr.*	*fr.*	*fr.*	%	*fr.*	%
1-5	10	34.5	-	4	2	4	9	69.2	29	48.3
6-10	12	41.4	1	4	-	3	3	23.1	23	38.3
11-15	6	20.7	-	-	-	-	1	7.7	7	11.7
16-20	1	3.4	-	-	-	-	-	-	1	1.7
Total	**29**	**100.0**	**1**	**8**	**2**	**7**	**13**	**100.0**	**60**	**100.0**

Total number of families in the village = 60, Total population = 390
Average number of persons per family = 6.5

9 families, one of Jagra and 8 of Koltas, who own land below 5 acres. Of the total number of families in the village, these 9 account for 15.8 per cent. There are only 2 families, one of Bajgi and the other of Kolta, owning between 0.5 and 0.9 acre of land of those whose holdings are of the size of 1.0 to 4.9 acres. There are 15 families (26.3 per cent of the total number of families).

The horizontal study of the table further shows that there are 15 families of Rajputs who own 5.0-9.9 acres, and 6 families owning 10 acres and above of agricultural land, forming 26.3 per cent and 10.6 per cent of the total number of their families. The vertical study of Table 4.4 reveals the position of different castes–that out of 32 Rajput families, 34.4 per cent, 46.9 per cent and 18.7 per cent own land of areas of 1.0 to 4.9 acres, 5.0 to 9.9 acres, and 10 acres and above, respectively. Thus, 65 per cent of the Rajput families own more than 5 acres of land. There are two Jagra families in the village with only very meagre land at their disposal. One family owns even less than half acre while the other falls in the group of 1.0 to 4.9 acres. Out of 2 Bajgi families, one owns less than one acre of land, while the other possess less than five acres of land.

Kolta Families

As far as Koltas are concerned their position is most miserable in this respect. Nearly half of the Koltas, i.e., 47.6 per cent (10 families) have no land. They earn their living by attaching themselves to some of the higher caste families in the village. Nine families own land of less than one acre each. Only 2 out of the 21 Kolta families (9.5 per cent of the total) have land between 1.0 to 4.9 acres. Kishiaru Kolta has the largest slice, 3.47 acres.

A large family can live when there is ample space. Lower castes have these space constraints, whereas the upper classes have no such reason to split the families. Therefore, the higher castes have larger joint families than the lower castes. Rajputs in Lohari have larger joint families than the Koltas who very infrequently have more than two to three persons in their families. Just as the higher castes own more land, so also they own more cattle than the lower castes. They are well off and can afford to keep a large number of cattle. They construct and maintain cattle sheds where needed. Table 4.5 shows the caste-wise ownership of the livestock in the village Baila.

Features of Different Castes

The horizontal study of Table 4.5 reveals some important features of the life of different castes in Jaunsar-Bawar. There is only one Brahmin family in the village Baila and it owns 18 cattle (6 bulls, 7 cows and 5 calves), other livestock, viz. sheep and goat total 42. Virtually it is the Rajputs who are the masters of land and cattle. Only 29 Rajput families possess 670 sheep and 635 goats, totalling 1,305, compared to 13 Kolta families which own only 58 sheep and 59 goats.

The number of Kolta families is nearly half; they possess only one-twelfth the number of goats and sheep owned by the Rajputs. The position with regard to cattle possessed by the Rajputs and the Koltas is not very different either. The former own a total of 346 cows, calves and bulls, while the latter have only 74 in all. There are 2 *sunar* (goldsmith) families in the village which do not own any cattle. It is only the Koltas or the lower castes who possess pigs and fowls.

Reading the table vertically, there are 735 sheep and 799 goats in the village. The total number of cattle is 540. Thus, the number of cattle is much less than the number of sheep and goats. The total number of pigs tamed by the Koltas is 28, while there are 63 fowls in the village. It is obvious that the lower caste families have to depend upon the high caste people of the village for their livelihood.

Family Budget

Taking a family of ten adults as the base, the daily food consumption comes to 15 seers, that is, some 140 maunds per year. This does not include additional expenditure during the festivals. Vegetables used are generally what grows in the jungles on the scorpion grass, but now a few of the families have their own kitchen gardens. Pulses are also grown.

Self-sufficient Economy

In the areas under study, the people are practicing a self-sufficient economy for most of their requirements. In the domestic economy of these hill agriculturists, a large part of their needs is met from the produce of their fields, such as the foodgrains and vegetables; fuel is available in the jungles and wool from the sheep. It becomes very difficult, if not impossible, to evaluate the different items of consumption in terms of money. The items of the family budget are foodgrains–wheat, rice, barley, *manduwa, jhanjhora* and other food cereals; pulses–*moong, urd, masoor,* and unspecified pulses; milk and fats–ghee, mustard oil, milk, butter, curd, whey; vegetables and fruits–green fruits and dry fruits; animal food–meat, fish, egg, pig and fowl; salt and spices–pickles; miscellaneous items–sugar, gur and tea. Clothing implies expenditure of three types–apparel, bedding and miscellaneous.

Women's Needs

A woman needs at least two *ghagras*, two *kurtis* and two *dhantu* per year, in addition to a woollen *jhoga* every third or fourth year. Fuel and light are not an expensive item, because most of the fuel needed for the family consumption is fetched from the jungles. It is only on kerosene oil and match-boxes that one has to spend money. They generally use small lamps and for only a few hours in the night, say from 7-30 to 9-00 p.m. Furniture and

Table 4.4

Land-Holding Among the Villagers of Lohari (1957)

Size of Landholding (in acres)	*Rajput*		*Nath*		*Bajgi*		*Kolta*		*Total*	
	*fr.**	*%**	*fr.*	*%*	*fr.*	*%*	*fr.*	*%*	*fr.*	*%*
Landless	-	-	-	-	-	-	10	47.6	10	17.5
Below 0.5	-	-	1	50.0	-	-	8	38.1	9	15.8
0.5-0.9	-	-	-	-	1	50.0	1	4.8	2	3.5
1.0-4.9	11	34.4	1	50.0	1	50.0	2	9.5	15	26.3
5.0-9.9	15	46.9	-	-	-	-	-	-	15	26.3
10.0 and above	6	18.7	-	-	-	-	-	-	6	10.6
Total	**32**	**100.0**	**2**	**100.0**	**2**	**100.0**	**21**	**100.0**	**57**	**100.0**

*fr. = frequency; % = percentage.

equipment are costly items, because they involve lots of labour to produce.

Although the *deodar* slippers are available to them from the jungles, the cost of transporting them up to the village, and then the wages of the carpenter become too much, and once a man resolves to build a house, it is usually seen that for the time being the family economy is completely upset. Utensils and pots are either purchased from Chakrata or from the traders who often visit the villages. Tobacco is used in large quantities by everybody, except by small children, no matter whether male or female. Tobacco is grown by the villagers themselves; only molasses, one or two tins, are purchased from the market.

People have developed a taste for cigarettes. Because cigarettes and *bidis* are easier to carry than tobacco, *chillum* and *agchyar*. They are widely used, at least on the fields and during festivals. Other sources of expenditure are recreation, festivals and social ceremonies, and drinks.

Table 4.6 gives the production of most important grains consumed by the villagers at Baila; the quantity is shown in local measures.

When it comes to cultivation and farming, it is only the Rajputs, the Brahmins who actually produce some surplus. Other castes produce only meagre quantities. The Rajputs produced 106 *bojhas* of wheat, while the Sunars, the Badis, the Bajgis and the Koltas together produced only 40 *bojhas*. Similar is the case with respect to the other grains, barely, rice, maize, *manduwa*, *cholai* and *kauni*. Naturally, when it is only the Rajputs who produce most of the grain of the village, they acquire a superior position.

Landless Koltas

The miserable Koltas hardly possess any land and have to slave for those who have the land and the produce. The two Sunar families in the village do not produce much,

Table 4.5

Livestock Owned by the Villagers of Baila (1957)

Caste	*No. of Families*	*Sheep*	*Goat*	*Cattle*			*Pig*	*Fowl*
				Cows	*Calves*	*Bulls*		
Brahmin	1 (1.6%)	7	35	7	5	6	-	-
Rajput	29(48.3%)	670	635	126	116	104	-	-
Sunar	2 (3.3%)	-	-	-	-	-	-	-
Badi	8 (13.3%)	-	21	21	20	19	-	-
Bajgi	7 (11.6%)	-	49	19	12	11	-	46
Kolta	13 (21.6%)	58	59	23	27	24	28	17
Total	**60**	**735**	**799**	**196**	**180**	**164**	**28**	**63**

because they earn their livelihood not through agriculture, but through goldsmithy. They own just two or three fields adjoining the village. The Badi and the Bajgi also get a major share of their cereal needs from those whom they serve. The Rajputs of the village say that they find it difficult to meet the requirements of other castes who depend on them for support. Besides this, on an average, a middle class family needs at least 40 maunds of grain (*manduwa* or barley) for distilling.

The zamindars who are the major producers, have to keep the grain reserved for festivals and social ceremonies. All this becomes too heavy a burden for the land to support, and the people have to depend on purchases from outside. Besides the grains, there are many other things which the villagers consume but do not produce; neither are these things available locally. Table 4.7 shows the purchases from outside either from Chakrata or from the village shops.

Dependence on Local Traders

There are many items of daily consumption for which the villagers have to depend on the Chakrata or the local trader. This is shown in Table 4.7. Other items of goods brought from are clothes, utensils, and other miscellaneous things. A very significant fact emerges when we compare the purchasing power of the Koltas with that of other castes. The Koltas are divided into 13 families, but their purchasing power is very low. Both the Bajgi and Badi who altogether constitute 15 families consume 13 tins of molasses while the Koltas (13 families) take only one-third of it, i.e., 4 tins.

Heaviest Consumers

The heaviest consumption of the various things bought from outside is by Rajputs; they make more than the total purchases of all castes taken together as far as the consumption of salt is concerned. As salt is needed for the cattle, it is purchased in large quantities.

Table 4.6
Production of Main Crops in Baila (1956-57)

Caste	*No. of Families*	*Wheat*	*Barley*	*Rice*	*Maize*	*Manduwa*	*Cholai*	*Kaumi*
Brahmin	1	5 Bojha	6 Bojha	8 Bojha	8 Bojha	4 Bojha	Bojha	-
Rajput	29	106 Bojha	159 Bojha	222 Bojha	180 Bojha	109 Bojha	4 Bojha	3 Bojha & 3 Patha
Sunar	2	1 Doon	2 Doon	2 Doon	2 Doon	1 ½ Doon	-	-
Badi	8	21 Bojha & 15 Patha	22 Bojha & 3 Patha	21 Bojha	13 Bojha & 3 Patha	9 Bojha	5 Patha	4 Patha
Bajgi	7	9 Bojha	21 Bojha	26 Bojha	32 Bojha	15 Bojha	2 Doon	4 Patha
Kolta	13	9 Bojha & 30 Patha	20 Bojha & 3 Patha	17 Bojha	31 Bojha	20 Bojha	22 Patha	6 Patha
Total	**60**	**150 Bojha & 53 Patha**	**228 Bojha & 3 Patha**	**294 Bojha & 22 Patha**	**264 Bojha & 19 Patha**	**157 Bojha & 12 Patha**	**7 Bojha & 43 Patha**	**3 Bojha & 17 Patha**

Approximate weights: 1 Bojha = 1 ½ maunds; 1 Doon = 8 Patha; 1 Patha = 1 ½ seers; 1 seer = 2.2 lb.

Dalloo gave a rough idea about the salt needed per month for the cattle and sheep: 5 seers per 50 sheep; 5 seers per 12 cattle; 5 seers per 50 goats. Thus, for 100 sheep and goats and 12 cattle, one needs at least 15 seers of salt per month. The Rajputs own a major part of the 735 sheep, 800 goats and 540 cattle in the village. The heavy consumption of salt is due to cattle and sheep.

Material Culture

Multi-Storeyed Houses

Bricks are not available in these tracts. Stone is there in plenty. The first and second storeys of the houses are invariably made partly of stone and partly of *deodar* (cedar) wood, while the uppermost storey is exclusively made of wood. A typical Jaunsari multi-storeyed house (Sayana Dev Ram's residence, Baila) is shown on Plate 1. The various storeys and apartments are described below:

(a) *Dobra* or *Dobri*. This is the underground apartment (basement) of the house and is used for storing grains, cereals and valuable possessions like guns, cartridges and swords. It is made of stone slabs. The inner walls of a *dobri* are usually white-washed with clay lime.

(b) *Obra*. Above the basement (*dobra*) is *obra*, often referred to as *obru*. Its walls are made of stones while the roof is wooden. This is because just above it is the uppermost or next wooden storey on the top. The height of *obra* is hardly more than 6 feet. Very often, but not necessarily, the people construct a gallery supported by carved wooden pillars around the *obra*. The breadth of this gallery is never more than 3 or 4 feet.

Obra is utilized for keeping *giltas* and *topra* (kinds of basket), *supa*, fishing net (if the family has any), ropes, bags, *parat*, *bantas* (water vessels), other extra utensils and pots,

Table 4.7

A Rough Estimate of Villagers' Purchases From Outside Baila (1956-57)

Caste	*No. of Families*	*Salt (mds.)*	*Gur (mds.)*	*Mustard oil (tin)*	*Kerosene oil (tin)*	*Molasses (tin)*	*Tea (lb.)*	*Remarks*
Rajput	29	45	15 mds.	9	3	29	3	Some other it
Brahmin	1	2	10 srs.	½	-	1	½	items of purchases
Badi	8	7 ½	3 ½ mds.	3	-	7	2 ¼	are spices,
cigarettes,								
Sunar	2	3	16 srs.	1	-	1	¼	matches, sweets,
etc.								
Bajgi	7	6	2 ½ mds.	1 ½	1 ½	6	½	
Kolta	13	7	3 mds.	2 ½	1	4	½	
Total	**60**	**70 ½**	**24 mds.**					
			26 srs.	**17 ½**	**5 ½**	**48**	**7**	

boxes, and other things not needed in day-to-day life. It is a sort of general store. A portion of the *obra* is meant to keep such corns and provisions as are to be used currently. This portion of the *obra* is called *kuthar*.

The rich people have their *kuthar* (store-room) separate from the main dwelling. In Lakhamandal, however, there is no such separate *kuthar*. When the *obra* is not used for storing grains and provisions, it is usual to keep goats and sheep there. A circular hole, usually one and a half feet in diameter on the roof of the *obra* in the corner just opposite the kitchen. The lower caste people, such as Badi, Bajgi and Nath, who are allowed to enter the house but not the kitchen, can go up.

(c) *Manjia*. The next storey is called the *manjia*. It is made partly of wood and partly of stone. The walls are made of thin slates, while the roof is wooden. It is not usual to have *manjia* except when one has large property, and many members in the family. This portion of the house is also utilized for storing grains and keeping family property. In the *manjia* are kept the beddings and extra clothes.

(d) *Baur*. It is the topmost apartment in a Jaunsar house. It is made exclusively of *deodar* wood. The walls are one and a half feet wide and kept hollow and partitioned for keeping the family property, beddings, clothes and other necessary things not meant to be shown to others. The *baur* is accessible through a wooden ladder from the attached courtyard (*angan*) of the house.

The *Baur* and the Kitchen

The guests and friends are entertained in the *baur*. Therefore, it is well decorated with artifacts depending on the financial status of the family head. As a rule, the kitchen is always in the uppermost storey projecting outside. The kitchen occupies a corner known as *rasora* or *chauka*. On the two sides of the *baur* are about a yard wide galleries called *ataris*. The *atari* at the back of the house is partitioned in two: one part is utilized for keeping the sacrificial goat in a closed apartment, as also the water vessels, and the other half of the *atari* is used as a bathroom. The front *atari* is reached by a ladder. If the family is large, this may be utilized for sleeping purposes.

The Front Gallery

This front gallery is decorated with carved images painted with different colours. It is in the *baur* that all the spices, ghee, and other edibles are kept. The beddings are also kept there. Parallel to each other, there are two raised platforms about 6 inches high on the remaining two wall-sides. They are utilized for seating and sleeping purposes. Whenever any guest or relative comes, he is seated on these platforms called *tekri*. The *baur* is a drawing, sleeping and dining room, all rolled into one.

There are two fixed wooden brackets in two of the walls of the *baur* on top of the doors. These are called *kedaru* where the idols of the family gods are kept. The walls and roof have small openings called *sindhai* or *tira* which serve the purpose of windows. They let in the light and allow the smoke to go out of the house. It is usual to refer to the roof-openings as *sindhai* and to the wall-openings as *tira*.

Two-sloped Roof

Rain and snow are frequent visitors. So that water flows down from the roof easily, it has to be sloped. With the square wooden structure, the roof of a Jaunsari house is always two-sloped, made of wooden slippers. The slippers are shouldered on very long bars of pine wood. These wooden slippers are covered with slate slabs, when they are available. At Lakhamandal, slates of very big sizes are available just in the vicinity, hardly a furlong away from the village. All the entrances and doors in the houses are very narrow and small. One has to stoop down before he can enter the apartment. Usually the dimensions of the entrances are 1 foot 9 inches by 3 feet 1 inch.

Expensive Residence

An average earning man who wants to build a house cannot afford *kura*. The wooden slippers are brought from the jungles far off, sometimes not less than ten or twelve miles from the villages. The Badis do the carpentry work. The day the Badi starts work, he gets his meals at the employer's house. An idea about the heavy expenditure involved may be formed by the following account of a (Darduna) cooperative labour which was needed for executing a formidable task with the help of villagers. Daya Ram Sayana of Baila needed some flat slate stones for the roof of his newly built house. He first asked a few Koltas to go to Chila top, prepare the stones required, and then pile them up. Finding the task beyond himself and his family members, he arranged for a 'Darduna'. Accordingly, the villagers were invited to cooperate. Those who did, belonged to the villages Baila, Bulad, Bagi and Didakheda. One man could make in a whole day only two rounds from Chila, a hilltop, up to the village; 26 members cooperated in this task.

5 from the village Bulad, 1 Brahmin and 4 Rajputs

2 from the village Bagi, both Brahmins

4 from the village Didakheda, all Koltas

15 from the village Baila, 9 Rajputs, 4 Badis, one Kolta and one Gurkha

Throughout the day the men were busy fetching slate slabs from the hilltop, while the women were occupied in the preparation of the dinner that was to be served to the 'Darduniya'–those who cooperated.

A Grand Dinner

The participants were given a dinner the same day, after which they danced and sang in the courtyard of the village temple. The dinner cost about Rs. 200.

All the Darduniya were served with two large spoonfuls of ghee. Those who did not take liquor were provided with one extra spoon of ghee. Meat was prepared in ghee, and served with ghee rice. The total cost worked out as follows:

Liquor 36 bottles	Rs. 72. at the rate of Rs. 2 per bottle
Ghee 8 seers	Rs. 32 at the rate of Rs. 4 per seer
Goats 2	Rs. 75
Rice and Flour	Rs. 21
	Rs. 200

Thus, the cost of covering the roof with the slates was Rs. 200. All the requisites for the construction had to be managed, partly by cooperative labour, and partly by the family. It is a difficult job to arrange for the stones and wooden slippers to be strong enough to support the storeys. The walls are usually one and a half feet in width. Daya Ram said that from its inception to the day when the first feast was given to the villagers after the completion of the house, it cost several thousand rupees.

Recent Changes: A Kolta can Own a House Now

Up to quite recent times, only the higher castes, and a few of the artisan castes who were well-to-do, could afford to own houses. Many rich Brahmins and Rajputs have two or more houses, but the Kolta could not afford to build any. Since the inception of the C.D.P., the Koltas have been given loans for construction of houses. They were granted 50 per cent of the total cost of the house, but the plan of the house had to be passed by the District Board, Dehradun.

School Buildings

A change in the design of construction has been brought about by the school buildings, Panchayat Ghar and Seed Stores, built by the District Board, C.D.P. and other Departments. The doors are bigger than the traditional Jaunsar doors. Even their design, windows, and roofs are different. In many cases the villagers have adopted these new styles. Permanand of Lakhamandal built his house very recently with long apartments, unlike the usual Jaunsari pattern, and kept big entrances, about 6 feet high and 1¼ yards in width.

Dress, Ornaments and Body Decoration

Jaunsaris are fond of good clothes. They are among the best dressed people in the Himalayas. The males and the females of course dress differently. The dresses for festivals and for daily use also differ. The altitude of the village counts for much. In the villages situated at comparatively higher altitudes, for example Lohari, Kandi, Kandoi, Chultad, Ghanta, Kuna, most of the clothes needed are woollen, as cotton clothes may only be used for two or three months in a year. On the other hand, the people of the villages situated on the lower reaches wear mostly cotton clothes, while woollen clothes are used only in the few months of cold winters. The male and female dresses are given below.

Men's Dress

(a) *Winter Dress. (1) Chola.* Also called *thalka* or *loiya.* A very big sized coat made by stitching together the narrow strips of woollen cloth woven from homespun wool. It is tailored by local tailors. Quite loose, without buttons, it is worn like a double breasted coat, tied to which around the waist is another very long piece of cloth.

(2) *Jhangel.* Made from homespun wool and stitched at home. It looks like the *chooridar pyjama* of the plains.

(3) *Safa.* Above the loose coat they tie around the waist a cotton or woollen strip.

(4) *Snow Shoes.* On the higher altitudes it is usual to wear a special type of shoe called *khursa.* Its sole is made of leather while the uppers are woven by the villagers themselves with woollen thread.

(b) *Summer Dress.* During the summer months, on the lower altitudes villagers usually wear the following.

(1) *Shirt.* This is quite long reaching down to the thighs. It is stitched by the village tailor and is similar in design to the shirt of the plains. It is called *jhoga.*

(2) *Jhangel.* Cotton *jhangel* is put on during the hot weather, or when one goes to one's relations or to markets. While working in the fields, the *jhangel* is removed, and instead a small knicker or loincloth is used.

(c) *Other Accessories.* (1) *Digwa* or Cap. *Digwa* is the traditional Jaunsari headwear made of woollen cloth. It is round and its edges are folded. Long hairs and *digwa* have been the tradition, but now because of their contacts with outsiders, Jaunsaris have started wearing Gandhi cap.

(1) *Shoes.* Shoes, either the *chamraudha,* or boot, are put on only when one goes to market or to other villages or to attend some social function, say a *mela* or a marriage.

(2) Whether winter or summer, a typical Jaunsari will always be found with his *chola* either on his shoulders when not wearing it, or put on in a decent manner.

Women's Dress

(1) *Ghagra*: A very loose skirt bordered with lace and *tul* cloth, resembling the petticoat, but it is not an under-garment.

(2) *Kurti*: Shirt.

(3) Dhantu: Net (*jali*) handkerchief used as headwear.

(4) *Khilka* or *Mekhra*: A woollen coat.

It is usual to have the *ghagra* of blue cotton drill and black *dhantu*, although the latter may be very often found in gay colours. For daily use, the *kurti* and *ghagra* are patched at many places but the ladies always keep one reserved for festivals and *melas*. Thus, a woman needs two *ghagras* and two *kurtis* per year. *Ghagra* needs 7 yards of cloth while the *kurti* can be made from three yards. *Mekhra* is made of homespun wool.

(5) Women also put on shoes made by the local cobblers. But these are used only when one goes to, or comes from one's husbands' village.

Children's Dress

Children wear only a shirt and *chora* in the summer and a woollen *jhangel* during the winter. It is usually seen that a child above ten years of age wears a cap.

Special Dresses

At religious and social ceremonies people wear a special dancing dress called *joda*. It is white and covers the whole of the body from neck to the heel and opens in front to be tied with laces after wearing. Similarly, the women folk have special dresses which they put on while dancing.

Time for New Dresses

Men, women and children prefer to get the new dresses tailored on the eve of Bissu, Dewali or Manr festivals. Mostly the tailors belong to the village.

Ornaments

The Jaunsari women have great fascination for ornaments. They are attracted by the ornaments so irresistibly that very often divorce is resorted to on the ground of the inability of a husband to provide ornaments for his wife. In Baila, Supa's daughter-in-law was not ready to come to her *shasurari*, parent-in-law's village, only because she was not given a golden nose-ring. It was only after she got it that she agreed to do so. Kammo (of Baila) is married in the village Buraila but refuses to go there because they are not providing her with the desired ornaments. Bardei of Lakhamandal also gave a similar excuse for not going to her husbands' village.

Table 4.8
Ornaments Worn by Women

S. No.	*Local Name of the Ornament*	*English Equivalent*	*Metal of Which it is Made*	*Approximate Weight*
1.	Sanutia	A number of hair-pins joined together	Gold or silver	4-5 tolas
2.	Utraya	Ear Studs	Gold or silver	5-6 tolas
3.	Labia or Mukri	Ear-rings	Gold	2 tolas
4.	Nath	Nose ring	Gold	3-4 tolas
5.	Bulak*	Nose pendant	Gold	1 tola
6.	Pulli	A kind of nose ornaments	Gold	3 As. To 4 As.
7.	Kanduri	Neck ornament	Silver	12 tolas
8.	Kanthi	Neck ornament	Silver	12 to 16 tolas
9.	Tabil or Tait	Necklace	Silver	40-60 tolas
10.	Bid	Locket	Silver	4-6 tolas
11.	Kangutye or Dhagutye	Bracelet	Silver	30-40 tolas
12.	Chura	Wristlet	Silver	30-40 tolas
13.	Churiyat	Bangles	Silver	20 tolas
14.	Pali	An ornamental ring worn on toes	Silver	½ tola

* In Bawar Pargana, women do not appreciate wearing 'Bulak'. Most of the ladies were observed not to have asked their husbands or fathers to get it. But in the lower Jaunsar region, it is as common as other ornaments—are, and goes hand-in-hand with 'Nath' (No. 4).

† Another point of note is that it is a custom to wear.

No Preference for Ornaments

Men do not like ornaments but sometimes one may find a man wearing an earring. Nowadays this is not favoured, although men still their earlobes perforated. They believe that if this is not done ghosts and other evil spirits are likely to perforate the ear after the die. Table 4.8 gives a list of ornaments worn by women.

It is said that about two or three decades ago men also used to wear certain ornaments, but the fashion has now disappeared. The ornaments which men used to wear were:

(a) *Kantha*–Ornament for the neck, made of silver

(b) *Murkiya*–Gold ear-rings

(c) *Kanguta*–Silver bracelets

(d) Gold chains fitted in *digwa* cap

But men are now very rarely seen wearing any ornaments. Rather, they feel embarrassed if they are asked to put on one.

Restrictions Lifted

Wearing gold ornaments, for centuries, was the preserve of high castes. Koltas could not wear gold ornaments. Even if they were prosperous and could afford to buy gold, they were not allowed to wear them. However, the times have changed. Now there is no restriction to their wearing gold, although in the Bawar region the people still stick to the convention. Invariably, the higher castes deprecate this practice on the part of the untouchables. The Koltas in Lakhamandal area who carry on the Chakla business wear golden ornaments. At first, the higher castes protested against this but no one listened to them.

Sri Chand, Pradhan of Gram Sabha of Nada, is quite intelligent. Realizing the social evil and looking up of money involved in the use of ornaments, he moved a resolution that people should stop wearing them. He argued that if the money blocked in ornaments was released for developmental purposes by purchasing capital goods for agriculture or cattle, it would add to their material prosperity. He was successful in his attempts at least in his village Nada, and most of the families abandoned the practice, but the effect was temporary only.

Food, Drink and Smoke

Food

Rice and wheat are the chief food crops, supplemented by coarse grains like *manduwa*, *jhanjora* and *kauni*. As a matter of fact, the Jaunsaris have a custom of taking coarse-grain preparation in the morning and bread of wheat flour in the evening.

The normal food items are about the same for all classes—rich, middle or poor, with the difference that the poor cannot afford milk, curd and butter, nor superior grains. Actually the preparations vary according to the seasonal crops. Since the people live a self-sufficient economy, they have to change the menu according to the availability of the grain and other cereals.

Meat is not commonly taken except at festivals or when a goat is sacrificed at the instance of the Pandit or diviner for the propitiation of some angry deity, or when some goat had died of an accident.

Dietary Routine

Three meals a day is the rule found among the villagers of Lohari and Baila, both in winter and in summer, whereas at Lakhamandal people often take four meals daily. The meals are known by local names, as shown below, together with their timings.

(a) *Kaliyari* (Morning Meal). It is taken early in the morning, or at about 7 or 8 a.m.

(b) *Dopahri* (Midday Meal). It is taken at noon, and is usually served in the field where one is working.

(c) *Tinoli* (Afternoon Meal). It is taken at about 4 p.m., when one comes back from the field or jungles.

(d) *Byai* or *Biao* (Supper). It is the dinner or the main meal of the day, and is the only meal in which all family members participate. It is served at about 8 p.m.

In the case of a three-meal routine, there are no separate meals as *dopahri* and *kaliyari*, but a morning meal served at 8 or 9 a.m., though those who go out for grazing or field work may eat earlier. The timings may vary slightly according to individual convenience as well as according to seasons. Children may be given food at an earlier hour, and they may also take more meals in a day.

It is a local convention that the 'Nahani', namely, one who had a sacred bath in the Ganga at Hardwar, and who is usually the eldest member of the house, takes only two meals—the *kaliyari* and the *biao*. If he, because of mistake or unavoidable circumstances, eats more than twice a day, he has to purify himself and to offer some *atta* (flour) or *roti* (bread of big size) to the village god.

No Set Pattern for Meals

Apart from that exception, there is no set pattern in the matter of number and timing of the meals. During the season for field work, they have to take four or even five meals in a day, otherwise they may be satisfied with three meals. Generally speaking, the *kaliyari* and *biao* are essential meals to all people and at all times, the *dopahri* is mainly meant for field workers, and the *tinoli* is usually a light refreshment. Not only the season in the year, but also the situation of the village calls for a change or modification in the schedule of the meals. The contents of the meals change as well, according to the varying altitudes and seasons, which affect the agricultural produce.

Food Items and Variations

That the cereals form the main and indispensable item in the menu for every meal was revealed by a sample survey of daily food habits of the people. Next come the vegetables and pulses, besides certain sauces (*chatni*) and pickles. Among the protein foods, ghee (clarified butter) and meat are the most desirable but not readily available delicacies. Instead of milk, whey (*mattha*) is frequently served at the table.

Preference in Cereals

Thick bread (*roti*) made of *manduwa* is found in all meals during all seasons; it is carried to the field for the *dopahri*, and taken with some sauce or vegetable. Wheat *roti* is occasionally prepared and often used at supper (*biao*). Rice is usually served at home in the *kaliyari* and *biao*, and is preferably taken together with ghee or meat, whichever is available. *Chura* (flattened rice) is also frequently used for the *dopahri* and *tinoli*.

There are various kinds of *roti*, such as:

(a) *Chiltra*–very thin bread made of wheat flour.

(b) *Dharoti*–paste made of *masoor* pulse and barley flour.

(c) *Sidi*–steamed wheat bread filled with *masoor*.

(d) *Karao*–fried wheat bread filled with some pulse.

(e) *Misiyar Kadwa*–bread made of maize or *manduwa* and stuffed with pulse, potato, etc.

Sources of Vegetables

Vegetables may be either collected from jungles, such as the scorpion grass (*kushka*) or procured from fields, such as *chaulai* and pumpkin. Potato may be used either as vegetable or as cereal. Onion is occasionally found at the table as a delicacy, but it is only available from the market and not from the fields. As a rule, a vegetable dish is prepared for the meal only when it is available. A *dal* (pulse) may be its substitute, and some sauces (*chatni*) or pickles are often used in the absence of both *dal* and vegetable.

As already mentioned, there is no categorical difference in the dietary routine between the upper and lower classes. A palatable meal may also be expected by a Kolta, as his due share from the high-caste master, whom he serves and from whom he gets his daily meals. Like other villagers, he may also supplement his diet with such items as game, liquor, fruits and some sort of jungle herbs. He is, unlike his social superiors, in an advantageous position in having for variety the flesh of pig and hen, which are often domesticated in his household.

Special Preparations

On day-to-day basis, the food is similar. However, when there are ceremonial occasions or when there are festivals, the type of food made available to the family is certainly different and of better quality. Every seventh day or so, and at the end of every month, when they celebrate the 'Sankrant', the villagers prepare special rice dishes and cook many types of *roti*, like the *ulwa, aska, maskuria, dhindka, chilra* and *khir*. The same things are also prepared whenever a new crop is sown or reaped, just as an offer to the gods. A meal thus prepared in the name of God is known as Nithai.

The Visit to Relatives

During the month-long festival of Magh (January-February) it is a custom in Jaunsar-Bawar to visit one's relatives. For the purpose of entertaining the season's guests, every family sacrifices at least one goat, which is cut into small pieces and hung on a rope in the upper-most storey of the house. It dries there without the use of salt on it. There are other occasions like Bissu, Manr, Dewali, etc., on which goats are sacrificed and used along with other special dishes by the members of the family and the guests together. Marriage is another grand occasion for the Jaunsaris to enjoy their best dishes.

Sanitation, Hygiene and Nutritional Status

However, it was realised during various studies that, climate and geography, belief, isolation and poverty influence attitudes towards health, and illness, to a very great extent. The factors affecting health of the *Jounsaris* can be divided into two. The first category includes the factors which are responsible for fostering diseases in the people and in the second category come all such factors which affect the health of the people in an indirect way including attitudes and customs and some demographic features of the population.

The natural resources that surround human habitations are agents influencing the state of fitness of a community. Use of available natural resources can be of benefit, but improper use or misuse of these will cause a number of problems. A survey of mountain water spring revealed that the *Jaunsaris* suffer from lack of clean water to drink, although water as a cleansing agent and for domestic purposes is obtainable and is not far from their reach. The water is probable heavily polluted due to wastes thrown in it. While the same water at one place is used for drinking, at a nearby place it may be used for washing. The same water resources are used for all purposes. The idea of purity of water conveys hardly anything to *Jaunsaris*, and they make no effort to preserve the cleanliness of drinking water. Therefore, it is possible that contaminated water could result in a number of water-borne diseases, e.g. cholera. Even when people are ill their faeces and vomit are conveyed to the same water resources that are used for all purposes; the clothes of patents are washed in the same water, sometimes their excreta and the dead bodies of cholera affected people, too, are thrown into the running water streams.

Housing

In *Jaunsar-Bawar* area, the houses are nucleated. Despite the abundance of space houses are of very small size, possible due to the cold climate and hilly topography. The houses have hardly any arrangements for light and air, though both are available in abundance. Poor lighting during night hours, absence of suitable exits for smoke, i.e. too much smoke in crowded and ill-ventilated houses may be the cause for prevailing eye troubles. Non-availability of fresh air during night time causes respiratory troubles. The traditional customs, ignorance, illiteracy and poverty on the one hand and the cold climate on the other are the main causes for *Jaunsaris* living in this fashion.

The lack of an efficient drainage system in *Jaunsaris* village causes spawning of germs of different bacterial diseases such as diarrhoea, dysentery, typhoid and paratyphoid fevers. Flies which also breed in the dirty water of ditches may carry the polio virus from sewage to food during the monsoon and this may be aggravated by the habit of defecation in the open. Since *Jaunsaris* do not have a clear idea that these insects are responsible for transmitting diseases, they do not take measures to check insect breeding, just as they do not bother to purify drinking water. *Jaunsaris* are also not aware of that certain diseases may be caused or carried to man through their domestic animals inside the house. So domestication of animals unconsciously plays a definite role in perpetuating an insanitary environment and certain infectious diseases are transmitted by animals through urine, faeces, wool, hair, saliva, etc.

Certain intestinal parasites like tapeworms (taenia) and roundworms (ascaris) complete their life cycle in two stage, (one within cattle and different other animals, and the other in man). In this way, these intestinal parasites infest man. The presence of these domestic animals certainly increases incidence of infection. The bacilli and spores of tetanus (lockjaw) have their natural habitat in the intestines of horses, cattle and certain other domesticated animals. Rabies and plague are known to be transferred to human beings from the other animals. Tapeworms and other intestinal parasites of hogs, cattle, dogs may secondarily infest man. When people cannot effort to spend adequately even on food and clothing, they just do not bother about environmental sanitation.

Here, however, rich and poor alike, do not feel the need to keep their surroundings sanitary and are oblivious that disease and minor ailments would be checked if greater importance was given to sanitation.

Disposal of Excreta

Improper disposal of night soil and human excreta are responsible for direct infection, the contamination of soil or of ground or surface water, and the possibility of disease transference through insect or animals. The habit of going outdoors for defecation is another factor responsible for hookworm infestation. The eggs of hookworms pass out with faeces and are deposited on the soil. These may be scattered to nearby soil by rains and wind. Where the soil is particularly sandy, moist and warm, these eggs may develop into larvae. These larvae usually find their way back into the human body through the skin of the bare foot. The retention of wet soil or mud between the toes greatly causes the larvae's entry into the human body.

Teeth Cleaning

The Jaunsaris tribals bother very little about basic hygienic practices. They appear to be less conscious of the utility of cleaning the teeth. As age increases, the regularity of cleaning the teeth increases with education. We can predict that literacy may bring about a change among Jaunsaris in dental hygiene. The habit of not cleaning the teeth is responsible for the foul breath from their mouth, and may cause tooth decay. Those who clean their teeth with neem *datoom* do not seem to have dental problems.

The habit of bathing, too, is related with climate, belief, and level of literacy. For *Jaunsaris* bathing is more a matter of ritual and means usually throwing a small quantity of water on the body. Due to the cold climate, it is rarely that they take a bath. Most of them do not bath for quite long. Most Jaunsaris do not use soap or any other cleaning agent. Poverty and ignorance are probably responsible for this. The frequency of bathing is higher with increase in education.

A number of skin diseases are often reported among Jaunsaris because they do not clean their skin regularly and properly, scabies and itch being most common. They do not use soap or any other germicide for washing the clothes which is necessary for removing the dirt and killing the germs. The *Koltas* and *Bajgis* who are at the bottom of the caste hierarchy (and economically weaker too) change their clothes once a fortnight or once a month. On the other hand, *Brahmans* and *Rajputs* (economically better of people) have sufficient clothes to change at least once a week. Due to ignorance Jaunsaris do not know the importance of sterilization of instruments used in shaving and hair-cutting.

Besides, other practises prevalent among the people are unhygienic. Jaunsaris always sleep inside the house and due to shortage of space, closed to each other. In such a situation, coupled with the low frequency of bathing, washing and changing of clothes, louse infestation is prevalent among Jaunsaris. Lice are known to be carrier of epidemic typhus and relapsing fever.

Nutrition

Some cultural "blocks" aggravate the basic dietary limitations of that region due to poverty. Among these "blocks" to adequate infant nutrition in West Bengal are those based on the classification of food as "hot" and "cold". Foods classified as *garam* (hot), which include eggs, meat, milk, honey, sugar, and cod liver oil, are not given to children during hot weather (which lasts during a large part of the year) or when children are lasts during a large part of the year) or when children are suffering from illness classified as *garam*. In all of these ways cultural practices add to the already serious limitations in nutritional possibilities open to poor village mother in West Bengal.

In the north Indian village of Chinaura, people "generally believe that it is the adequate quantity of food that is important. The idea of quality is restricted to certain foods recognized to be strengthening...... No distinction is made between protective and energy producing foods. A major gap in the traditional dietary wisdom of tribal and peasant people is their frequent failure to recognize that children have special nutritional needs, both before and after weaning. Too often children are considered, for nutritional purposes, simply as little as adults. For the *Jaunsaris* it is necessary to eat a good quantity of food to maintain their health. They believe that those who do not eat much food will grow weak. A good appetite is directly related with health may any kind of illness restrict or curtail their diet. Sometimes illness, may only partly result in the withdrawal of some food items from their diet. During the lactating period, foods are selected carefully not because of their positive nutritive value, but because they will not give pain to the mother or illness to the child through mother's daily diet milk. The Jaunsaris are non-vegetarians, but the frequency of eating flesh is very low and the overall situation is that the items of their daily diet are derived mostly from plant foods, mainly cereals, pulses, vegetables, oil and fats. The *Jaunsari* diet generally includes cereals while foods which contain protein, such as meat, fish or egg enter rarely into their diet. Among vegetable foods, pulses and nuts are the known rich sources of protein, but *Jaunsaris* do not take an adequate amount of pulses, too, and their diet is unbalanced. The food of most of the people is deficient in protein, certain mineral elements, particularly calcium, and vitamin A, etc. On the other hand, they get a sufficient amount of carbohydrates and fat in their diet, which is necessary for hard and prolonged labour in a cold climate.

The local geography plays an important role in determining the dietary habits of the *Jaunsaris*. Their diet includes all those vegetable foods which are grown in the area, varying from season to season.

Meat is a special delicacy reserved for religious festivals when they may eat meat daily during a month. The children and mothers are given special foods for very limited periods. The semi-solid and solid foods which are given to a child in the initial phase continues upto the age of three years, thereafter they are considered, simply as grown up people and the same items are given with no special nourishing foods added. Pregnant and lactating *Jaunsari* women do not regularly eat food rich enough in vitamin A (milk, eggs, green leafy vegetables, carrots, fruits e.g., papaya and mango are best source of vitamin A) ; vitamin C (oranges, lemons, tomatoes, guava, pawpaw, mango and green vegetables contain a lot of vitamin C) ; and vitamin D (liver, milk, eggyolk, fish liver oils are foods rich in vitamin D) and calcium.

The food eaten by them is low for their nutritional requirements, they do not get the required amount of calories, protein and vitamins in food. Some special dishes given to lactating women, only for a few days after the delivery of the child, also do not fulfil their special needs. Traditional food habits, and poverty are the main causes responsible for an unbalanced diet. Their diet includes seasonal foods which to some extent effect a balance in the diet, but in fact they do not eat sufficient quantities of seasonal foods to make more than a marginal difference. They eat meat regularly in the festive season (and rerely during the rest of the year) not from the nutritional point of view but because it is their custom. Withdrawal of food items from ill people's diet without nutritive substitutes may also be responsible for deficiency.

For example, during stomach ache while a liquid diet is given and coarse cereals are avoided there is no strengthening supplement included. When a person suffers from cold, curds, rice, etc. are avoided and eggs and tea as warming foods, are given according to their classification of hot and cold foods, but not keeping in mind nutritive value. Similarly, in case of heat stroke the patient is given cold food items, e.g. *sharbat*. Special diets, which are given to the children and women could balance the diet to some extent, but actually they do not get it for a reasonably long period, e.g. children are given such foods which are easily digestible, mostly semisolid food upto three years of age and lactating mothers are given nutritive food but for too short a time.

Drinking Liquor

Drinking of home-made liquor, is common among the *Jaunsaris*. While alcoholic drinks are strongly disapproved of by the *Brahmans*, and their intake is regarded as an offence (due to superstition), still *Bajgis*, *Rajputs*, and *Koltas* are addicted to liquor. Among these people, it is held that the use of alcohol or liquor tends to develop a permanent increase in the body activity and a moderate use of liquor increases the power of endurance of the drinker. In fact alcohol is not a stimulant. It depresses all vital organs. It does not stimulate intellect. It does not remove physical tiredness. It causes heat loss. Alcohol is not necessary for any normal human activity. The risks of alcoholism are increased by low-protein high-carbohydrate diet and general habit of over-eating, high incidence of parasitic infections of liver, climatic conditions and strong social disapproval.

In a contrary statement Elwin has written of the NEFA tribals, that "while rice beer is a thing which should not only be banned, but should actually be encouraged, for it is nothing more than a nourishing and palatable soup with a kick in it, there can be little doubt that distilled liquor, which has been positively supported by governments in order to inflate their revenues, is injurious".

Further, that "there are many people, greatly admired by society, who have devoted their entire lives to robbing the tribal folk of what little they have. They turn them into vegetarians and thus take from them an essential item of their diet and give nothing in its place. By introducing prohibition among them they rob them of a *much needed tonic*.." Hence a regular and moderate use of local beer among the Jaunsaris may act as an appetiser, and counteract the effect of highly contaminated drinking water, help to check stomach diseases and keep the digestion healthy. On the other hand, the excessive use of distilled liquor is bound to be injurious to health and responsible for the prevalence of disease. There is a *Jaunsaris* belief that excessive drinking is responsible for tuberculosis.

Smoking also has a causal relationship to lungs cancer and other cancers, cardiovascular diseases, respiratory diseases, gastro-duodenal ulcer, etc. Heavy smokers are over 20 times more likely to develop lung cancer than non-smokers. The risk is 10 times more for average smokers. Several studies have shown that the children of parents who smoke are more liable to chest illness than the children of parents who do not smoke. The risk increases with the number of bidis smoked daily by the pregnant women. Smoking of *bidis*, *hukka*, *chilam*, as well as cigarettes is quite popular among the *Jaunsaris*. Not only males, but females and children smoke abundantly.

The habit of smoking *hukka* is comparatively less harmful than the smoking of bidis or cigarettes, because a part of the nicotine is absorbed by water. They not only smoke outside the house but inside too. In this way, the spread of the 'habit' may be likened to a communicable disease, the agent being cigarette or any other smoke. All those who smoke are carriers and endanger the unaffected, i.e., non-smokers. The habit of smoking among pregnant women is a risk to unborn children. Thus, a number of *Jaunsaris* suffering from respiratory diseases may be due to excessive smoking. There is a folk belief that tuberculosis can be caused by excessive smoking, still they do not give up smoking, even after having contracted the disease.

Curing through Magic and Sorcery

According of Jaunsari beliefs the causes of illness are classified into these categories:

(1) Diseases produce exclusively by supernatural powers including divine wrath e.g., wrath of gods and goddesses, sins, crimes, disobedience of religious laws, evil-eye, witch and sorcerer and non-divine wrath e.g., evil spirit and ghost intrusion.

(2) Diseases produced by natural and non-supernatural means.

A "health care" system is concerned with the ways in which people organize to care for the patients and to utilize disease 'knowledge' to aid the patient. This system involves the interaction of number of people, minimally the patient and curer. Diseases recognized to be produced by any of the three means" viz. supernatural, magical, natural (non-supernatural) are cured in different ways and the cures are found to be very effective in such cases (Table 1).

In case of illnesses caused by supernatural means, gods have to be placated by burnt offerings and sacrifices and the machinations of evil spirits have to be counteracted by spells. The practice of this medicine has mystical, and religious elements, they are an essential part of the armoury of the quack and faith healer.

Table 1 : Cures Seen/Heard for the Diseases Caused by Supernatural and Magical Agencies

Sl. No.	*Name of illness*	*Cures seen*	*Heard*
1.	*Matri* (evil spirit)	196	104
2.	*Jimbhoot* (evil spirit)	195	105
3.	*Opra* (evil sprit)	190	110
4.	Chaad rooiain (evil sprit)	192	108
5.	Bhoot paret (ghost intrusion)	196	104
6.	*Raag* (evil-eye)	196	104
7.	*Dankan* (witch)	190	110
8.	*Pishaach* (sorceress)	190	190

Thus, it is clear that the diseases cured by offerings, sacrifices, mystical and magical means have been seen cured by a great number of people. There are also persons who have themselves only heard of them. In case of diseases caused by magical means, *magical medicine* has been utilised for cures. In most of diseases recognised to be produced by natural means specific indigenous medicines (herbs) are commonly used. Some of which are really quite effective. *Jaunsaris* have an extensive knowledge of drugs which they gained by bitter experience (many men must have died in the process).

Their faith in drugs was probably strengthened with recoveries from illness, many times in succession. *Jaunsaris* individually are usually not very clear in their ideas of health, disease and treatment. They depend upon the advice of their village elders, etc. and advice from several persons may be solicited simultaneously. Thus, their health care system is an informal and indefined system, with no individual cures for many ailments. Isolation of patient and special arrangements for ill people are almost never prescribed. Interviews between curer and patient, or exclusive treatment directed by the curer are also rarely seen. Among these people in fact most of the customs and practices with regard to health and disease have no modern scientific basis, yet indigenous medicine is successful in a limited manner. If the patients are cured by indigenous medicine the credit is given to the treatment applied; if it fails, the reason is not that the treatment was wrong but that the patient was beyond help.

The effectiveness of the indigenous medicine in the area may be because a number of effective factors are found in it e.g., massage, blood-letting, bone-setting, and certain efficacious *materia medica* of flora and faunal origin. It carries with it certain psychotherapeutic qualities because treatment is a process not merely of consultation of specialists but relatives and friends, who assemble and whose presence helps to cheer the invalid and make him feel that he is not isolated from his society. Another important explanation for the success of folk medicine is that 75 per cent of those falling ill may be cured automatically because the body is usually strong enough to ward off ordinary maladies, but all the same they need some treatment whether it is blowing and conjuring or wearing of charms or amulets or a decoction of some herb. Indigenous medicine, gives great psychological satisfaction to the patient just as pills, capsules and injections help urban and literate patients.

Child Mortality

Child mortality is very high among the *Jaunsaris* as compared to other rural and urban population of the country. But those who survive live longer and the average life expectancy for *Jaunsari* men is 70 to 80 years, and for women 60 to 70 years which is contrary to world life expectancy for the two sexes. The people live in insanitary and unhygienic conditions which could have been responsible for illness in greater numbers, but surprisingly they do not suffer to the expected degree from illness. This may be due to their strong physique or the effect of a healthy climate. The area is hilly and forested, air pollution is not as much as in other rural and urban plain areas, and the effect of fresh air is an aid to their fitness. Most of their manifestations of illness are due to indirect factors, i.e. supernatural or magical causes, which cannot scientifically explain illness. Since they believe in supernatural and magical powers a number of diseases in their daily life are believed to be caused due to these mysterious forces, they do not know or think that surroundings, hygiene and dietary habits may produce disease.

Chronic diseases were not the usual ailments that people suffered from. In fact, the majority of the *Jaunsaris* were found to suffer from a number of affection which can be overcome without any treatment, e.g. stomachache, headache, bodyache, etc. Further, social factors have a profound influence on the tolerant acceptance of many disorders. However, in spite of potentially unhealthy ways of life many *Jaunsaris* are not in chronic ill health and most people who survive serous illness keep quite fit.

For most diseases thought to require treatment local medicine men are consulted. Allopathic doctors are consulted only when either the cause of the disease is not understood, or there is a vague feeling of not being fit.

The failure of western medicine in this region is due to the following facts : (a) that the medical facilities are very meagre; (b) medical facilities are at great distances from most of the villages; (c) villages in the interior do not have medical facilities; (d) the existing medical aid centres do not have sufficient stocks of medicine or other equipments;

and (e) most of the older people refuse or reject western medicine and dissuade the young from consulting modern medical practitioners. In evaluating how far modern scientific medicine has been accepted by Jaunsaris, it is important to remember that they spend very little money (and sometimes nothing) on the treatment of illness either by priests or through herbalists, because payment is indirect, in the form of kind. Indigenous medicine do not have to be purchased, as they are being prepared from common plants found in the region.

Bibliography

1. SNH Rizvi, *Medical Anthropology of the Jaunsaris*, Northern Book Centre, New Delhi, 1991.

5

Himachal: Arts and Manufacturing

The embroidery of Himachal is unique in quality. The one that is done at Bilaspur is of much more superior quality than anywhere else. The craftsmen there have been working for centuries on this without a break Bilaspur embroidery is much more delicately stitched and better in execution.

Metal working generally is rude and elementary. Small brass idols which resemble Polynesian figures, are found in the temples, and are said to be of local make, though I have been unable to trace them to their founder. A curious brass pen and ink case contrived to be thrust in the girdle like a dagger, is occasionally seen. But most of the brass in use is brought up from the plains. Some of the necklaces worn by women are pretty.

Art Manufacturing

Referring to the art manufacturers of Kangra Mr. Kipling says:

The art manufacturing of Kangra are few. Nurpur has for year been declining in importance as a seat of *pashmina* manufacture, which indeed would appear to be waning throughout the province at Kanga. Silver ornaments, such as finger and toe-ring's, necklaces and ornaments for the brow, head and ears, connected by chains, are decorated with dark blue and green enamel. The patterns sometimes include figures drawn with the Polynesian rudeness which seems to characterize all hill work, but the distribution of the parts is very good, and there is a distinct and not unpleasing character in the work. It is not unlikely that at some former period, Kangra produced better work than any now seen there.

Kangra ki Qalam

Kangra ki Qalam is a phrase occasionally heard among native draughtsmen who profess to be able to distinguish the *qalam*—meaning touch or style in this case of a sort of school of illumination and picture—painting that is supposed to have flourished at Kangra, the enamelled silver is now the only product that shows artistic skill. Tinsel-printed cloths are a speciality of the place and they are certainly more neatly done here. The good warm blankets are necessities of life and they are well made, but not for exportation.

Strangeness in Ornaments

Many of the ornaments worn in these regions are interesting from their strangeness, more than for any art qualities. Large lumps of rough amber and blue and white beads of large size are strung together for necklaces. The turquoise is the favourite stone, and sometimes large ornaments square in form, set with this gem in a pattern of chased or filigree silver, are met with. In one case each turquoise is sewn on its surface. It has been said that the eligibility, of a marriageable girl was determined by the number and size of the turquoises on her perak. In addition of this, woollen or silk is also intertwined with the hair in a long tail. Such brass work as in wrought appears to be rude and elementary. Neatly-made tobacco pipes in iron are not uncommon.

Folk Art

For centuries different people have been coming into Himalayas. They came and settled in the valleys, keeping their culture in tact. Their art and sculptures stayed isolated from the mainstream of their adopted country. From Ladakh to Burma (now Myanmar), they have provided sheltered valleys with a relatively unmolested environment. They are unique because they have, for political and geographical reasons, escaped much attention. In the western Himalayas, the areas comprising Spiti, Lahaul and Ladakh are a typical example of isolated valleys which preserve a Buddhist culture.

Artistic Talent of Pahari People

The artistic talent of Pahari people of Himachal Pradesh is a many-sided living reality with them. Imbued with the innate desire to add gaiety and colour to their arduous life, the people give expression to their religio-aesthetic urge in the form of painting on leaves, floors, walls and paper. Leaf painting is done on 'arvi' (colocasia esculenta) leaves. On some festivals, ladies paint in red vermilion, rice solution or *makol* (white earth) animal, human figures and cosmic bodies in accordance with the legends.

Like plain Hindus, on "Hoi Asthami," the image of goddess "Holi" is painted on the wall. Women paint the goddess in different forms according to their aesthetic vision. Many a times, this gets transformed in art forms, mostly in painting, sculptures and embroidery.

On Diwali, women exhibit their creative faculty in a most independent manner. The pathway is profusely decorated with 'makol', 'golu' or rice solution and other pigments.

Resemblance with other Regions

If one looks at these decorations carefully, one would notice in them the *Rangoli* of Maharashtra, *Mandana* of

Rajasthan and *Alpana* of Bengal in theme and style. If one considers the isolated life these people have been living, one wonders how these decorations reached all corners of the country. It must have taken centuries for these to percolate and reach other regions. A connubial painting on paper or cloth called *Kauhara* or *Dehra* is executed on the wall during marriages. In *Kauhara* marriage scenes are highlighted along with other features pertaining to the married life ahead. The *Kauhara* is a miniature form of epic *Citrashala.*

The temples of *zhakharg-soma*, *gsum-thsog*, *rNamparsnag-Mdzad*, *Lo-tsa-bai*, and *Jamd-Byarg* contain frescoes and figures which are unique in the whole of India. The three colossal standing statues of *Matreya* or *Gyalva Chamspa* in the *gsum-thsog* temple are extraordinary examples of the Kashmiri craftsmanship. Hundreds and thousands of miniature paintings furnish proof of the supreme patience and skill that the devoted artists possessed.

Creative Genius in Golu

In addition, Pahari folk art is also amply visible when they decorate the interior and exterior of their homes in various floral designs with *golu* (grayish earth) or *makol.* Cowdung decoration on the floor, called *Hangaiyan*, is really fascinating. All these things glorify the creative faculty of Pahari folk. They employ the humblest of materials in a very artistic way in a bid to divest life of all drabness and monotony. Obviously, these paintings and drawings unfold a vast panorama of Pahari folk creativeness and aesthetic sense.

Temples

The existence of temples and shrines shows the bend of the people of any area. Himachal that way is lucky that its people are worshippers of the Divine. This State is endowed with temples, some of which date back to 7th century A.D. Evidently, the inscriptions show that at least 3 of the 4 important temples were built by one master craftman Guga in the time of Raja Meru Varman who ruled over Chamba A.D. 680. The temples suffered to a great extent at the hands of the Kira invaders in the later 8th century. The wounds inflicted by the invaders under King Khirsrong Idebtsan are still visible in the loss of an ear and tail of the Nandi bull standing before Mani Mahesh temple as well as the disappearance of feet and legs of Ganesha.

Archaeologists are of the view that only the Lakshna temple still remains in its original form although it was repaired several times. The other temples of Mani Mahesh, Ganesha and Narsinghji are believed to be of later date although they house the original statues. The inscriptions throw a flood of light on the history of Chamba and the students of ancient history have been able to derive their own deductions from the temples and their inscriptions.

Jawala Mukhi and Bajesari

Jawala Mukhi and Bajesari are famous temples in Kangra district. For a fuller appreciation, a perusal of the "early wooden temples of the Chamba" by Herman Goetz is a rewarding labour. There all in all 84 Shiv temples of big and small *lingas* in the Chaurasi area of Brahmaur. The temples in Brahmaur that deserve mention and that are historically important are only four. They are: Mani Mahesh or Harihar temple along-with its bull, Ganesha, Lakshna and Narsinghji.

Mani Mahesh

Mani Mahesh temple is unique in the sense that it has a huge *Shiv linga* on a huge stone *Yoni.* The size shows that the temple was erected over the idol. The door of the temple is too small to let the idol through it. It is built in stone and stands on a big rectangular platform facing the north. There are no inscriptions and it is difficult to say when it was built, but the local belief is that the idol (symbol of fertility) dates back to Meru Verman although the temple over it was built later on. In front of the temple and at distance of about 20 yards from the platform, stands the brazen bull 5 fee high and 5 feet 10 inches long from nose to tail. It is made of a mixture of *ashtdhats* and is of massive structure.

Nandi

Lord Shiv's *vahan* is Nandi. Nandi is His inseparable companion. In this temple Nandi stands on a pedestal 13" high and the pedestal carries an inscription said to be in Sharda script which states that it was cast in the reign of Menu Varman by Gugga. The cast shows the cover cloths with embroidered hem and an ornamental chain made of dises and bells. It lost one ear and the tail during Kira invasion and the people say that the invaders damaged the statue because they thought that it was made of gold, but is escaped total destruction when it was found that it was not gold. The bull now has a shed over it with wooden seats running around it.

This statue differs very much from the bulls of hill breed found in this area and obviously the craftman prepared the casting with eye on some far away bull of Shiva which they had seen in the plains. This also signifies that the craftsmen of yore had been moving to other regions in search of work or ideas. This should presumably account for some of the disproportionate parts of the statue as its nose and hoofs are not in proportion to the rest of the body. *Puja* is performed twice in this Hari Har temple and many devotees collect to sing hymns in praise of Shiva.

Ganesha Temple

Ganesha temple is situated just behind the Mani Mahesh temple in a small ill lit shrine. The dol is again made of *ashtdhat* and is 3' high and sits on a pedestal 14" high. It also carries an inscription of Raja Meru Verman. It is a 4 armed statue with a pot belly body. For the usual sacred thread the idol has a snake. It is an awful inspiring figure and is much respected. It is believed to have been destroyed during general destruction of Brahmaur by Kira invasion. *Puja* of the idol is performed twice a day.

Lakshna

Though at many places it is written in big bold letters "Pracheen Mandir", it is not always so. Many temples are of recent origin. However, of all the temples of Brahmaur, Lakshna temples is supposed to be the oldest and original. It is a small unimposing structure with a beautiful carved wooden gate leading to the entrance. Inside the sanctuary, is the fine brass statue 3'-4" high of Lakshna Devi which is a form of Durga depicting her as *Mahishasur Mardini*—killer of the buffalo demon. It is a beautiful statue with fine features executed by the same craftsman Gugga as the inscription at the foot of the idol shows. The temple of Lakshna has marvellous wooden carvings on cedar wood (cedrous deodara). The richly carved entrance gate has been damaged on account of its exposure to the rains and shows of 13 centuries, but the *mandap* inside and richly ornamented panels are well preserved. A description of the temple as given in the Chamba Gazetteer is worth reproducing—

"The plan of the Lakshna Temple differs from that described above in that in front of the shrine we find an ante room, the two being enclosed within a solid wall of rubble and wood masonry which has replaced the verandah. The facade of this building is of particular interest, as in the style of its decoration it exhibits a close affinity to the architecture of Kashmir and *Gandhara*, and indeed, shows traces of classical influence peculiar to the monument of the North West. Under the ridge beam of the roof we notice first of all the triangular pediment with the trifold arch, a characteristic feature of the Kashmir temples. The seated figure in the arch is not Kali, as supposed by Cunningham but Surya the sun-god, as is evident from the position of the legs. His twelve arms, holding various attributes are presumably indicative of the twelve months of the year. The seven crouching figures along the basis of the triangle probably represent the seven days of the week.

Gandhara Art

Here, as well as on the architraves between the pediment and the doorway, we find an arrangement frequent in the Graeco-Buddhist art of Gandhara, rows of figures in arched niches, separated by dwarf pilasters. In the lower most row the figures are amatory couples which can be traced back to Graeco-Bundhist examples. We notice also a row of supporting, crouching figures, frequently met with in Gandhara sculpture and corresponding to the Atlantes of classical art.

The ornamentation on the lintels and jambs of the doorway is of a purely Indian type. Over the entrance we find a double row of garland-carrying flying figures, presumably meant for Gandharvas. In the upper row each of these figures is accompanied by the female-figure seated on its hip. Along the jambs standing figures are placed which are difficult to identify owing to their decayed state. On both sides of the threshold the river goddesses Ganga and Yamuna (i.e., the Ganges and Jamna) are still recognizable, each holding a water vessel and a lotus stalk, and standing on their vehicles the crocodile (*makara)* and the tortoise. Finally, I wish to draw attention to the winged dragons rampant which adorn the upper corners of the doorway".

Gugga, the Craftsman

Gugga was the craftsman of his time. He built another wooden temple on an ambitious scale at Chhatrari in honour of another aspect of Durgashakti Devi–and the temple is accordingly well-known throughout the area as Shakti Devi temple, but the design and execution of carvings in the Lakshna and Shakti temple are essentially in the same and the *ashtdhat* idols also more or less carry the same features in different postures. On the right side of the entrance of Lakshna temple is housed the Keling *devta* in a small *mandap*. Keling *devta* is regarded as *wazir* of Shiva.

Many goats or sheep are sacrificed in the name of Lakshna, but a greater number of sacrifices are made to Keling because of its position as minister to Lord Shiva he has to be well appeased. Because of the vast number of sacrifices made to this god, an outsider humorously described it as *'killing devta'*! The people of Brahmaur have great faith in its miraculous powers and its *chelas* who wear a sort of red cap as distinguishing mark, are in great demand. The killing of goats and sheep within the Chaurasi area is disappearing and all killing has to be done somewhere-else.

Narsinghji

Facing the temple of Mani Mahesh towards the southern side of Chaurasi area, is the stone *shikhra* temple of Narsingh, a manifestation of God Vishnu. The idol carries a head of lion over a stout and sturdy human body and has 4 arms. According to Hindu mythology, Vishnu had to appear in this form to save Prahlad from the murderous intentions of his father Hiranyakashyap. Hiranyakashyap was granted a boon that he would not be killed by any man or animal and hence Vishnu had to manifest himself in this form–half human, half animal. The temple is smaller than Mani Mahesh temple and according to a copper plate issued by Raja Yugakar Verman, it was built by his queen Tribhuvan Rekha Devi in the 10th century. The image does not go back to Raja Meru Verman's reign, but is believed to belong to the reign of Ajay Verman.

Narsinghji Baba

The *ashatdhatu* statue compels one to bow one's head in reverence. The people of the village believe that the *murti* has miraculous powers and no one would dare take a false oath before it. (It was revealed by a local; young man, who was a college student at Chamba, that he vividly remembered 3 persons (one of them his uncle) taking false oaths before Narsinghji *baba* as the *murti* is called and all of them had to pay the death penalty for this sacrilege). He also stated and some others corroborated him that the parties prefer to get their disputes settled through a court of law than by an oath taken before Narsinghji *baba*. The *puja* is offered twice a day in this temple too. This temple was damaged in the earthquake of 1905 and was repaired at State expense.

Jawalamukhi

Jawalamukhi is a famous temple of the goddess Jawalamukhi. She has a flaming mouth. It lies in the valley of the Beas and is built over some natural jets of combustible gas, and is believed to be a manifestation of the goddess *Devi*. Another legend says that the flames proceed from the mouth of the demon Jalandhara, the *Daitya* King and who gives his name to the Jalandhar Doab.

Temples

The building is modern, with a gilt dome and pinnacles and possesses a beautiful folding door of silver plates, presented by the Sikh Raja Kharak Singh. The adjacent village is surrounded by remaining which attest its former size and wealth.

The interior of the temple consists of a square pit about three feet deep with a path way all round. There is no idol of any kind, the flaming fissure being considered as the fiery mouth of the goddess, whose headless body is said to be in the temples of Bhawan.

Bajesari Temple

The temple of the Bajesari or Vageswari Devi at Kangra is perhaps the most famous in the District. It is said to have been founded by the divinity of that name at a famous Aswamedh which was held on the spot. When Mahmud of Ghazni invaded India, his first and foremost calling was to destroy any temples that came in his way. He had invaded this district also and along with other temples destroyed the temple of Vageswari Devi. On this site he built a mosque. The material retrieved from the temple was used in the mosque. Perhaps a century or so later the mosque was removed and temple built again. During his reign, Emperor Akbar along with Diwan Todarmal visited the temple.

Akbar's toleration went so far that he is said to have presented a golden image himself, in an attitude of prayer, to the temple of Jamlu at Malana in Kulu.

Folk Dances and Songs

Folk dances are an essential part of life of the tribals. Among most of them, life without music, love or rhythm has no zest. Dance is a kind of sport in which their creative faculties find a new expression, during hours of leisure or slack season. The origin of dance is an expression in movements of the feeling of joy. In other words, it is a means of enjoyment reaffirming social unity and occurs on all occasions which have some social bearing. It is a sole expression of the aesthetic sensibility of the folk people through rhythm and enchanting group formations.

In a man's life, events like child birth and marriage inspire special type of music, dance and songs. This is what the anthropologists say. After these, religion and magic also have a very important role to play. Among tribals and rural communities, the faculties of "trance" and its magical effect on disease is often implicitly accepted. A tribal dance has its origin in harnessing labour for the good of the community. That is why several folk songs and dances are associated with sowing, harvesting, threshing, hunting and vanquishing the enemy, etc.

The Lama Devil Dance

The tribals living in the valleys of Kinnaur district, have a rich tradition of folk dances. Of these, the Lama Devil Dance is one of the most attractive. The dancers are masked. Two of them are dressed up as a lion. The dance depicts the taming of the lion which represents evil spirits. The orchestra consists of drums, long lama horns, Shehnai, etc. Emotionally frenzied, folk dancers abandon all but the thought that there must be peace, prosperity and happiness all round. At the sound of the drum they swing and sway rhythmically in unison—backward, forward or diagonally.

Chohara Dance

Chohara is another joyful folk dance of the Kinners and Mahasu people. It is performed on almost all important festivals by the village community. Both men and women participate. The dancers move with rhythm and to the tunes of instruments. While dancing, they sing their tribal songs. The tempo increases as the climax is built up by the orchestra. There is a short pause before a new song is started.

Jhanjar Dance

Jhanjar dance is performed in Chamba Valley on every festive occasion. Mostly Gaddis male and female dancers participate. The dancers stand in two rows. As the dance progresses, the two groups interchange their positions. The tempo of the dance is slow in the beginning and gradually rises to an exciting climax.

Gaddi Dance

The folk dance of Gaddi tribe is of uniform pattern and is performed by a group of dancers. They move in circle, sway their bodies half way round at each step in an easy and graceful manner with the arms alternatively raised over the head and hanging down. The men and women dance in separate circles and do not intermingle. The dancing of the men is vigorous and boisterous. The women clap their hands on regular intervals and at every 2 or 3 steps sit down on their hunches facing each other. The dance is accompanied by beating drums and singing the songs of a metrical setting of old legends.

Shun and Shaboo Dances

The snow covered district of Lahaul and Spiti is full of gompas and monasteries. After his family, religion occupies the top position in a man's life. Sometime it has the foremost position. To pray, people dance. *Shun* and *Shaboo* dances are performed inside a monastery in praise and memory of Lord Buddha. Songs in praise of Buddha are sung by three members who participate. It is a community dance which takes place after the harvest. *Shehnai, Duf, Dhol* and a violin like instruments are used as musical accompaniments.

Shabo dance of Lahaul-Spiti is performed on festive occasions and gives an expression to the joy and love of the village folk. There is no rigid pattern but moods and formations differ.

Japro Dance

Hangrang Valley in Himachal Pradesh is a land of rich folk dances. Whenever fair is held, there is a Japro. The gaiety and confidence of the people residing there, find expression in their dances.

The Japro dance is a special feature of auspicious occasion. Both men and women participate. Their rendezvous is the 'emerald lake' near village Nako which becomes a vast white frozen patch during winter.

In fact, the forms of life have evolved in the surroundings and under conditions in which the tribals lived. Rituals have sprung up, traditions formed and man thus started to sing and dance to appease the deities or to forget the hardships of life.

Dodra Kawar Dance

Dodra Kawar is an isolated and remote area of Mahasu district. Like their neighbours, the people of this district find ample opportunities to sing and dance. They are easygoing people, therefore these opportunities are there in plenty. Fairs and festivals provide the occasion for the dance. The people dance, and their gods dance with them. The whole atmosphere is of gay abandon. The multicoloured dresses of the people and their typical ornaments lend peculiar charm to the celebrations.

Kulu Valley Dances

Kulu valley is known for its rich product of apples but it is equally rich in its colourful folk dances. Dances here consist of various types viz., *Kharait*, *Ludi* and *Banthda*, *Phili*, *Pheti* and *Basahri*, *Lahuli*, and *Ujagjama* and *Chadhgebrikar*. These folk dances are named as 'NATI'.

Other Dances

Kharait is performed with swords, *Ludi* and *Banthda* have a fast tempo. *Phili*, *Pheti* and *Basahri* are performed during village fairs. *Ujagjama* and *Chadhgebrikar* represent the climax of the dances with fast tempo. Both men and women participate.

In India, no folk dance can be performed without a drum. The drum is the life of the folk dances. Piper stringed instruments and long trumpets add charm and make the dances picturesque. Perhaps it was the *damroo* which inspired Lord Shiva to dance. Cosmie dance of Shiva—the chief Himachalists is obviously the fountain-head of rhythm in life.

Nataraja

Ananda Coomaraswamy says that among the greatest of the names of Shiva is *Nataraja*, Lord of Dance. The cosmos is His threatre, there are many different steps in his repertory. He is himself actor and audience:

When the Actor beateth the drum

Everybody cometh to see the snow

When the Actor Collecth the Stage properties

He abideth alone in his happiness

The Himachal dancers have to be well-clad because of the cold climate. They, like nature, are colourful in their costumes and evergreen in their minds.

Folk Songs

A study of Himachal folk songs reveals a rich emotional life of the people. Natural atmosphere, good diet and a hardy existence have combined together and produced a race of people who have a healthy and cheerful approach to life. A song of the Gaddis goes—

I weep profusely
while washing clothes, O Kunjua
come and speak to me, please
come and talk with me.

In your hand is a silk handkerchief,
O' Chanchalo,
and my ring is on your finger,
as a token of our undying love.

My lustrous black eyes, O Kunjua, often
admired by you, are now filled with tears
and sorrows,
symbols of our hopeless love.

On your fair arms the red bangles quiver,
and among them, O Chanchalo,
is the bracelet I gave you
In token of my adoration.

Do not come to me at midnight, O Kunjua,
there are five loaded rifles in my house
itching to fire at your heart.

I will surely come at midnight, O Chanchalo,
what harm can five rifles do
to my importal love for you ?

You are going far away, O Kunjua,
give me a ring as a token of your love.
do not bother about such trifles. O Chanchalo
in Chamba there is gold in plenty
and I will deck you with ornaments.

Do not leave tomorrow night, O Kunjua
do not leave me,
I would sacrifice my every life to keep you here.

I must go tomorrow night, O Chanchalo
I must go for I have pressing work which
I cannot ignore.

The Wail of a Woman

The sorrow in a women's heart on the demise of her lover and the gap which it leaves in her world is graphically described in the following song:

If the husband dies
One may wander;
If the lover dies
How can you live ?
If a blanket is torn
We may put on a patch
But if the sky is torn
How can you sew it.

Song for a Beautiful Woman

The beauty of the Himachal women is the theme of many a hill-song. She really looks like a queen of the mountains. In Chamba and Kangra districts of Himachal Pradesh, the following song is very popular and depicts the unique beauty of the women folk:

'Gori da Chitta lagga
Chambe diyan dharan
Chambe diyan dharan
Pain Phuharan
Gori da Chitta lagga
Chambe diyan dharan
Ghar-ghar bindaloo
Ghar-ghar tikaloo
Ghar-ghar bakiyan naran
Gori da Chitta lagga
Chambe diyan dharan'

The woman is deeply in love with the Chamba hills, its rivers and streams. She does not want to leave this beautiful land. In every home there is a *bindlu, tiklu* and a comely bride. This is, obviously, the land of beauty and nature's paradise. Life is lovely among the dear ones.

A Kinner (half man half horse) is another handsome community living in Kinnaur district. The substance of a Kinner song is:

Tipsi was an attractive girl
Her beauty a magic band
The mad dancers like her
She was a queen of beauty
Usha, another girl could not tolerate it
She had some divine power
She used it
Tipsi lost all her beauty soon
And She died
Alas ! The beauty killed
Another beauty.

Other Songs

There are many songs composed on domestic life, the love tiffs between the young bride (*bhabi*) and the husband's younger brother. Tyranny of the mother-in-law over the young daughter-in-law is also depicted in a touching language in some of the songs. A woman recollects her old days and requests the Dholadhar hills to bend a little so that she can have a glimpse of her parent's home:

O, Mother Dhauladhar
Bend a little
O, bend a little
On this side lies my mother-in-law's place
On the other side lies my father's place
Bend yourself a little
Bend a little
O' Bend a little.

Most of the songs are sung by the women or shepherds while tending their sheep and goats. They are sung with an amazing clarity of expression. Each line is repeated several times before passing on to the other line. They sing these songs in chorous. The menfolk place their right hand on their right ear to sing a song in a high pitched voice. Many of the folk dances have been copied and orchestrated in Hindi films. Likewise, much of the folk music has been adapted into film music. Folk songs have also been included here and there in Hindi film songs, some in full, some in snatches.

6

Aspects of Cultural Ecology : Sikkim

SECTION-1
INTRODUCTION

Geographical Setting

When a people migrate from a place and settle somewhere else, in the beginning they do not realize that the geography of their new settlement is going to have a great bearing on how they and their generations are going to live. In fact, the geographic settings have played a major role in the demarcation of the boundaries of nations and states and the cultural regions within them. The geographical setting has also had its profound impact on historical impulses and human ecology of the residents within a cultural region. The geography of Sikkim lends itself to one major culture region, with three sub-cultural regions within its boundaries. While the Dongkiala and Singalila ranges demarcate the eastern and western limits of the state, the Chorten Nyima range in the trans-Himalayan region demarcates the northern boundary.

Traditional Trade Routes

The traditional trade routes from Tibetan plateau into Sikkim were either through the Lachen or Lachung valleys in the north Sikkim, or through the Nathu or Jelep passes on the Dongkiala range in east Sikkim. The Kanchendzonga Massif was a major geographical barrier leading to commercial isolation of southern and western districts of Sikkim. The Upper Rangit Basin in particular, wedged between Kanchendzonga Massif, Singalila range and Mongbrue watershed supported almost an independent sub-cultural region. Thus, the commercial activities, communication path ways, and altitudinal elevations divided Sikkim into following three cultural sub-regions:

(a) Northern Sikkim sub-region north of Mangan where the sparse population adapted to harsh and cold Tibetan type of climatic conditions.

(b) East Sikkim, which became a commercial trade link between Tibet and main land India.

(c) South and West Sikkim, where agro-economy and spirituality were more pronounced. Perhaps its geographical isolation presented itself as secure from political and military interference from outside, prompting the first Chogyals to establish their capitals of Yuksom and later Rabdentse in vicinity of the present township of Gyalshing.

Historical Inputs

The Upper Rangit Basin is a study in contrasts. Historically, Upper Rangit Basin had boundaries with the Limbuana country to the west, and Mongbrue watershed to the east. Culturally, it formed a part of Limbuana (Subba[1] 1999). Accordingly Limbus, Rais and Gurungs form a major part of population in Rathongchu watershed. The Bhutias who arrived later, became the ruling class, the

Chogyals being Bhutias themselves. The other Nepali castes, and Lepchas formed the remainder population in the area. The Lepchas, who are regarded as the autochtones of Sikkim, were animists and followers of Mon faith prior to their amalgamation into Mahayana Buddhist faith on arrival of the Bhutias. With the passage of time, cultural diffusion gathered momentum. The cultural diffusion has resulted in:

(a) Though the Bhutia, Lepcha and Limbu tribes have their own languages, Nepali has become the *lingua franca* in the regions.

(b) The Hindu temples have begun to hoist the prayer flags, which are original to the Tibetans Buddhist cultural form. Many gods and goddesses in the Hindu temples and Buddhist Gompas are common, (Sakya 1989).[2]

(c) Names of all natural features, and human habitats originate from languages of all constituents of the population, mainly forming the Lepcha base (Thakur, 1988).[3]

(d) Ideas were borrowed from each other for rituals during shamans, and celebrations systems of festivals (Subba, 1999).[4]

(e) Methodology of food preparation and consumption patterns were learnt from each other, thus modifying the earlier practices of respective ethnic groups (Tamang, 1998).[5]

(f) In Nepal, various sub-groups such as Gurungs, Sherpas, Tamangs, Chettris, etc. are settled in their respective traditional geographic areas. They have their caste and groups considerations. But in Sikkim the Nepali immigrants, barring the original Limbus, have settled collectively as Nepalis. There is no caste consideration. That is how they are known. This has resulted in a mixed Nepali culture, wherein cultural inputs have been borrowed from all constituent sub-groups. Intermarriages have further amalgamated the cultural mix.[6]

In the year 1788-89 Nepali Gurkha General Jahar Singh had invaded Sikkim, and captured areas upto the western banks of Tista river. The area was under Nepali control for 29 years upto 1817, when the Titalaya treaty was signed. The then Chogyal of Sikkim Tenzing Namgyal was forced to abandon his capital Rabdentse and retreated to safety beyond the eastern banks of river Tista and Tamlong. The captured territories, less the Darjeeling hills sector south of Rangit river were restored to the kingdom of Sikkim, while Darjeeling was merged with British India for good. J.C. White, the political officer chose Gangtok for constructing his residence, and at his instance the Chogyal shifted the capital from Tamlong to Gangtok during 1885-86.

Chogyal Stays put at Gangtok

The restoration of lost territories of the Rangit Basin however did not prompt the Chogyal of Sikkim Tsugphud Namgyal to return to his original capital. The new capital city of Gangtok had now come into being and it continues to be the state capital till date. Eastern Sikkim and Kalimpong divisions had enjoyed the historical and traditional commercial bliss till the year 1962, when the Indo-China conflict put a stop to the trade links. The area however housed the capital city of Gangtok, and commercial centres of Rangpo and Singtam, resulting into continued economic, educational and urban development. The National Highway 31A, which passes through eastern Sikkim, helped the district authorities in setting up infrastructure for industrial development.

When National Highway became operational, it immediately impacted the life of people living along it. The West and South districts did not prosper much in economic terms. However, from time immemorial they have been rich in spiritual and cultural ecology. The ethnic and folk culture thrives in this pocket. The present day ethnic and folk culture is pronounced by:

(a) *Folklores.* These include tales, songs, lores, beliefs, superstitions and customs that have been passed from generation to generation. The folklore and faith regarding the wishing lake Khechopalri deserves a detailed account. A detailed account of the same is given in a separate section in this chapter. Accounts of certain other folklores appear in the chapter on spiritual ecology.

(b) *Shamans and Spirit Possession.* Shamans, *Jhakris* and spirit possession are encountered in all parts of the world. The Himalayas and other hill regions however have more cases of these kinds. Small case studies of various types of Shamans encountered in the study area have been analysed and described in later sections of this chapter.

Cultural Fusion and Identity

For centuries Sikkim continued to maintain its identity as an independent state under the Chogyals. The isolation of the kingdom helped the prospering of culture and spiritual related aspects within and outside the monasteries. Though the population percentage of Nepalese, most of whom are Hindu by religion is larger, the culture of the Mahayana Buddhist Lamaistic faith continued to be the state culture. The merger of Sikkim with India had its direct and indirect affects on the Sikkimese population.

Their proportions depend upon the economic status, level of education and exposure to the world at large. The people in high income and higher education bracket may appear highly westernized in external behaviour but they are very much conservative at heart. They go for western education but strictly adhere to their religious and ritualistic practices at home. The mass participation of them in Sikkimese festivals, such as, Losoong, Bum Chu, Pang Lhabsol, etc., amply exemplify their adherence to the traditional culture. The upper class Sikkimese hardly show any interest in mainland Indian culture.[7]

Sikkimese Middle Class

The middle class Sikkimese is comparatively less conservative. They have accepted both Indian and western cultures along with their virtues and vices. They are highly influenced by the glitz that reach them via audio-visual devices and glossy magazines. The influences are manifest in their speech, attire and home décor. English being the medium of instruction in educational institution, the young generation is leaning towards Anglicized life style.[8]

The people who are least educated and have a low economic status are understandably least exposed to the influences—Indian or Western, whatever the case may be. Even when there are less reservations, normally they follow their age-old traditions and practice whatever they have learnt from their ancestors. They are often found to adopt the food habits, clothings, and even means of recreation brought to them by the village traders who are mostly from the plains. The areas where everything from salt to sari come from India, are bound to have the influence of Indian culture.[9]

Traditional Sikkimese Culture

However, the Kazi landlords were not forgiving as far as culture was concerned. They used a heavy hand. As a result, the villages located at the strongholds of the Kazi landlords have preserved their traditional Sikkimese culture under the strict vigilance of the landlords or the priests. Very recently, there was uproar over the construction of the Rathong Chu Hydel Project in Upper Rangit Basin at Yuksom on the issue of encroachment upon religious sanctity and culture. The protestations were so vehement that the project was scrapped mid-way. There are ample grounds to believe that the project has been scrapped toward off the plainsmen who were supposed to construct the power plant, and in the process would pave the way for Indianization.

SECTION-II
CONSERVATION THROUGH CULTURAL LEGACY AND TRADITIONAL ECOLOGICAL KNOWLEDGE: KHECHEOPALRI LAKE—CASE STUDY

Sustenance of Ecosystem

Life in pastoral societies was organized around a highly refined awareness of environment. Long ago these societies were convinced that ecosystems sustain themselves in a dynamic balance based on cycles and fluctuations, which are nonlinear processes. Present day science has facilitated the study of these balancing patterns through field and laboratory research methodologies. Ecological awareness however only arises when we combine our rational knowledge with the traditional folk knowledge of the indigenous people. Such intuitive wisdom has been a characteristic of traditional cultures, such as the Sikkimese ethnic groups.

The Sikkimese of Upper Rangit Basin residing in the 'spiritual and cultural pentagon' formed by the five monasteries of Dubdi, Khecheopalri, Pemayangtse, Tashiding and Ralang have had a symbiotic relationship between their traditional spiritual culture and the environment.

Ecological Knowledge

The traditional ecological knowledge has been acquired over centuries of trials. In general it differs from current scientific ecological knowledge in a number of ways: (Inglis, 1993).[10]

(a) Traditional Ecological Knowledge (TEK) is mainly qualitative as opposed to quantitative.

(b) TEK has an intuitive component (as opposed to being purely rational).

(c) TEK is holistic (as opposed to reductionist).

(d) In TEK, mind and matter are considered together (as opposed to a separation of mind and matter).

(e) TEK is moral (as opposed to supposedly value-free).

(f) TEK is spiritual (as opposed to mechanistic).

(g) TEK is based on empirical observations and accumulation of facts by trial-and-error (as opposed to experimentation and systematic deliberation for accumulation of facts).

(h) TEK is based on data generated by resource users themselves (as opposed to that by a specialized cadre of researchers).

(i) TEK is based on diachronic data, i.e., long-time series on information on one locality (as opposed to synchronic data, i.e., short-time series over a large area).

Merging with Nature

The TEK is markedly slower-paced than scientific push. It is based on human experience, not on knowledge of tool and machines-based experiments. That is why in contrast to ecology, it does not aim to control nature. The arrival of scientific development has to some extent, already shown signs of environmental degradation in this region. The modern housing techniques, the hydel projects, the electric power etc., have accelerated both—human development, and natures', and cultures, disintegration. The construction of roads and stone queries have resulted in frequent soil erosion and landslides. The electric power based saw mills have led to faster clearance of the forests. Though, in Rangit Basin the situation is still manageable, but the degeneration needs to be checked.

Social and Cultural Context

In social and cultural context, the TEK of the ethnic habitat in Upper Rangit Basin includes:

(a) Symbolic meanings through history, place names, and spiritual relationships between natural objects. Most rivers, lakes and mountain tops here have spiritual relationships, Mount Khanchendzongpa being the "Guardian Diety", and "Khecheopalri" being the wish fulfilling lake.

(b) A distinct cosmology of worldview based on the 'Wheel of Life' and 'Mandala' add on of their conceptualization of environment, as opposed to the Western science (Govinda 1960).[11]

(c) The human and environmental relations of all ethnic groups is based on reciprocity, and obligations towards, both, community members and other beings. This in the wider sense is also the essence of 'deep ecology' which is essentially biocentric.

(d) The 'Four noble Truths' and the 'Middle Path-Madhyamika' or 'Eight Fold Path' essentially seek understanding and provision of means to support the humans along with the balance of the biodiversity in the region.

Application of Culture and Tek on Khecheopalri Lake: Celebration of Bum-Chu Festival (From 12 to 13 March 1998)

The Lake Region

Sikkim is land of lakes. These are situated at elevations ranging from tropical to alpine. Till some years back, no figures were available as to the number of lakes in the State. The majority of its lake ecosystems are of glacial origin and are located in the North District, while the South District has the least number. All recreational or other activities such as boating, water sports, and irrigation, etc. are restricted in these lacustrine systems, as a result of which the lakes of Sikkim have fared differently from the other lakes in India. Most lakes in Sikkim are considered sacred and are revered due to ancient mythological connections. Lake Khechoepalri is one among them. Although very few studies have been undertaken in general in the lacustrine systems of Sikkim Himalaya, notable reports on the various aspects of Lake Khecheopalri have been published by Venu et al.(1990)[12], Roy and Thapa (1996,1997), Roy *et al* (1998).[13,14,15]

Multinomial Names

Like other lakes in Sikkim, Lake Khechoepalri has multinomial names among the different ethnic groups of the state. Located within 27° 19' 15" N latitude and 88° 15' 06"E longitude at elevation of 1831 m, near Tsozo village in the West District, it has the outline profile of a human right-foot. A cursory observation shows the original area of the lake to have been much larger in the past, and to have been later reduced to about a third of the open water area by the gross encroachment of marginal vegetation and by eutrophication. The lake has two permanent inlets and one outlet. Besides ground sources, water is also fed into the lake through two temporary inlets from surrounding hill-slopes over the monsoon. The rock in the lake area belongs geologically to the Sikkim group of granite-gneciss, schist and phyllites (Raina and Srivastava, 1981; Bose, 1989).[16,17].

Melas and Festivals

Sikkim is a mystic land of extraordinary beauty where a series of festivals are held and these annual festivals are commonly called "Melas". Some of the remarkable melas are the Khecheopalri mela, Saramsa mela, Rishi mela and Tashiding mela and the like.

The Khecheopalri mela in the West Sikkim is perhaps the largest and most significant of its kind. It was held near the Khecheopalri lake monastery on the occasion of "Maghe Purne" from Mar 12 to 13, 1998 and attracted pilgrims from all over Sikkim. Not only Indians, but foreigners also attended it. It had a special gravity. The pilgrims worshipped the spiritual power and offered various food-material into the lake to appease God. They used the lake's water as a "Prasad". From an ecological point of view, whether this Khecheopalri mela was also an important contributor to the environmental degradation or depletion of aquatic biodiversity of the lake, is being assessed.

Purpose of the Festival

The Bum Chu festival got initiated at Tashiding monastery which is about 24 km away from the Khecheopalri lake. The festival generally coincides with Maghe Purne every year. There was a holy water-pot inside the monastery filled with water to the brim while prayers continued overnight. In the early hours these pots were uncovered in the presence of High Lama by the monks. If the water showed ripples, that year could prove to be bad for Sikkim and vice versa. Since, Khecheopalri lake is the gift of Goddess Tara Jetsum Dolma (according to mythological view), pilgrims assume the lake to be represented by the pot and used the lake's water as "Panchamrith". They pray and offer different products so that the lake will not dry and if it so happened people are doomed.

Pilgrims

One cannot believe that an enclosed lake will have no leaves on its surface. But this happens to be true in case of Khecheopalri lake. It is an ethereal and venerated lake situated amidst dense temperate forests, with no floating leaf on its surface. People of Sikkim believe that Lord Shiva existed in solemn meditation inside the lake. They also believe that the level of lake water increased during the festival which originated from the Head of Lord Shiva. Bearing these feelings pilgrims pay their visits to this holy lake during festival period from different corners of Sikkim and even neighbouring district of West Bengal. They come here to forget their sufferings and return home with the blessing of God. People from all religions' Nepalese, Buddhist Bhutias and Lepchas, were seen during the occasion.

Description of Festival

The Bum Chu (*Bum* means pot; *Chu* means water) festival was celebrated near Khecheopalri lake only for two days namely, from March 12 to 13, 1998. People from all over Sikkim and other parts of India including foreigners attended this spiritual festival.

There were about 32 make-shift shops and restaurants including some grocery shops. All the shops were constructed using bamboo and katus (*Castonopsis* sp.) leaves. There were some hotels serving food-items, like; chicken rice, mutton rice along with hot momos, thukpa and kinema (fermented soybeans) (special local food). Liquor (both local and IMFL mode) were up for sale. Beside these, villagers sold their local edibles like, Ghar tarul, Simbal tarul, squash tarul Ban tarul (local tubers) and sweet potato. Other vegetables were also being sold.

Most of the pilgrims were piously engaged in their puja. Many pilgrims were in ebriated condition. The shop-keepers were busy with preparation of food-items. An unexpected accidental fire in one of the stalls was noticed. These were the pilgrims activities on the first day when the pilgrims number was about 1000.

The second day of the festival was started by Lamas' prayers. Pilgrims reached by all modes of transport. The level of pilgrims increased and some state ministers visited lake accompanied by officials at about 12.30 p.m. It was the peak level of pilgrims about 2000 in number.

Pilgrims Activities at Prayer Station on Wooden Ramp

People of Sikkim believe that the lake Khecheopalri has some divine power to release the people from distress. They appease God by offering some materials. Even the temple offerings in the form of flowers, incense sticks cast into the lake's water every day takes its toll. It was seen that pilgrims offered different types of fruits, milk, raw rice, fried rice, mustared oil, Dalda (dehydrogenated oil), biscuits, bread sugar and the like into the lake. The amount of these religious materials was maximum during the festival. This is taking its toll. All this material added to the lake water in the name of prayers and beliefs is polluting it. There was a time when people used to take water home as Shiva's *prasad*. Now only occasionally anyone does it.

Moreover, they released many bamboo-boats with burning Dalda and khadas (sacred scarves). This is the recent phenomena by the pilgrims. Animals, especially dogs (ferals) were seen relishing the proteinous offerings. Many officials including police and military personnel were also observed tying khadas to the offerings. Once scene, very peculiar, was that of some pilgrims offering these materials to the water body and others consuming lake's water at the same time for their good health at this spot. Some washed hands unnoticed by the pilgrims who consumed the water.

Lake Khecheopalri

The last day of the festival was a very significant day. Lake Khecheopalri, a renowned water-body of Sikkim has many mythological tales. A team of monks (lamas) reached the wooden ramp to prove the reality of the lake's myths. There was the Khechu-Rinpoche, about 8 years old (believed incarnation) and a Cherechi Rinpoche, about 70 years old among them. The old monk folded few khadas spelling some spiritual words and threw them into the lake. The water of the lake then started bubbling after a few minutes. This was astonishing. Hence it was assumed, that the reality of living God existed in the Khecheopalri lake. It was the early morning feature on the final day.

Activities of Avifauna during the Festival

Nine species of avifauna were observed during the festival. They were little grebe *Podiceps ruficollis*; common merganser-*Mergus merganser*, large cormorant—*phalacrocorax carbo*; little cormorant- *Phalacrocorax niger*; common teal-*Anas crecca*; tufted duck- *Aythya fuligula*; white breasted water-hen-*Amaurornis phoemicurus*; moorchen- *Gallinula chorophy*; and crane brown-*Amaurornis* bicolor. All these avifauna gathered at the centre of the lake early in the morning and then dispersed due to human activities.

Stall Construction

There were about 32 stalls constructed using bamboo and katus (Castonopsis sp.) branches collected from nearby dense forest. Each stall used about 50 kg biomass (total of approximately 1.7 tons of biomass including fuel-wood). The tree branches also served as fuelwood.

Sanitation

Pilgrims defecated where ever they could (especially in the South and North slopes surrounding the lake). This definitely did not match with the sanctity in which the lake is held by the pilgrims, due to the shortage of proper sanitation facilities.

Waste Materials

About 5 kg of waste paper, plastic and polythene bags was detected after the festival, on Mar 13, 1998 by a weigh-balance. The number of pilgrims was about 3000 during the entire festival duration. Each pilgrim carried about 15 gm offering materials. Thus, it was assumed that about 45 kg of materials was deposited into the lake.

Discussion

There is no doubt in anybody's mind that Sikkim is nature's paradise in the lap of the eastern Himalaya. Bum Chu is an annual festival held around Khecheopalri lake and it is perhaps the most significant annual festival of Sikkim. Undoubtedly, fairs have great importance in our social life. But the fact was that the pilgrims in the festival helped accelerate the ecological degradation of the lake in the following ways:

(1) *Outwash:* Outwash (mainly triggered by activities of pilgrims) that was produced around the periphery of the lake during festival was observed as a pollutant of the once crystal clear lake. It is being accelerated due to heavy rainfall.

(2) *Cattle-grazing:* This is also a detrimental factor polluting the lake's water through excreta and is a common phenomenon surrounding the lake.

(3) *Religious offerings:* Addition of offerings to the lake reduces the water-quality as found through the observations and results. This is a constant phenomena, but the highest level was during the festival.

(4) *Loss of biomass:* Most of the shop-owners used the tree loppings with leaves from the surrounds for temporary construction which affected the lake's environment indirectly and decimated the biodiversity.

(5) *Sanitation and hygiene:* There were no proper toilet facilities. Subsequently pilgrims used the surrounding areas (especially, south and north-east corner) of the lake for human defecation purposes. The pollutants would percolate into the lake's water during the monsoon and alter the ecological balance of the lake.

There is no provision of water-sports, but pilgrims throw several products into the lake's without being noticed which certainly disturbed the biodiversity of the lake.

(6) *Water quality:* The pH of lake water showed signs of being more acidic in nature. The possible reason for this could be leachates generated by the decomposition of waste materials.

Pollution and Water Quality Degeneration

The human interference with nature is taking its toll. The concentration of dissolved oxygen decreased with increase in temperature found after the festival. This is probably by increase in biochemical reactions due to addition of offerings which consume dissolved oxygen at a rapid rate and its concentration tends to decrease just after the festival. This was an important indicator of pollution. Low content of dissolved oxygen just after the festival reflected the presence of organic matter in water offered during festival.

Chlorides are readily soluble in water. Changes in chloride contents between pre- and post-period of festival, may be related to salts generated from the surrounding area through the activities of pilgrims. This also was an indicator of population levels.

Iron and Ammonia

The concentration of iron and ammonia increased and the high concentration of these also support the pollution of water. Some planktons like *protococus* and *Tetraspora* also supported this.

Therefore, the impact of monitoring of lake water chemistry indicated that the offerings and other activities influenced the water quality by way of pollutants loading of the lake Khecheopalri. Hence, the lake Khecheopalri is faced with slow and certain pollution.

Proposed Remedial Measures

1. Afforestation of areas degraded by forest fires in 1970s should be undertaken.
2. Instead of prayers being offered at the lake proper, pilgrims should be encouraged into conducting prayer ceremonies at the monastery.
3. The management plan for the lake should be implemented through the Khecheopalri Development Authority formed by local people.
4. Education on the importance of lake ecosystems should be initiated, especially for school children.

5. Construction of houses, slash and burn agriculture and grazing in the lake catchment should be stopped.
6. The festival committee for the annual Bum Chu festival should be authorized to collect and administer funds for proper sanitation, and provision of drinking water, parking facilities and garbage bins.
7. Anthropogenic outwash and agricultural runoff into the lake should be checked, along with landuse practice which contribute to degradation.
8. Human offering to the lake changes the chemical composition of water. The offerings some time help weeds to germinate and sprout. With the help of local community, mechanical and manual checks should be applied to control invasion of the lake by weeds.

SECTION-III
SPIRIT POSSESSION, SHAMANS AND JHAKRIS IN UPPER RANGIT BASIN

Introduction

Lepchas and Bhotias who migrated to Sikkim believed in animism. Therefore, spirit possession in Sikkim is not unique. It has been there for centuries. Social researchers and anthropologists have encountered it throughout the world. This section of the chapter on cultural ecology is an attempt at understanding some of the sociological and cultural implications of spirit possession with in the setting of Upper Rangit Basin. Mystical experiences are common in the Himalayas. Most people believe in spirits, and therefore fear the possession by the spirits.

There is also the religious angle to spirit possession. The concept of Mahayana Buddhism within Sikkim is based on the Tibetan lamaistic rites and the Mun Lepcha animistic rituals. The Limbus and the other Hindu Nepali caste have their faith in the ancient Hindu Tantric order mixed with animistic rites. The diffusion of the Bhutias, Lepchas, Limbus and the other Nepali groups have however given an almost uniformly common platform to the phenomenon of spirit possession. Cultural borrowing of shamans is common.

Human Ecology Angle

From the point of view of human ecology, there is a close relationship between spirit possession as an altered form of consciousness and parapsychology. In speaking of the social function of human behaviour and in situations, it is useful to adopt the distinction between 'manifest' and 'latent' function. Manifest function has to do with intent while latent function is frequently unintended. In often used linguistic and anthropological terminology, manifest function is 'emic' while latent function is 'etic'.

Throughout Sikkim, spirit possession is cited as a source of discontent as well as a means for resolving discontent. Illness and misfortune are attributed to a variety of supernatural forces such as attacks by witches, sorcerers, forest divinities, spirits of deceased individuals and angry gods or goddesses. People frequently recognize that human neglect is usually at the basis for supernatural discontent. For example, the failure to propitiate household or village gods and goddesses is frequently cited as the source of their anger, or as among the Limbu, human envy and jealousy leaves the individual or family open to attacks by witches or evil spirits.

Living Metaphors

Through human failure and neglect supernatural forces are unleashed and bring chaos, disorder and disaster. These forces are combated, held in check or defeated by individuals who are capable of 'seeing' and identifying them. Such individuals receive their power primarily through successful encounters with supernatural forces in the past Frequently, these encounters are violent as in the initial possession of the *jhakri.* Invariably, the contact is loaded with danger. The eventual control of this contact imbues the individual with power to diagnose, cure illness and rectify misfortunes that are caused by similar encounters. They become 'living metaphors', through controlled spirit possession, or contact with supernatural power.

The system of cause, effect and cure, is thus a circular and enclosed system of knowledge. The cause is spirit, the effect is spirit possession, and the cure is controlled spirit possession. This system of knowledge provides the manifest function of explanation and control in the face of disorder, chaos and inexplicable circumstances. The social function here described is adaptive. It (spirit possession) is the basis of 'social stability' in potentially unstable and disruptive social circumstances. It has the similar function that witchcraft beliefs, have for many societies. It functions to 'explain unfortunate events' and thus stabilize social relations where doubt serves to disrupt them.

Meanings and Definitions

Shaman. In some of the general dictionaries and anthropological textbooks, the term 'shaman' is defined so generally that no elements differentiate it from words referring to many other religious practitioners. For example, in the *The Random House Dictionary of the English Language* (Stin 1973: 1310) '*shaman' is defined as a medicine man; one acting as both priest and doctor who works with the supernatural* Keesing (1958) in a general anthropology textbook, defines 'shaman' as an individual religious expert' (Hitchcock and Jones, 1994)[18].

Spirit possession. The invasion and control of a person by a spirit, demon or god. Spirit possession is characterized by a change of personality and behaviour on the part of the possessed. In some societies illness is regarded as a form of spirit possession.

Jhakri

In Sikkim the common name for all shamans in general is 'Jhakri'. The shamans in the Sikkim community context are outlined as under:

(a) *Limbu shamans.* Limbus recognize five kinds of shamans whose names are 'yeba', 'yema', 'samba', 'phedangma' and 'mangba'. The differences are minute. All perform at weddings funerals, harvest rites and periodic rituals for the welfare of households. The differences are more pronounced when it comes to the diagnosis and cure of disease and the prevention of misfortunes and other calamities that have supernatural causes. 'Yeba' is male while 'Yema' is female 'Samba' is a specialist in oral literature and mythology. 'Mangba' is a specialist in dealing with the spirits of those who died through violence.

(b) *Sunuwar.* 'Punimbo' and 'ngiami' are the shamans of Sunuwar community. Their numbers in the Upper Rangit Valley are very few though.

(c) *Rai.* The Thulung Rai community belonging to Tibeto-Burman (Kirata) sub-group refer to their shamans as 'saleme', while Nepali speaking Rai community refer to them as 'bijuwa'.

(d) *Sherpa.* Sherpa shamans are known as '*hal-wa*' meaning 'god one', or 'mindung'. The female shamans are called *do lo ma,* meaning 'woman who has been to hell and returned back'.

(e) *Kami.* The Kami *jhakris* are most numerous. They are some time addressed as *dange.* The wife of a *jhakri* is called *jhakrini*, while a *jharini*, is a female shaman.

(f) *Tamang.* Tamang *jhakri* is called *bon-po.* The head dress of Tamang shamans, and other gear has a similarity with other *jhakri* groups.

(g) *Gurung.* There are two categories of Gurung shaman, the *pajyu* and the *khepre.* Both traditions incorporate pre-Buddhist Bon rites. Aspects of lamaism and Nepali Hinduism are both detected in ritual style and paraphernalia.

(h) *Lepcha.* The chief functionary of their indigenous beliefs is the *bon-thing*, who is a kind of intercessor. The female is *mun.*

Shamans and caste system. Within Hindu community the caste system and ethnic pluralism operate to deny many individuals self-respect and prestige in the village setting. This is especially the case with lower castes such as metalworkers, tailors or leatherworkers. Frequently, these castes provide the village shaman or religious specialist who combats disease and misfortune through controlled spirit possession. In respect and prestige spirit possession in all its forms is not limited to any particular class or caste. It is a sociologically 'open' system. This is not to say that it occurs with the same frequency among all classes and all castes, but simply that it is open to all. It is a recognized and frequently institutionalized means for social advancement (Field study).[19]

In this fashion, the beliefs and institutions surrounding spirit possession fulfill the function, or providing 'a culturally approved means for the resolution of inner conflict (between personal desires and cultural norms)'. Within the Hindu caste system many people are denied access to goods, wealth and prestige as a result of culturally prescribed norms. The institution of spirit possession within different contexts serves as a means for the satisfaction of personal wants and desires. Thus, on one level it provides an explanation for social dissatisfaction and on another it channels it according to prescribed norms.

Female shamans. The spirit possession in general occurs more frequently among those categories of people who are denied social statuses and traditional means for social advancement in society. This is especially in the case with women, who more frequently than any other social category, find themselves relegated to inferior positions in society with little or no hope of social and institutional advancement. Women of lower castes and tribes would by definition be in relatively inferior social positions to women of higher castes who, through marriage and education, are in positions of respect unmarried women, widows and women in servants positions are more likely to become possessed by spirits than married women with children, a family and a successful marriage. Spirit possession, as pointed out by Lewis (1971), provides an 'oblique aggressive strategy' to such socially deprived categories of people.

Male shamans. Similarly, men of lower castes, or men without lands, titles or positions of authority seem more inclined to spirit possession than those of higher castes, with wealth and social position. Spirit possession again provides an approved means for 'social protest'.

Distinction between shamans and priests. Shamans are generally distinguished from priests by the following attributes:

(a) Shamans are part-time professionals and seldom make their living solely through their religious occupation, as does a priest.

(b) Shamans do not inherit their status or succeed to it, but acquire it by divine intervention, which generally occurs in adolescence as a result of the trance or a state of possession. The priest, on the other hand, lacks the psychodrama of the shaman and generally acquire his position through inheritance, study or other channels of succession.

(c) Shamans are primarily curers and healers, while priests seldom diagnose disease and misfortune but instead limit their activities to prayer, worship and religious offerings to supernatural beings.

(d) Shamans generally shy away from set rituals having to do with the life cycle, planting, harvesting or temple worship, while these are the stock in trade of a priest.

(e) Shamans are controlled ecstatic who assume a trance or become possessed, and in that state they serve as mediums through with supernatural beings, make their wishes known, and display their power in a dramatic style.

Case Studies

Case studies on certain specific shamans, *jhakris* and *bon-thins* encountered during field study are enumerated in succeeding sections of this chapter.

SECTION-IV
SHAMANS PRACTICE AMONGST LIMBUS

Introduction

Western district of Sikkim has been historically and culturally very closely associated with the Limbuana cultural centre of Nepal. Limbus consider themselves to be autochthones of the area. Limbu shamans are common in general are a Yuksom, and areas West of Rathong Chu. Various kinds of Limbu shamans have been described in the proceeding section of this chapter.

That people's lives are intimately linked to a world of supernatural beings. That world consists of numerous gods, goddesses, ghosts of the dead, and spirits associated with animals, plants, the forest, the home and other animate and inanimate objects of nature. The Limbu shamanism rests on this firm belief. The Limbu Shamansim rests on this firm belief. Not every Limbu believes the same way or in the same things, nor as in most other cultures, does every Limbu believe in supernatural forces with the same intensity. I encountered many Limbus who were confirmed agnostics, while other could be classified as 'true believers'. In general, most Limbus accepted the idea that disease, misfortune, crop-failure, death and other unexplainable events had supernatural causes. In order to understand these causes and to rectify unfortunate circumstances, they seem to depend with profound faith on the shamans or *jhakris*.

Limbu Shamanic Costumes

Over the centuries, many contrasts have occurred in different Limbu shamans. They are now defined by their their respective costumes and shamanic paraphernalia. Both the *yeba* and *yema* wear a costume consisting of skirt (*jama*), feathers headdress (*wasang*), *cowrie* shell bandoliers (*aplak*), and garlands of acorn seeds, *rudraksa* beads, bells and the like. They frequently wear a leather or canvas belt (*pett*) on which are strung a series of bells. The *yeba* and *yema* do not use the traditional shamanic drum found throughout Nepal, but instead during a state of trance or possession they beat a brass plate (*thal*).

In contrast, the garb of the *phedangma* and *samba* is much less dramatic. Noticeably absent are the feather headdress and cowrie shell bandoliers. Only on a rare occasion, depending, on the teachings of one's *guru*, did I see a *phedangma* or *samba* wear the shaman's skirt (*jama*). The key instrument in the ritual activities of the *phedangma* and *samba* is the two-headed drum, the *dhyanro*, and both wear garlands of *rudraksa* beads and bells in curing ceremonies.

Brass Plate

It is important to note that shamans of all types seldom use the drum or the brass plate in life-cycle rituals birth, marriage, and death—or harvest rituals. Their activities during such rites parallel those of a priest, while their powers as shamans are used as a means for summoning spirits and tutelary deities, as well as maintaining power over these supernatural beings. These powers are undesirable when making offerings to gods and goddesses who are neither angry nor displeased. The *mangba* uses both the drum and the brass plate, but does not wear the feather headdress, skirt or cowrie shell bandolier.

The Yeba

Over time, all shamanic practices in Sikkim have got diffused. This is evident from costumes, which they wear and instruments they use while performing worships. This is especially evident in the garb of the *yeba*. During the course of field work, I attempted to witness and check a full costume of the *yeba* and *yema*. One Limbu informant took me to a Tamang shaman (*bon-po*) who owned such a costume. He was an old man of about seventy and no longer practicing his art. The headdress was almost identical to the ones seen elsewhere, with the exception that the Tamang headdress (called by the same name, *wasang*) consisted of peacock feathers, while the *yeba's* headdress included the feathers of a number of other species of birds. Both headdresses displayed a headband decorated encountered a female shaman (*yema*) who owned a similar headdress but refused to wear it. The type of headdress under discussion closely resembles those of the *jhakri* found elsewhere in Sikkim.

The *yeba* told me that the kinds of feathers used were not of extreme importance although the wild species of birds were preferred to domestic fowls. The feathered headdress of the *yeba* is symbolic of celestial flight, characteristic of classic Nepali and Sikkimese shamanism, which explains the preference for feathers of wild birds, especially wild birds of the high Himalaya.

Other Instruments

Other instruments of the Limbu shamans parallel the common tradition. The two-headed drum (dhyanro), oval, or occasionally diamond or triangular shaped, resembles many of the drums used by other shamans. Although the hides of goats and water buffalo are occasionally used in making drumheads. The most preferred skins are of deer and elk. Drum heads are occasionally painted with drawings of the sun and moon, which are symbolic of the shaman's celestial origin and flight during the trance. Similar motifs are frequently carved with images representing helping spirits or Limbu deities, including the Limbu high goddess Yuma Sammang, the earthly counterpart of Tagera Ningwaphuma, the creator. A number of species of animals are carved on drum handles—birds, elk, deer, and snakes are the most frequent. Most of these animals are symbolic of his journeys through the sky during a state of ecstasy. Also, frequent representations of the 'cosmic tree' are either painted on the drum head or carved in the handle.

Drums are used by Limbu shamans to achieve a state of ecstasy and control helping spirits as well as to gain power over those that do harm to the living, or the spirits of those who died by violence. Although the *yeba* does not use the shaman's drum during a séance, preferring the brass *plate*.

Divination and Curing

During course of field work I spent a day with a Limbu shaman Purna Bahadur. He explained his methodology of divination and curing during shamanic rites.

Limbu shamans divine in a number of ways. The techniques he uses are related to the different situations of illness and misfortune. The most frequent technique used for minor aches and pains is rice divination. The patient or client presents the shaman with a coin, which he places in a brass plate. He then takes a handful of rice, covers the coin, and separates the rice into six small piles. I was told that four of these represented the direction and two of them Limbu deities. In one case, the shaman told me that two of the piles symbolized Yuma and Theba Sammang. The shaman then counts the grains of rice in each pile, even numbers signifying one thing and odd numbers another. In this way, he is able to determine the severity of the illness, its cause, the direction from which it came, and the course of action to be taken.

A second form of divination, used in cases of extreme illness, requires the shaman to take articles of clothing from the patient and place them at an altar erected for Yuma Samang or other Limbu deities. The shaman then chants the *mundhum* and goes into a trance. He learns the nature of the illness by divination in the presence of the clothes and seeks help from his tutelary spirit. The details of this form of divination were never explained to me, but it is used in most major seances where the shaman constructs an altar and goes into a trance.

Tamphungma

Occasionally he would take the pulse of a patient and determine the illness. At a wedding he attended, one of the guests fainted. Two shamans were present. One held the patient and took his pulse beat. After a few moments, he declared that the man had been attacked by Tamphungma, the jungle spirit. He chanted a few *mantra* to this spirit and gradually the patient revived. He told me this would not free the man from the grasp of Tamphungma, but was only a temporary measure. On returning home, the man would have to call in a shaman who would perform a *puja* to Tamphungma on his behalf.

Causes of Illness and Misfortune

In Bhotia and Lepchas beliefs, all illness and misfortune are thought to have supernatural causes. In extreme cases, the divination and cure require elaborate preparations on the part of the shaman and are expensive for the patient. The patient and his family must feed the shaman while he is in attendance. They should also supply him with liberal quantities of chhang liquor and tobacco. The payment of the shaman follows the cure. I was told that unsuccessful cures required no payment but that a successful cure would sometimes require as much as hundred or more rupees. The amount would be determined according to the time the shaman spent with the patient. Sometimes payment is in cash, but more frequently, it consists of goods such as clothing or grain.

Becoming a Shaman

One becomes a shaman as a result of possession by a deity. The most frequent possession seems to involve Yuma Sammang. At first, possession is involuntary, and the victim seeks a cure by consulting a shaman, who will attempt to pacify the deity with offerings. Should he be unsuccessful, the victim may take this as a sign that he is learn the art of shamanism in order to eventually control his possession.

Many times, the state of involuntary possession continues for years, or in rare cases, throughout one's life, without the victim becoming a shaman. Simple possession by a deity is not the only sign that one is to become a shaman. One must acquire a teacher, or rather, more accurately, the teacher must discover the patient and learn the will of the deity. Limbu insist this knowledge comes to the teacher as a result of the deity's own wishes, not the patient's or the teacher's. The teacher might learn this in a dream, or in a state of trance, or though some other divine omen. He then pays the victim a visit, informing him of the wishes of the deity.

The teacher, who is himself a practicing shaman, then begins to teach the patient the *mundhum* and the techniques of his art, which include divination, the construction of an altar, and how to make and use the shamanic paraphernalia—the costume, the drum and the various fetishes. Invariably, the patient rejects the call to become a shaman. Few desire to become shamans but, at least consciously, would rather be cured of their possession than to take on a trade which requires much time and effort and few rewards. I never met a wealthy Limbu shaman. The practicing shaman is frequently taxed both physically and mentally. During major festivals, such as Dasain, he is in great demand and often goes days without sleep. Frequently, his own family is neglected, as well as his fields. The remuneration for his services seldom equals the losses that he suffers as a result of neglecting his own agricultural work. Furthermore, most of the shamans I met had large families. One shaman had eight children. The value of a large family is great, once the children have reached the age where they are able to help in the field, but while they are young, they only represent more mouths to feed.

Spirit Possession

Spirit possession indicating the call to shamanic apprenticeship usually occurs at an early age. One shaman, a *yeba*, was first possessed at the age of eight by the spirit Samdonogma Yejuli, a household spirit of his mother's brother. His family called a shaman on a number of occasions, with the intention of curing the boy, without success. Finally a *yeba* learned of his plight and visited the boy, telling him that he was to become a *yeba*. He taught him the *mundhum* and how to control the Yejuli spirit. At first he rejected the idea, but after much coaxing from his *guru*, he decided that he would become an apprentice. His apprenticeship was short, not lasting more than two years. He then began to call the spirit at will and have success in curing people who became ill. Occasionally, however, even today, he has difficulty in controlling Yejuli, and sometimes the deity 'comes on him' without being summoned.

Yuma Sammang is frequently the goddess that possesses an individual and forces him or her to become a shaman, but it may also be a spirit of one's mother's brother's patrilineage, or the household deity of one's mother's brother, which are believed to be female deities as well. It may also be the spirit of one's maternal grandfather or grandmother, there is a widespread idea that the tutelary spirits of Limbu shamans are 'inherited' in the matrilineal and are feminine. Being called by a spirit, through possession, does not always mean that the individual will become a shaman. One man who lived near Yuksom would occasionally become possessed by the spirit of his maternal grandfather, but he did not become a shaman. I was told that a *guru* never came to him and he never learned the art. It was emphasized that, if the *guru* did not take up the individual as an apprentice, the individual could never learn to control his helping spirit.

The Guru

The *guru* is essential to the practice of Limbu shamanism. He is the one who has learned to control his possession. He teaches this art to his apprentice and instills in him the confidence that is needed in dealing with supernatural powers. In this way, the *guru* also teaches his apprentice the causes of illness, the ways to diagnose, divination and the means of curing. Without a *guru*, a person possessed is merely a person that is ill.

Conclusion

Limbu shamanism is not just a matter of teaching and learning the procedures. Without the call through possession by a spirit, a person can never become a shaman, regardless of how much he learns about divination and curing rituals. Possession and teaching are both essential to the profession.

SECTION-V
THE LEPCHA—*BON-THIN* OF TASHIDING

Introduction

In Tashiding area, the Lepchas adopted Buddhism only in the seventeenth century. Earlier, for centuries they had been living in the shadow of animism. Even Buddhism could not force them to give up their earlier religious traditions. The chief functionary of their indigenous beliefs is the *bon-thin* who is a kind of intercessor. He is chosen by the tutelary god *bon-thin rum* from a family where there have been *bon-thin* for many generations, and he is initiated after a long illness which serves as a kind of preparatory phase. The occupations of the *bon-thin* are the same as those of other villagers. He cultivates his field and looks after his goats, cows and oxen. Because of his religious position, he possesses a high social standing in the village.

The well-intentioned divinities are called *rum* in contrast to the divinities of evil intent, the *mun*, who are the cause of disease, death and disaster. The most important of the propitious divinities is *ta-se tuk-bo-thin*, also called *ta-se-thin*. Many of the propitious divinities take the form of female spirits (*mit*) inhabiting springs and *chus*. The evil divinities, the *mun*, are innumerable, haunting forests, bogs, torrents and rocks. Being very powerful, they are liable to interfere at any time in the life of the Lepchas and obstruct their projects. Only repeated sacrifices can satisfy their greed for flesh and blood.

Case Study

A double religious function devolved upon *bon-thin* Purbu who was my informant. In the role of propitiator he had to attract the attention of the chief god *ta-se-thin* and other well-intentioned divinities by means of offerings; as intercessor he had to appease and drive away the *mun* through blood sacrifices.

Periodically the *bon-thin* burns incense and recites the following prayer:

'O great god, protect us from illness, influenza, winds of the south and lightning. Protect us from the evil which can come from those who practice magic against us. You, too, king of demons, restrain your followers'.

Invoking Deities

The most important religious ceremony (*rum-fat*) takes place once a year after the harvest. The *bon-thin* makes an offering to all the divinities with whom he has contact. The villagers bring rice, millet, eggs, butter and fruit of all kinds. These offerings are placed on a stone on a hill-top well in view of *kno-cen cu* (Kanchandzonga), the mountain deity which dominates the whole region.

The Bon-thin

The *bon-thin* invokes successively the different summits of the mountain, which are identified with the following divinities: *Kon-cen cu* and his wife *kon-lo-cu*, *pun-dim* and *pun-zon-cu*, their son and daughter *ra-tat* and *ra-yot*, there grandson and granddaughter, *sin-mu* and *ko-lin-mu-cu*, their male and female servants. The offspring and the servants are the lesser summits on either side of *kon-cen cu*. Next the *bon-thin* addresses the spirits of the earth and the protectors of the village places, *tsen-gog* a mountain divinity, *ta-lyan-do* divinity of the heights above the village, *so-mon-pon-di*, spirit of the hamlet.

To these divinities, whose role seems altogether rather obscure, he offers rice, millet and oranges. In the third place the *bon-thin* requests the chief of the demons to restrain his followers. Of these *tam-nok-mun* and his partner *lyan-ser* were mentioned as the most powerful. This pair of black demons comes from the plains; having no children they are particularly self-willed and so more difficult to control than the others who are named *tsen-dut* and his mate, *tun-kun-mit,lun-li*, and his mate *lun-lun-mun*, dwellers in caves, rocks and streams. The *mun* receives offering of chhang and rice.

Sacrifices

Offerings are given at regular intervals. Cocks are also sacrificed and offered, but the *mun* still manifest themselves by causing diseases. The *bon-thin* is called upon in these cases to identify the dissatisfied *mun*. By means of divination he determines the kind of sacrifice required by the demon. A serious illness often necessitated a sacrifice of an ox. Before killing the animal invocations were made to the demons *gie-bu-mun*, *co-gye-mun*, *tsen-dut* and *me-so-mun*, who takes the life of men. While the animal was being killed, the sick man was attached to it by means of a cord, and he beseeched the demon to accept them, praying that they may cease to cause illness of all kinds: headache, stomachache, pains in the limbs, etc. The sacrifices of the ox are on a wane these days.

Functions on Death

Finally the *bon-thin* has an essential function to play at the death of a man. Since the soul of a man must return to the place of its origin, it has to find its way to the ancestor's *ti-kun-tik* and *ni-kun-nal* in the sacred land *rum-lyen*. In order to make the soul take the right path the *bon-thin* has at his disposal suitable spells. If a man is killed in the jungle or eaten by an animal, this causes special difficulties. Great efforts are made to retrieve his body, for if his soul has not been properly dispatched, it will hang around troubling members of the family. My informant also told me that the soul is judged by the god *co-ge pe-no* and is sent either to heaven or hell.

Mun

Mention was also made of the *mun*, the feminine counterpart of the *bon-thin*, but none is to be found now in Tashiding. The *mun* whose office passes from grandmother to granddaughter, is inspired by a tutelary divinity similar to *bon-thin rum*. According to the Tashiding villagers, these *mun* have power over the divinities of streams and mountains. Their supernatural power is characterized by the following stories which are often told in the village.

Folk Tales on 'Mun'

'Two brothers had become enemies after quarreling about a piece of land. The younger one appealed to a *bon-thin* in order to avenge himself on his brother. The elder one fell soon afterwards, and so his family called upon a *mun*. By means of divination she discovered the cause of the illness. A pig had been buried in the field which was the cause of the dispute. This pig was still alive, and the *mun* ordered that it should be dug up and placed near the house of the younger brother. Four days later, he died, together with seven members of his family'.

Earlier Practice

In earlier times, the *mun* shared with the *bon-thin* the power of guiding the souls of the dead to *rum-lyan*. Moreover, they could forestall the future and hold conversation with the dead.

'Three Lepchas went fishing. One of them left his companions and disappeared. His friends looked for him and found his corps in the river. On returning to the village, the two men, although innocent, were accused of this death. A *mun*, who was consulted, asked the soul of the dead man how he had died. He replied that a *mun*, whom he had offended by cutting bamboos in a forbidden place, had pushed him into the water. Through the mediation of the *mun*, the drowned man asked his father to release his friends and also revealed the place where his savings were hidden. The parents found in fact eleven rupees and some paise in a bamboo near the hearth. The dead man entrusted his child to his parents and requested his wife not to marry again'.

Conclusion

The *bon-thin* and the *mun* are different from the other *jhakris* in the sense that, these also carry out the tasks of the priesthood. Though, since the merger of Lepchas within Mahayana faith, the dependence on the lamas and the monks has become more pronounced, the traditions of the *bon-thin* and *mun* continue.

SECTION-VI
FOLKLORE RELATING TO JHAKRIS

Introduction

In the medieval times, there was no word like 'folklore' in any English dictionary. When the Europeans went out to Africa and the Americas, what they saw there was nothing like they had seen back home. To them everything they saw and did not understand looked primitive. Whatever they came across in villages, in jungles, they referred to them as 'popular antiquities'. It was only in 1864 that WJ Thomas replaced this expression with folklore – literally meaning the 'learnings of the primitives.' It has established itself as a generic term. It comprises nearly all animistic beliefs about the world of nature, animate and inanimate, about human nature and things made by man, about a spirit world and man's relations with it: about witchcraft, spells, charms, amulets, luck omens, disease, and death. It further includes customs and rites as a marriage and inheritance, childhood and adult life, and as to festivals, warfare, hunting, fishing, cattle keeping etc.; also myths, legends, folk tales, ballads, songs, proverbs, riddles, and nursery rhymes. In short, it covers everything (Burne 1914).[20]

The subjects comprehended under the name of folklore may be arranged in three principal groups with sub-headings as follows (Burne, 1914)[21]:

1. *Belief and Practice relating to:*

(a) The Earth and the Sky.

(b) The Vegetable World.

(c) The Animal World.

(d) Human Beings.

(e) Things made by Man.

(f) The Soul and Another Life.

(g) Superhuman Beings, (Gods, Godlings and others).

(h) Omens and Divination.

(i) The Magic Art.

(j) Disease and Leechcraft.

2. *Customs*

(a) Social and Political Institution.

(b) Rites of Individual Life.

(c) Occupations and Industries.

(d) Calendar Fasts and Festivals.

(e) Games, Sports, and Pastimes.

3. *Stories, Songs and Sayings*

(a) Stories: (i) told as true; (ii) told for amusement.

(b) Songs and Ballads.

(c) Proverbs and Riddles.

(d) Proverbial Rhymes and Local Sayings.

Sikkimese Folklore

Stocks (1926)[22] and Kotturan (1989)[23] have given detailed accounts of Sikkimese folklore, most of which are, at least in numbers, dominated by Lepcha folktales *Jhakris*, shamans and *bon-thins* form an integral subject within the arena of folklore and customs. Almost all subjects described in introductory paragraph above form the vast assemblage of folktales.

The folktale described here is conspicuous by the fact, that it encompasses within itself the Hindu Gods, and the Buddhist Bhutia Lama. The tale also to a great extent explains the diffusion of the shamanic rites within the region. It relates to the origin of the *jhakri* system, and as to, who was the first *jhakri*. The ethics to be maintained by the jhakris are also amply brought out in the tale.

Folktale of First Jhakri

Majority of persons agree that Shankar Mahadev Bhagwan was the first *jhakri*. Mahadev and a Bhutia Lama met on Mount Kailash in the Himalays. The two competed to draw forth from the jungle, using nothing but 'Mantra' the following objects:

(a) *A gorin.* A necklace made of beads. This type of necklace is also used in Tantric ceremonies. Each *jhakri* possesses several of these.

(b) A *rudraksha Mala.*

(c) *Dumsi ko karo.* These are the porcupine quills.

By the same *mantra* power they also tried to fill an empty vessel with water and reach the sun. Mahadev produced a *ghoirin* and *mala.* Mahadev filled the vessel with water. The Lama drew a prayer wheel. Mahadev arrived half way to the sun, but everything became dark, and he could no longer follow the path. The Lama arrived at the sun. Mahadev constructed a drum and danced and played with it. Since Lama reached the sun, it was agreed that Lama would perform *puja* during day, whereas Mahadev would perform at night. Mahadev and Lama then separated and each settled down in different parts of Kailash.

Mahadev Drum and Siran Shikari

The story continues on making of Mahadev's drum. Mahadev sent the porcupine into jungle to bring *sinaro* wood from the jungle to make the drum frames. A deer skin was brought for making drum heads. Mahadev closed the drum by attaching a handle. A *rudraksha mala* and other articles were placed inside the drum. A hen was brought, which laid an egg. A red dog arrived by itself. The dog irritated the Lama, who killed it. The dog's spirit assumed the role of guardian of the drum and the egg. In Mahadev's absence the dog's spirit protected his gear. Mahadev produced bow and arrows for the dog to function effectively. From that day on the dog became *Siran Shikari.* This was the first *shikari.* Today traditional distinguishes 16 *Shikaris.* Their names and characteristics are :

(a) *Ekle shikari.* The lone hunter. He is the assistant to the others.

(b) *Lawari shikari.* The colour-bearer. He leads the *shikari* troupe, carrying the seven-coloured flag white, red, blue, green, yellow, light blue and cream. *Lawa* means 'flag'. It is made of a long cherrywood staff, surmounted by an iron spearhead. Various coloured cloths are attached to an iron ring at the base of the tip. The whole things is called barcho.

(c) *Bagali shikari.* The guardian of the troupe. *Bagalimu* means 'to group together'.

(d) *Chamung shikari.* This one is bad. If seen at the time of a *puja*, he may jeopardize the *puja's* success. The name is perhaps related to *chamkanu*, 'to be insolent'.

(e) *Khurma shikari* throws needles out from the earth. Inflicts illnesses such as sciatica (khuro means 'pin').

(f) *Namrun shikari* found under fruits and flowers. He protects. He is good.

(g) *Bajra shikari* lightning (*bajra* = lightning).

(h) *Chalena shikari* makes fun of people. He is at once good and *bad*. (*chale* (*adj.*) = 'to pretend').

(i) *Kheluwa shikari* plays everywhere (khelmu = to play).

(j) *Sarma shikari* bends people by inflicting attack of paralysis.

(k) *Sama cherin chatmaghe shikari* if he is not properly worshipped, he inflicts fatal pains of the stomach and heart.

(l) *Raktaban shikari* causes internal haemorrhage. (*rakta* = blood).

(m) *Ban shikari* moves about like the wind and knocks people over. The paralysis is said to be caused by jungle spirits who shoot the sufferer. *iban* = arrow).

(n) *Kali shikari* black, like a black *bhut* (ghost).

(o) *Solasarma shikari* if people speak badly of him, he immobilizes them on the spot.

When men are sick, the *jhakri* must name the 16 *shikaris* and designate the one responsible for sickness. A cock may be sacrificed on such occasions.

Summary

A *jhakri* does not live in isolation. It is noticed that *jhakri* though does not fully embrace the same world of relationships as classical Hinduism, the *jhakri* and his clientele are more or less Hinduized, but are also influenced by Tibetan Mahayana Buddhism, the Mon and the Bon rites. In these accounts of cultural diffusion also, many folktales are prevalent. The overall integration of cultural diffusive knowledge becomes definitive only when the *jhakri* integrally transmits his knowledge to a pupil, an exceptional event for the society as a whole. It seems clear that the pupil in turn interprets and embellishes the material in terms of this own competency and experience, and so it goes from generation to generation.

References

1. Subba, J.R., *The Limbus of Eastern Himalayas: With Special Reference to Sikkim.* SYMS, Gangtok, 1999.
2. Sakya, J.B., *Buddhism and Hindusism in Nepal.* Handicraft Association of Nepal, Kathmandu, 1989.
3. Thakur, R.N., *Himalayan Lepchas.* Archives Publishers, New Delhi, 1988.
4. Subba, J.R., *ibid.*
5. Tamang, J.P. and Tamang, N. *Sikkim Biodiversity and Eco-Tourism Project*, Tadong, Sikkim, p. 31, 1998.

6. Field Work in Upper Rangit Basin.
7. Field Work in Upper Rangit Basin.
8. Field Work.
9. Field Work—Ravangla Folk Market.
10. Inglis, J.T., (ed.) *Concept and Cases: Traditional Ecological Knowledge.*
11. Govinda, L.A., *Foundations of Tibetan Mysticism*, B.I. Publications Pvt Ltd, New Delhi, 1960.
12. Venu, P., et al, 'Limnological Survey of Water Bodies of the Sikkim Himalaya, India.' *Journal of Human Ecology*, 1(2), 1990.
13. Roy, B.N. and Thapa, M.P., 'Limnology of Lake Khecheopalri', *Journal of Hill Research*, 9(2), 1996.
14. ——, 'Limnology of Lake Khecheopalri-II', *Journal of Hill Research*, 1997.
15. Roy, B.N., et al, 'Studies on Biological Diversity of Lake Khecheopalri' paper presented in International Conference on Wet Lands, New Delhi and Bharatpur, 1998.
16. Raina, V.K., and Srivastava, B.S., 'Tectonic Evolution of Sikkim Himalaya'. In A.V. Sinha (ed.), *Geoscientific Research in Himalaya*, Dehradun, 1981.
17. Bose, P.N., 'Geology and Mineral Resources of Sikkim'. *The Gazetteer of Sikkim*, Nature Conservation Foundation, 1989.
18. Hitchcock, J.T., and Jones, R.L., *Spirit possession in the Nepal Himalayas*, Vikas Publishing House, Pvt. Ltd., New Delhi, 1994.
19. Field Study in Upper Rangit Basin.
20. Burne, C.S., *The Handbook of Folklore*, Sidgwick & Jackson Ltd., London, 1914.
21. *Ibid.*
22. Stocks, C.D.B., *Sikkim : Customs and Folklore*, 1926, Cosmos Publications, Delhi, Reprint 1975.
23. Kotturan, G., *Folktales of Sikkim*. Sterling Publishers Pvt. Ltd., New Delhi, 1989.

7

Tradition as a Factor in Modernization—A Case Study of Bhutan

Tradition as Factor in the Process of Modernization: A Case Study of Bhutan

In this paper I propose to trace the process of modernization in Himalayan Kingdoms of Bhutan. But before I come to the main subject I think it proper to define the term modernization so that my theoretical parameters may become identifiable.

Modernisation and Tradition: A Theoretical Discussion

Modernisation, more often than not, is regarded as something analogous to westernization. It is in the countries of the West that development of science and technology has made long strides and the whole life has got revolutionised in the process. The theoretical construct of modernization assumes a modicum of modernity as an ideal type and it is in relation to it that any individual, nation, society, institution or pattern of life is adjudged as modern or behind it. As rationality is said to be quintessence of modernization, faith in religion has not only grown feeble but it has also materially changed values of life.

Pure rationality, or what the sophisticated call 'scientific temper' has even led to the absolute denial of God and soul and with an increasing number, absolute non-belief in God and Soul is sometimes taken as a sign of modernity.

Extent of Religion Faith

Modernity should not mean all that. In no case should it be considered synonymous with westernization. Scientific temper cannot be equated with western thinking. What has been invented since the advent of industrialization does indicate that the society is responsive to the use of science and technology, which can, in turn, improve prospects of material happiness. But likewise there can be long strides in the sphere of emotion and spirit which are as much a part of human life as reason. To banish faith and thus to conclude that the extent of religious faith in a people is the measure of its traditional back-log and a sign of backwardness is not necessarily true.

Modernity

In spite of its rather loose use in the literature, modernity can be considered inclusive of one or more or all of the following dimensions:

(a) Pattern of life and values, including faith of the people.

(b) Mode of transport and communication.

(c) Pattern of Education.

(d) Ideas and Idiologies.

(e) Laws of the lands.

(f) Socio-economic system.

(g) Administrative system and practices.

How far and by what process modernity has penetrated in a particular society is a question that cannot be examined in all cases purposefully in the spheres mentioned above because indices of measurement and more particularly, their operational forms vary from country to country and time to time.

Three Tests

If one becomes westernized, knows about science and technology, has he become civilized? There is lot of talk about modern civilization and to be reckoned among civilized nations a society has to be modernized. This clearly will lead to the conclusion that the concept of modernity can be equated with the concept of being civilised. At this moment one is reminded of what C.E.M. Joad said, "To be civilized means making and liking beautiful things, thinking freely, living rightly and meeting out justice equally between man and man." One may or may not fully subscribe to the views of Joad, but it does atleast indicate that modernization is not something concerned with superficialities but with a life pattern in which basic attitudes and aptitudes, whether of an individual or of society, are such as have aesthetic sense developed, are prone to free thinking and right living and which make no distinction between man and man in meeting out justice. Thus, one test of modernity is the attitude of people in general, not just utopian, but translated in to action in the various spheres of life mentioned above.

Natural Sciences and Technology

One very important characteristic of the modern age that draws a line of demarcation between it and the ages prior to it, is the unprecedented development in the field of natural sciences and technology. So the second test would be an advancement in these and the degree of their judicious application in the relevant spheres of life. The adjective "judicious" is significant. Science and technology are neutral as far as their use and abuse are concerned and as such the idea of judicious use becomes relevant. Rationality is the very essence of science. And when we are well aware that sheer and reckless limitation is suicide, rationality demands that in different spheres of human activity in a given society in a particular-setting whether as regards topography, climate conditions, level of socio-economic development and the like, adoption of everything that has come into vogue in the developed countries of the west would not be considered a case of judicious use of technology and science.

The third test concerns values. Is there a change in the values of the people as a whole and, if it is, to what extent and in what direction? Is man more happy now than he was before the invention in science took hold of him? Here, also, rationality would demand that change is consistent with the happiness of man in society and that also in all its dimensions—material, human and even emotional and spiritual.

On Tradition

Let us now turn to tradition for a while. According to dictionary meaning, any continuing practice is a tradition. Thus, tradition can refer to practices that are, by all accounts modern, tradition is not something necessarily confined to the ways, methods and practices of pre-modern times. Terms like traditional methods of production in factories, or traditional way of teaching in modern schools and colleges are in common use, signifying that the latest methods and ways have not yet been adopted. Thus, it is difficult to draw a purposeful line of demarcation between modernization and tradition.

Tradition and Modernization

However, one could argue that a tradition is a continuing practice, while modernization is a continuing process. What is termed modern today, may fall in the category of tradition a few years hence. Modernization in any society, therefore, may assume any of the following forms:

(a) Adopting something for which a tradition did not exist.

(b) Giving a pre-modern tradition a modern shape.

(c) Modernising a modern tradition.

(d) Innovating something by self-effort.

Bhutan and the Modernization Process

I shall now turn to discuss the role of tradition as a factor in the process of modernization Bhutan against the background of mentioned theoretical discussion.

Of the two kingdoms, Bhutan is much smaller and according to the Census of 1971 its population is only 13 lakh. The interior is also cut up by mountain ranges and the northern parts are far too cold in winter so that the residents there migrate with their goods, cattle and charttle to the southern parts. Out of its twenty districts, thirteen are cut up from one another by mountain ranges, thus forming not only administrative but also geographical divisions. Moreover, it seems to have been designed by nature to lead an isolated existence owing to its inaccessibility from all sides. It was after the eight century A.D. that it came under the influence of Tibet. Prior to it, it was a part of Kamrup Kingdom of Assam.

Contact with Tibet

Bhutan has been more under the social and religious influence of Tibetan lamaism than of Indian Hinduism. Hindu influence did not account for much till Nepalis started migrating to Bhutan in the nineteenth century. Long extending contact with Tibet accounts for its impact on the religion of its people and the overpowering influence of Lamaism, which in Bhutan has elements of Animism mixed up with it. It is in the light of all these factors that the process of modernization has to be viewed in the small Kingdom of Bhutan.

In Bhutan, concentration of population in any area is prohibited by nature. Influences of outside world, in such a situation, are very slow to come even if there are no artificial impediments–internal or external. The pace gets very much accelerated if and when there is government support for these influences. In the eventuality of the government attitude being neutral, private agencies, such as missionaries and social reformers, play their role in making people conscious of the need of change. Elite also play their part.

Monarchy and the People

In Bhutan, the king is the symbol of supreme authority in the state. With the event of modernity, one of the expectations is that absolute powers of the King would yield place to some sort of a participatory system. In Bhutan there are four stages that can be clearly identified through which a change in this direction have taken place:

(i) In stage one the King was the supreme authority in all matters–temporal and spiritual- wielding power for the establishment of Dharma.

(ii) In the stage two during the middle ages–the authority got divided between two heads–Dev Raja and Dharma Raja, the one supreme in matters temporary and the other in matters spiritual. Both of them had equal ranks.

(iii) In stage three—when the hereditary Kingship was established in 1907, the Dev Raja became the supreme authority. An interesting feature is that the change came about by unanimous consent of all the penlopes or regional heads.

(iv) In stage four—the King at the time of his coronation, decided by his choice, to get the hereditary king confirmed by election in 1974, signifying that even though hereditary, he was there to rule by the consent of the people expressed through members of the National Assembly who represented the will of different sections of population. The blending of the elements of heredity and election in the institution of Kingship is a unique feature and presents a rare example of modernizing a tradition according to the genios of the people.

Internal Conditions in Bhutan

It is not very difficult to understand the differing religious situations in Bhutan. The population of Bhutan is to a great extent homogeneous at least in matters of religion because Buddhism or Lamaism of the Bhutanese brand does not recognise any caste distinction. The masses in Bhutan have remained uneffected by the winds from democratic India on account of its inaccessibility. Bhutan's ruler partly influenced by the western ideas, which he imbibed during his education in England and partly to entrench himself at the very outset, took the sagacious step of associating the people to win over the reluctant members of the National Assembly in his side and to keep the power of Lamas in check. It is thus obvious that, even though they spread of modern education in Bhutan has been through the agency of the government, their attitude towards it has been negative rather than one of encouragement.

Hostility towards Modern Education

The hostility of the Lamas in Bhutan and of the old styled Brahman class in Nepal also contributed to the nourishing of this attitude. At least in Nepal the pressure of circumstance however feeble and of those few elites who were influenced by forces that were taking shape in India and the need to respond to the British ruler's emphasis on education, compelled the Rana Prime Ministers to introduce modern education. As stated earlier also, the pace of its spread remained slow due to several reasons–the attitude of the Rana government, topography of the country, resistance from traditional life situations in which the recipients of modern education found themselves a mis-fit at least to some extent and the cold reception given to it by traditional pattern of education. Gradually the economic prospects titled the balance in favour of imparting modern education. It was not a case of modernizing a pre-modern tradition but of supplanting the old pattern by a new system. The Christian missionaries who had been pioneers in other countries in this field had no role to play here. In both Nepal and Bhutan it was through the agency of the respective governments that the process got started. In Nepal the take-off stage has almost come but in Bhutan it has also to go a long way.

Communication Network and Modernity

Easy means of communication and transportation, roads, railways, aerodromes, posts and telegraphs are another feature of modernity. As stated earlier also, in Bhutan it was only after the closure of the trade-route with Tibet in 1959 that economic pressures prompted the Bhutanese rulers to look for trade routes through India and agree to the speedy construction of Indo-Bhutanese roadlink. Since then the relations between the two countries, particularly, after the Chinese invasion of India in 1962, have grown more and more cordial. Topography of Bhutan militates against rail construction to any great extent. Development of road communication and construction of small aerodromes at district headquarters to overcome the problem of internal inaccessibility are practical propositions. The natural barriers would be broken thereby. There is no tradition to stand in the way of this programme, which is underway with multi-lateral foreign aid.

Already there is a small aerodrome constructed in the capital town of Paro. So modernization process is having its way in this respect. Traditional methods have been employed in the construction of roads and thus it can be argued that tradition has helped rather than hampered the process of modernization, foreign aid, government's positive attitude under an enlightened ruler, and enthusiasm of the people who clearly see prospects of better living conditions in the wake of improved means of communication should accelerate the process of this respect. It is a case of adopting modernity for the well-being of the pepole, for giving boost to trade and commerce, for bringing the people of different areas closer to one-another and effecting administrative compactness.

Modernization process in Bhutan can be identified at Domestic and External levels:

At the Domestic Level

Planned Economic Development in Bhutan started in 1961 when First Five Fear Plan was launched with the cent-per cent economic assistance of Government of India. Thus, the barter economy of Bhutan changed into industrial economy. Presently, Bhutan is on the way of completion of 7th Five Year Plan and 8th Five Year Plan is to start. Since 1961, Bhutan has become an open Trading Economy.

Forced transportation through India, due to closure of trade through Tibet, has made Bhutan an open trading economy. The evolution between medieval Bhutan (prior to the late 1950s) and modern Bhutan is underscored by its integration with global economies. To show the extent of globalization and integration of the Bhutanese economy with others, in 1991 exports amounted to about 29 per cent of GDP, while imports were 36 per cent of GDD. India is by far the most important trading partner for Bhutan. It accounts for 90 per cent of Bhutan's exports and is the source of 85 per cent of Bhutan's imports. Bhutan's main exports are electricity, processed wood products, minerals and cement. Exports to India have risen from Nu. 380m in 1986 to an estimated Nu. 1472m in 1991. However, at the same time, imports from India have risen from Nu. 861 m in 1986 to an estimated Nu. 1961 m in 1991.

Development Plans

Today, educational institutions which numbered only a few in 1959 have increased to 328 in 1992, providing education and training to more than 70,000 Bhutanese youth. More than 67 per cent of Bhutan's children of school going age are attending schools, and literacy rate has reached 54 per cent in 1991.

Other Achievements

There are also several other notable achievements relating to human development. A modern health infrastructure has expanded from 15 centres in the early 1960s to 174 centres and 350 outreach clinics by 1992. Currently, 90 per cent of the people have access to primary health care. In 1990, the Royal Government and its development partners were able to achieve Universal Child Immunization. In addition, as the bulk of the population live in rural areas, concerted efforts have been made to direct the benefits of modernization to the rural population. Extensive programmes have been launched to deliver safe drinking water, improved sanitation and electricity to the people.

Today, 40 per cent of the population has access to safe drinking water. Satellite based telecommunications and international air-links have also been established making Bhutan more accessible to the outside world. By the end of the Seventh Plan the whole country will be linked by a digital micro-wave telephone network.

The speed at which this transformation has been achieved has not been seen anywhere else in the world.

This transformation from the medieval to the modern has been achieved in just 31 years.

At the External Level

The basic premises of Bhutan's foreign policy can be observed through the remarks of the young ruler Jigme Singye Wangchuck of Bhutan who once said:

> "Our aim continues to be threefold: Firstly, we are committed politically to a strong and loyal sense of nationhood to ensuring the peace and security of our citizens and the sovereign territorial integrity of our land. Secondly, to achieve economic self-reliance and the capacity to begin and complete any project we undertake and thirdly to preserve the ancient religious and cultural heritage that has for so many centuries strengthened and enriched our lives".

Bhutan subscribes fully to the charter of the UNO, NAM and SAARC and has accordingly continued to play an active and committed role in both these international organizations. The foreign policy of Bhutan is thus based on the principles of peace, friendship and non-alignment. To quote the Bhutanese King "We have based our policy of non-alignment on our determination not to align ourselves with one bloc and to hate the other or to play power politics with both. Never in this world does hatred cease by hatred, it ceases with love. This is the law eternal."

Bhutan Foreign Policy

Bhutan foreign policy pursuits are characterized by subtle but significant initiatives. Such initiatives have been in two broad fields: (a) in relation to neighbouring countries, and (b) with regard to regional and international organizations and forums like SAARC, the UNO and its associated agencies and the NAM.

With skilful diplomacy and surprising maturity, Bhutan has so far succeeded in harmonizing an inherently contradictory situation by pursuing its threefold strategy of consolidating the home base, correcting the Indian connections and seeking new friends abroad. The two Asian giants–China and India–situated in the north and south of Bhutan respectively are so vital in geographical terms that their attitudes towards this buffer state as also their relative capability distribution in the Himalayan region and in South Asia will always determine practically all foreign policy considerations of Bhutan. It hardly needs to be stressed that Bhutan is strategically important for both its big neighbours because of its location. This is the most compelling reason for both China and India to strive for special and friendly relationship with the Buddhist theocratic state.

International Personality

The leadership in Bhutan is very clear about its goal. This is surprising for a country, which is taking its first tentative steps towards integration with the comity of nations. Although hesitant in the face of world diplomacy, Bhutan made cautious and calculated moves to diversify its diplomatic contacts into the world beyond the Himalayan context. With a slow but steady approach Bhutan has prudently and selectively initiated diplomatic thrust in order to step into a new phase of political evolution.

In its search for establishing an identity, distinct and separate from India, efforts are visible in two directions. Till 1971, economic dependence on India was total. Today international agencies like UNO, the World Bank, the Asian Development Bank, the Kuwaiti development firm and others are involved in Bhutan's economic progress in a fairly significant way. Though Indian aid is still the largest (65 per cent) the dependence has been reduced purposefully. All the benefits have been achieved in a very cautious manner without unduly upsetting India whose interests are critical in this area. None of the political links with India have been devalued on the surface so as not to give offence or invite an hostile response.

New Trade Contacts

Over the last five years or so there has been a further expansion in Bhutan's external contacts. Bhutan has opened new trade contacts with countries in South Asia like Bangladesh and Nepal. In 1983, Bhutan and India signed a new trade agreement replacing the earlier agreement of 1977. The new agreement simplified the procedures to facilitate Bhutan's trade with third countries. Some of the countries, with which Bhutan has trade contacts are Bangladesh, Nepal, Singapore and Hong Kong.

Diplomatic Missions

Bhutan has also been making quick advances on diplomatic front. It opened its first diplomatic mission outside India in 1978 in Bangladesh. In 1982, it appointed honorary consuls in Singapore and Hong Kong. In 1983, Nepal and Bhutan established diplomatic relations. In 1985, diplomatic channels were opened with Denmark, Switzerland, Netherlands and the EEC. The most important development was, of course, the opening of direct border talks between Bhutan and China. In 1984, a Bhutanese delegation visited China and held talks on the question of the settlement of their boundary dispute, and since then ten rounds of talks have taken place in Thimphu and Beijing by rotation.

Bhutan and China

The event of 1984 is significant for two reasons. Firstly, it marks the opening of direct contacts, though for a limited purpose, between the two countries. This may pave the way for the establishment of full-fledged diplomatic relations. Secondary, and perhaps unfortunately, it is evident that henceforth the Bhutan-China border issue will not be considered an internal part of the Sino-Indian boundary dispute. In this context one of Nehru's remarks can well be recalled: "The Government of India is the only competent authority to take up with other government matters concerning Bhutan's external relations. As such if any rectification was to be made regarding their boundary it must be discussed along with the boundary of India".

Since, the events of 1984-85 it is clear that Bhutan has no longer adhered to the implications of the treaty of 1949 ; indeed they have a more liberal interpretation of the words and incorporated in the treaty. On its part, the government of India has also not taken much note of the deviations from the terms of the treaty. Bhutan's admission to the UNO on Sept. 21, 1971 and NAM in 1973 marked the international endorsement of its sovereignty and integrity as a nation. This was universally welcomed in Bhutan as one of the achievements of the country's foreign policy. Moreover, the opening of the permanent mission at the U.N. in New York in 1972 had several immediate consequences. For one thing, it provided Bhutan with an alternative channel of communication to the outside world. Bhutan's dependence upon its intermediary for linkage with the outside world has thus been substantially reduced.

Indo-Bhutan Treaty

While the provisions of the 1949 Indo-Bhutan treaty still hold good, the manner in which guidance is provided by New Delhi has undergone modifications. According to Bhutanese sources, India has now accepted Thimphu's interpretations of the treaty namely that Bhutan is obligated to seek India's advice on foreign policy questions but is not necessarily obliged to accept it. New Delhi has never publicly acknowledged this but appears to operate on this basis as a general practice.

The other indication that Bhutan asserted its position as an independent nation came at the Non-Align Summit Conference at Hawana in 1979 on the question of the admission of Kampuchea. While Bhutan supported the claims of the ousted Pol Pot regime of Kampuchea, India was in a favour of keeping the seat vacant. That Bhutan did not vote identically with India on a world issue did not happen for the first time. In fact, both in the UN and NAM, Bhutan had voted counter to India on the Issue of the rights of the land-locked countries. To the credit of the Indian Government it can be said that not once did it criticise the decision of Bhutan to vote counter to its wishes.

Bhutan and SAARC

Though Bhutan did not take much initiative in the establishment of the SAARC, once the idea was articulated and put forward by Bangladesh, it enthusiastically viewed it as a forum to project its aspirations and pursue its other regional initiatives. Bhutan was choosen as the co-coordinator of the working group on postal services, which was in fact a recognition of the great strides, this small kingdom has made in the field of postal services. Bhutan later hosted a number of meetings of the technical committees including the one on the postal services in Thimphu. Thimphu was also one of the venues where preparatory talks for the launching of the SAARC were held. Bhutan also organized a coaching camp in Table Tennis as part of its commitment of the SAARC cooperative training activities. Furthermore, Bhutan was also chosen as the meeting ground for the diplomats seeking to resolve the ethnic problem of Sri Lanka. To quote Bhutan's official Weekly *Kuensel*, "Bhutan is emerging as an 'Eastern Geneva', a venue for peace-making efforts in South Asia". Bhutan attaches great importance to the opportunities SAARC will provide for more beneficial economic relations with countries other than India.

Concept of Economic Cooperation

Bhutan's keenness to promote the concept of economic cooperation in South Asia is compatible with its efforts to increase its capabilities through internal growth and foreign trade as a means to counter its military and political vulnerability. Not that it has any danger from both the big nations in the north and the south. The trade agreement with Bangladesh signed in 1980 is another significant step. Not only does it establish Bhutan's right to trade with third countries, It obtained transit rights and customs facilities from India. The trade agreement of 1983 with India recognizes Bhutan's rights to trade directly with other countries. To the mutual interest, the Bangladesh trade agreement gives reciprocal transit privileges to Bangladesh through Bhutan to Tibet despite Indian reservations.

Air Communication Linkages

Air communication linkages have also been established between Dhaka and Thimphu. Thus, Bhutan has made considerable headway in establishing its links with its immediate neighbours both politically and economically. SAARC framework may lead to a wider network of collaboration in Bhutan's bid to steadily diversify its trade and economic ties with the regional countries. Bhutan is gradually putting in efforts to reduce her over-dependence on India. Consequently, in recent years, there has been a notable dynamism in the foreign policy of Bhutan.

Finally, it may be observed that Bhutan is evolving her foreign relations with extreme caution. With the intention to contribute constructively in all international forums, Bhutan has apparently restrained herself from opening up abruptly to all and sundry international forces and become a cockpit of power politics. One may conclude therefore that a policy of modernization combined with the diversification of dependence is perhaps suitable to meet the domestic needs and pressures of a country like Bhutan.

Summing Up

The people in Bhutan are neither uneasy for change nor they are absolutely no changers. They will stick to their traditional ways of life in matters of food, marriage customs, festivities, beliefs, faith in God and so on but at the same time welcome modernity if it does not appear to be absolutely hostile to their established beliefs. Thus, these two countries are forging ahead on the road to modernity in its basic essentials if it is not too narrowly, and perhaps wrongly also, interpreted to mean just westernization, industrialization and an anti-religious stance.

At every level, development in Bhutan has been extremely rapid ; so much so that nobody in the 1960s would have envisaged the rapid progress and change that has come about in the last three decades. A few examples could perhaps illustrate the quantum leap Bhutan has taken from the medieval ages to the modern era. Before 1961, there were virtually no proper schools, hospitals, post offices, telephones, motorable roads, electricity and so forth. All of these facilities are not only available to the people today, but they are subsidized heavily by the government. Both airline services and a satellite communication system linking Bhutan with the outside world have been around for some years and advanced technologies are being introduced in many areas. A network of microwave transmission is being installed around the country and within this plan, all the districts in Bhutan will be connected by the latest telecommunication system.

Bhutan has achieved tremendous progress in just three decades, without losing its rich cultural heritage and unique national identity. These achievements have been possible because of an enlightened leadership which has inspired a pragmatic, result-oriented and corruption free government and administration. The Bhutanese people look towards to the future with great optimism generated by the achievements of the past three decades.

References

Planning Commission, Royal Government of Bhutan, Fifth Five-Year Plan 1981-87, Main Document, Druk Sherig Press.

Planning Commission, Royal Government of Bhutan, Sixth Five-Year Plan, 1987-92, Royal Government Press, Lungtenzampa, Thimphu.

Planning Commission, Royal Government of Bhutan, Seventh Five-Year Plan (1992-97) Vol. I, Main Plan Document, Tashi Chhodzang, Thimphu, December, 1991.

Planning Commission, Royal Government of Bhutan, Bhutan; Towards Sustainable Development in a unique Environment, National Environmental Secretariat, Thimphu, February, 1992.

Karan, Pradyumma P. Bhutan: A Physical and Cultural Geography, Lexington, 1971.

Nagendra Nath Sarmah. Bhutan under King Jigme Dorji Wangchuk: A Study of External interactions, 1952-72, a Dissertation submitted for the Degree of Master of Philosophy, centre for South South-East and Central Asian Studies, School of International Studies, Jawaharlal Nehru University, New Delhi, 1973 (unpublished).

Nari Rustomji, Enchanted Frontiers, Sikkim, Bhutan and India's Northeastern Borderland, Oxford, 1971.

R.C. Misra, *Emergence of Bhutan*, SAN-Darbh Prakashan, 1989, Jaipur.

R.C. Misra, *Parvatiya Rajyon ki Rajniti Main Bhutan*. Rajasthan Prakashan, Jaipur, 1983.

Parmanand, *Politics of Bhutan*, Pragati Prakashan, Delhi, 1993.

Proceeding of Bhutan's National Parliament (Thimphu) from 69th to 72nd, published by Royal Government of Bhutan.

8

Art and Painting: Uttarakhand

Art and culture reflect the socio-economic and cultural life of any people anywhere. Paintings of Kangra, miniatures of Bundi and Kota, Madhubani paintings of Bihar, all these in a way showcase the life people live in these regions. This is so also in Uttranchal. The silver mountains, the sparking streams, vivid green valleys and the cool climate have attracted many into the hills of Uttarakhand for peace, tranquility and meditation. It is the beautiful land of Uttarakhand which inspired the great writers to write *Mahabharata* and *Ramayana* in the peaceful atmosphere of these hills. Maharishi Balmiki and Kalidas had great attachment for these hills. All this laid the ultimate foundation for the literary treasures in Uttarakhand including painting and art. Over the centuries, the tradition of folk art has remained unaffected in this region. Sultanate had taken complete control in the plains but due to inaccessibility and difficult terrain, the invaders could not move into the hills.

Ramganga Valley

It was along the Ramganga valley where Buddhism and Hinduism flourished in the hills of Uttarakhand. Dwarhat was the first important city in the hills which tells the story of the regions past. From Dwarhat cultural activity moved to Kausani and the valley of Garur and Bageshwar. The temples of Garur are said to be very close to Pala art and architecture. The temple of Katarmal, now in a ruined condition, about ten miles from Almora, displays skill and craftsmanship of a very high order. The art of Garhwal and Kumaon can be divided into five parts, i.e., temple architecture, wood-carving, Painting (Garhwal school of painting and Aipana, Peeth, Patas, Bar-boond of Kumaon), Dekhara and Ornaments.

The rulers of the region being *Vaishnavs* had temples and Hindu deities in their minds and hearts. Whenever there was peace in the kingdom, the rulers tried to promote temples. In Garhwal and Kumaon region, temple architecture was promoted and patronised by Katyuri, Panwar and Chand rulers. Temples of big size stones were erected with beautiful stone or metal idols of numerous Hindu god and goddesses. Temples at Lakhamandal, Adi-Badri, Dwarhat, Bageshwar, Baijnath, Gangolihat and Champawat are some of the example of temple architecture. Kings of Katyuri dynasty also constructed many temples of stone including Kedarnath and Tungnath in the higher reached of the Garhwal Himalayas. The other temple which clearly display the original Art in temple architecture of the region are Kamleshwar temple at Srinagar and Nanda Devi temple at Almora.

The ruins of palaces and temples in Champawat district are the proof of rich temple architecture promoted by the wealthy and powerful king of Garhwal and Kumaon. The salient features of the temple architecture are: lotus shaped roof, Lion over elephant projected over lower Shikhara normally covering audience hall and outer walls. The temples are either in 'Panch Rath' or 'Sapt Rath'. Pattern which provide cylindrical shape to temples. The main temple is invariably surrounded by a couple of smaller temples which house deities of lower hierarchy. The old temples of stone are being replaced by modern temples made of cement, bricks and steel leaving behind traditional temple architecture are part of history.

Wood Carving

Wood carving must have been started to give a good look to the façade of a house. The main gates of the houses everywhere in Uttranchal are made of wood. To give a good look to the façade, the main doors are generally decorated and carved.. Along with temple architecture, the craftsmen of Garhwal and Kumaon hill region also pursued woodcarving. This main entrance in also known as 'Kholi' in local language. The size and ornamental wood-carving also indicated the social and economic status of the family. Small images of human beings, flowers, birds and animals could be seen carved in the windows and doors of the houses. At Katarmal, one can see the famous carved doors which perhaps is the finest work of single piece wood-carving. Wood carving could be seen on every door of the house till only half century ago. In addition, wood-carving can be seen in hundreds of temple all over Uttarakhand. The remains of architectural work have been found at the following places in Uttarakhand.

1. Champawat king, Gangolihat temple, Patal Bhuvneshwari temple, Someshwar temple of Ranikhet in Almora district.
2. Chandpur fort, Temple of Srinagar, Pandukeshwar near Badrinath, Devi Madin near Joshimath, Devalgarh temple-all in Pauri Garhwal and Chamoli district.
3. Dhikali and Kashipur in Nainital district.

Period of Inactivity (Before 18th Century)

Over the centuries in India, painters did not work in isolation; they painted at the behest of their patrons. Unfortunately in the seventeen-century, activities in the field of art in Uttranchal came to a halt. It is quite possible in this period the interest of patrons waned in paintings or was diverted to some other activities. As the population kept on increasing, the main occupation began to be agriculture. The people thus remained contented with folk songs and dances. There is also a historical reason for the halt in the development of art in Uttarakhand. The region was divided into small fortresses particularly in Garhwal region and therefore there was little or no development of art and painting. However, the folk art continued to exist both in Kumaon and Garhwal region.

Garhwal School of Painting (18th and 19th Century)

A study of the Garhwal School of Painting has shown that it was during the later half of the eighteenth century and the first half of the nineteenth century that the art re-emerged and regenerated in the hills of Uttarakhand. It was during the period of emperor Aurangzeb that artists moved into the hills with their chiefs and rulers from Delhi and Agra. Some of them moved to Kangra where Raja Sansar Chand patronised these artists. In spite of the prosperous and peaceful times conducive for the development of art in Garhwal under Mahipati Shah, the origin of miniature painting at Srinagar is attributed to the reign of his son, Prithvi Shah (AD 1631-1664). For that, the irony of medieval Mughal polity is held responsible. Soon after Shahjahan fell ill in AD 1657, a war of succession started among his sons—Dara Shukoh, Shuja, Aurangzeb and Murad. Besides, his two daughters, Jahanara and Raushnara also entered the fray with their brothers. While Jahanara sided with Dara Shukoh, Raushnara supported Aurangzeb. Although, such struggle had become usual after the death of every Mughal emperor and lasted until the fittest was left, yet that one had definite and far-reaching consequences for the efflorescence of the imperial Mughal art and architectural mannerisms in the provincial and feudal centres in north India. In that war of succession, Aurangzeb emerged triumphant. He deposed his father and proclaimed himself emperor in AD 1658.

In order to make his position unassailable, he eliminated all his brothers and potential opponents, but his nephew, Sulaiman Shukoh, son of Dara Shukoh escaped his dragnet. Chased by the hounding army of Aurangzeb, he ran from place to place for his life. Ultimately, he reached Srinagar in Garhwal in August 1658 with the hope that the king, who had already defeated the Mughal army at least twice, should be bold enough to protect him. The reigning king of Garhwal, Raja Prithvi Shah (AD 1631-1664), upholding the honour of a Rajput to protect a refugee seeker, provided him and his entourage of seventeen retainers full hospitality and protection. It is most likely that among the people who accompanied him from Delhi were many artisans, were left jobless and insecure by the puritanical and bigoted rule of Aurangzeb, a sadistic and orthodox Sunni Muslim. Among those refugees, the names of two, Sham Das and his son Har Das are known through the writings of their later descendant, Mola Ram, the famous poet-painter of Garhwal. Both of them had been the retainers of Sulaiman Shukoh in the imperial Mughal atelier at Delhi. Mukandi Lal regarded them to be the patriarch of the Garhwal School of Painting on the authority of Mola Ram. The names of others are lost in obscurity, but the circumstantial evidences do indicate that the entourage of the fugitive prince also had more painters and artisans of other persuasions.

Even at Srinagar, as late as AD 1878, forty-five years after the death of Mola Ram, Mukandi Lal recorded at least five families of the traditional, painters, of which only two descended from Mola Ram and the remaining three belonged to different ancestry. The claim of Mola Ram, and on his authority of Mukandi Lal, that his ancestors founded the Garhwal School is, therefore, subject to the serious doubts. Furthermore, Sulaiman Shukoh is believed to have introduced the *Salimshahi* footwear in Garhwal. That would indicate that some cobblers also accompanied the fugitive prince and they stayed back at Srinagar even after the prince was deported. Subsequently, that footwear became popular among the nobles and the royalty at Srinagar. The local cobblers at Srinagar still manufacture them in yellow leather. It appears that Mukandi Lal, who pioneered research on the Garhwal painting, and the subsequent scholars who relied upon him, have conveniently overplayed the Mola Ram factor in tracing the origin and development of painting in this mountainous kingdom. In fact, Mola Ram prized himself more to be a poet than a painter. With an exception of one painting, *Mastani* where in the colophon, he designates himself as *kavi molaram musavar*, i.e., poet Mola Ram painter, nowhere he else calls himself a painter. It was natural for a poet to glorify his ancestry as the founder of a school of painting in Garhwal notwithstanding the fact that there were other unnoticed artists also at Srinagar. What in the whole gamut intrigues is the fact that despite being an accredited *musavar* (painter), he called himself a *sunar* (goldsmith) to establish his ancestry from the Sunar professional caste. The reason for that may be that a *chitera* or *musavar* has been considered under the category of *tarkhan* (carpenter) and regarded low-caste in the traditional Pahari society, whereas a *sunar* (goldsmith) was regarded as a caste person. In an identical case, the painters of Guler house, who belonged to the tarkhan professional community, added 'Pandit' or 'Raina' prefix or suffix to their names in an attempt to upgrade themselves in the caste-ladder, as Pandit Seu and Chandu Lal Raina. It is perhaps for that reason that Mola Ram, though working as painter in the feudal court of Srinagar, projected himself as the poet and was acknowledged as a poet in the feudal court.

This fact is revealed from an instance during reign of Jaykrit Shah (AD 1780-1785), which Mola Ram recorded in his *Garh Rajvansh ka Itihas*. The king asked him to abandon his worthless atelier *("molaram kam taji javo, chitrasal nahak vanavo. Chitrasal likhi him kya save, hamko dushtan aan dabayo")* and draft a fervent poetic petition seeking military help from Raja Jager Prakash (AD 1773-1792) of Sirmaur. While Sulaiman Shukoh, after having stayed at Srinagar for more than two years was deported on the 1211 December 1660, many of his companion-artisans chose to stay back in Garhwal. Among them were also Sham Das and his son Har Das, the two miniature painters of the imperial Mughal court. Prithvi Shah employed them as the *tasbirdar* (the picture-makers) in his court. Thus, a satellite atelier was established at Srinagar and the Sham Das-Har Das duo came to be regarded as the pioneers of the Garhwal School of Painting. Mola Ram, the leading figure of that school was one of their descendants. Now, when did the painting school originated in Garhwal, cannot conclusively be known. While there are definite evidences on the existence of an art activity during the reign of Mahipati Shah, the scholars regard Sham Das and his son Har Das, the ancestors Mola Ram as the founders of the Garhwal School during the reign of Prithvi Shah, thanks to Mola Ram.

Was there really a 'Garhwal School', is a contentious question. Presently, let us discuss the origin of the art of painting in Garhwal from the ancestors of Mola Ram, notwithstanding the fact that the painting already flourished in Garhwal even before them. One Banarasi Das, from whom the line of painters related to Mola Ram started, lived at Delhi. Nothing beyond name is known about him. He was a goldsmith in the Mughal court and his association with the painters in the Court might have provided him an opportunity to put his son Sham Das under the tutelage of an accomplished court painter. When Sham Das acquired proficiency as painter, he was employed as a retainer in the Imperial court. He also inducted in son Har Das into the profession of painting in the Mughal court. Both of them were the retainers of the prince Sulaiman Shukoh and worked as painters in the Imperial Mughal Court around AD 1658, when Aurangzeb proclaimed himself the emperor. When Sulaiman Shukoh escaped to Garhwal, both of them, Sham Das and Har Das accompanied him. They stayed back at Srinagar even after the prince was deported. Allegedly, that father and son team was responsible for the establishment of an independent school of painting that came to be identified as the Garhwal School.

Mola Ram states in his *Garh Rajvansh ka Itihas* that the reigning king of Garhwal, Prithvi Shah employed the painter-duo in his court as *tasbirdar*, i.e., the picture-maker. Possibly, Sham Das and Har Das might have produced some miniatures in the Mughal diction at Srinagar, of which nothing has survived. They also might have painted some frescoes in the royal palace at Srinagar; about which Moorcroft has made a casual remark in his description noted a short while earlier.

Whether the son and grandson of Har Das, Hira Lal and Mangat Ram (c. AD 1700-1770) also adopted painting as a profession, in not known. Possibly, they reverted to their ancestral profession of goldsmithery. Nevertheless, Mukandi Lal chanced upon two old and slightly soiled miniatures done in the Mughal style in the possession of Tulsi Ram, the great-grandson of Mola Ram in 1949, one of which he acquired. One painting depicted toilet scene of a queen and he reproduced the other, entitled *Manini*, in his monograph. Manini depicts a woman seated annoyed on the terrace of the royal palace at Srinagar. Her companion is trying to placate and soothe her feelings. Tulsi Ram believed those miniatures to be the works of either of Hira Lal or Mangat Ram or Mola Ram. Those painting, according to Mukandi Lal, could be the works of the early Garhwali painters, i.e., either of Hira Lal or Mangat Ram, but not of Mola Ram. It may suggest that none of the two completely abandoned painting, but took it casually. Mukandi Lal also published an inscribed line drawing done by Mangat Ram that depicted the artist in conversation with someone. Mangat Ram is regarded more as a designer than a painter. He designed sword-handles, scabbards, images and woodcuts incorporating floral and faunal designs. French saw three woodcuts in the collection of Balak Ram (addressed as Balak Ram Shah by French), who attributed them to Mangat Ram. French acquired one of them, *'Stag being pulled down by Panther'*, during his visit to Srinagar in AD 1930. The other two included *'Woodcut of floral design'* and *'Woodcuts of Fox and Lion Design'*.

However, Mola Ram, the son of Mangat Ram, was an accomplished painter. It is generally held that he had a long life. No precise date of his birth is known. According to Rahul (Garhwal, p. 133), he was born in AD 1740 and lived until AD 1833. Mukandi Lal originally fixed his date of birth as AD 1760 assuming that a portrait of Mola Ram said to be inscribed 'aged 73' was made in the year of his death, i.e., AD 1833, but he later ruled out that possibility. Mukandi Lal later changed Mola Ram's date of birth to c. AD 1743 assuming that when in AD 1771 he painted Mastani (inscribed with verses), he must have been at least of about thirty years of age. Later, K.G. Archer felt that "the figure of thirty seems unnecessarily high-twenty would be equally appropriate—c. 1750 is here suggested as his date of birth." There is no dispute on the date of death of Mola Ram in AD 1833. If at all Mola Ram had a long life, as Mukandi Lal indicates, the c. AD 1740 (or 1743) should appear to be reasonably correct, because that makes him really live longer, for plus ninety years. There is an unexplained gap of about a century between the time when Hat Das became too old to paint (or died) and when Mola Ram started painting. Possibly, the conditions at Srinagar remained too volatile and disturbed for the painting to flourish during that interregnum.

Nevertheless, painting flourished in the kingdom at Dehradun during that period, for which possibly not the king of Garhwal, but the imperial Mughal edict was responsible. The walls of the Guru Ram Rai *Durbar* were embellished with elaborate wall paintings. Possibly, some of the painters from Srinagar also migrated in search of jobs to Dehradun to take up jobs at the Durbar and elsewhere in search of jobs. The art of painting had virtually vanished from Srinagar when Mola Ram was born in AD 1740. Most of the professional painters had shifted to the Tarai area, where they could find jobs to embellish walls of houses of the wealthy people, dharmshalas, gurudwaras, temples, etc. Mola Ram had inborn urge for art, especially for poetry and was an avid collector of paintings. He possessed a good collection of miniatures done by several painters of different schools, besides his own works in similar style, all inscribed in Mola Ram's handwriting and notable for their harshness and crudity, writes Archer. From the large collection of paintings of other artists in his collection, of which his own works formed only a fractional part, the personality of Mola Ram emerges out more as a collector and connoisseur rather than an artist. He, therefore, abandoned his family profession of goldsmith and opted for poetry and painting. When did he start painting himself is not known, but it is certain that he had to go away from Srinagar to learn it at various centres.

Some of his early paintings bore influence of the decadent Mughal style. That may suggest that in the beginning he learnt painting under some Mughal painters, who were none else but the ones who had settled in the Tarai region from Srinagar. Later, he visited Kangra in about AD 1763 and possibly Guler as well. Those places were at that time the flourishing centres of painting. At those centres, he not only learnt the delicate techniques of painting from the Pahari masters, but also acquired miniatures for his collection. Mola Ram probably could not carry on well with Pradeep Shah (AD 1717-1772). On the reverse of a painting, Consoling the Queen, he inscribed four verses, one of which is dated samvat 1826 (AD 1769), bitterly lamenting over the treatment meted out to him in the royal court of Garhwal. His position in the court might have remained insignificant until Jaykrit Shah (AD 1780-1785), who acknowledged his scholarship and artistic talent and accorded him a place of honour in his court. Jaykrit Shah even appointed him as his advisor in the political affairs. Mukandi Lal says, "Mola Ram and his ancestors received a jagir of sixty villages and a daily allowance of five rupees from the Rajas of Garhwal".[1] It is, however, improbable that such endowment was available to his ancestors. Because, none of the predecessors of Jaykrit Shah or he himself, was the patron of art (painting). Jaykrit Shah regarded painting as a worthless effort *("chitrasal nahak vanavo. Chitrasal likhi tum kya pavo"* from *Garh Rajavansh ka Itihas* of Mola Ram).

Nevertheless, Mola Ram developed painting as his carrier and evolved a distinct style of his own by imbibing stylistic influences from different schools of paintings that he observed and assimilated them into his own diction.) Mola Ram had an occasion to interact with the painters from Guler at Srinagar and acquaint himself with some techniques in painting. Guler artists had came to Srinagar on the marriage of Praduman Shah (reigned in Garhwal from AD 1785 to 1804) with a daughter of one Ajab Singh of the ruling house of Guler in AD 1781. Understandably, the Garhwali prince received some Guler miniatures as the wedding gift on that occasion. The arrival of painters from Guler on that occasion may, however, appear a bit intriguing, for the fact that neither Jaykrit Shah nor Praduman Shah was the lover of painting nor was that a royal wedding on the Guler side. How than artists from Guler happened to be at Srinagar on the wedding occasion? The plausible answer to it may be that Mola Ram, placed at an important position in the feudal court of Garhwal under Jaykrit Shah, could have been instrumental in asking for the painters from Guler on that occasion. That matrimonial alliance was, indeed, a very important event, because the Garhwali painters could not only acquire refinement and delicacy in the use of line and colour, but also the thematic versatility and complaisance from those painters.

Garhwal School, therefore, owes considerably to the Guler and Kangra schools. Had it not been so, it could have ended up as a decadent offshoot of the provincial Mughal style. Mola Ram made his mark in the feudal politics of Garhwal and fully exploited the opportunity that his poetic and artistic talent offered him. At the request of Jaykrit Shah, he not only drafted a poetic petition addressed to Raja Jagat Prakash (AD 1773-1792) of Sirmaur, but also made a painting for the Sirmaur king. That letter and the painting were delivered to the Raja by one of his assistants, Dhani Ram. The Raja of Sirmaur felt so delighted by the poetic letter and the painting that he sent out a force in support of Jaykrit Shah.

Later, when Garhwal came under the Gurkha control, Mola Ram befriended Hastidal Shah Chauntariya, the Gurkha governor of Garhwal. He wrote the history of Garhwal—*Garh Rajvansh ka Itihas*—at his bidding. Hasti or Hastidal, figures in that work in various contexts. The significant benefit of that friendship was that Mola Ram could hold the jagir that Jaykrit Shah had granted to him even during the unsparing and oppressive Gurkha rule. Mola Ram had a very long, eventful and productive inning of nine decades in the world. He lived through the reigns of ten Garhwali kings—Prithvi Shah (AD 1631-1664), Medini Shah (AD 1664-1675), Fateh Shah (AD 1675-1716), Dalip Shah (AD 1716), Upendra Shah (AD 1716-1717), Pradeep Shah (AD 1717-1772), Lalit Shah (AD 1772-1780), Jaykrit Shah (AD 1780-1785), Parakram Shah (AD 1785) and Praduman Shah (AD 1785-1804). Mola Ram's Garh *Rajvansh ka Itihas* reveals that many of those rulers patronised poetry, but none of them are known to have favoured painters or encouraged painting. The endowment that Mola Ram received from Jaykrit Shah was for his role in the Garhwal politics and for his scholarship and poetry, but hardly for painting. It may probably be for that reason that one finds a very few Garhwali rulers depicted in the paintings and almost no miniature depicting a court scene is available. In one of such miniatures Praduman Shah and his brother Parakram Shah are shown seated. From the general treatment, it appears to be a work of some novice. In his article, 'Garhwal School of Painting' Mukandi Lal reproduced a miniature *Ruler entertained by dancing-girl.* He claimed the king depicted in the painting attired in the typical Mughal dress with well-trimmed beard to be Lalit Shah, but Archer refuted that identification. Archer's contention stands vindicated by the fact that Lalit Shah sported long flowing beard and a turban like a Sikh ruler, as may be affirmed from the painting of the king done by

Mola Ram[2], on which the name of king—Lalit Shah—is inscribed. There is a valid reason to believe that Lalit Shah adopted Sikh dress to appease his Sikh tormentors, whereas in the former painting, the king is attired in the typical Mughal dress, with the well-trimmed beard.

Mola Ram was witness to the collapse of dynastic Garhwali rule, rise and fall of the tyrannical Gurkha hegemony through which he could steer well, and the British dominance in Garhwal. The upheavals through which the Garhwal kingdom passed during those days are most authentically recorded in his *Garh Rajvansh ka Itihas*. This work of Mola Ram covers the history of Garhwal from the period of Sham Shah (AD 1550-1569) to the tyrannical days under the Gurkhas and British rule. Interestingly, Mola Ram has been rather restrained in criticising Gurkha rule, but very critical about the British occupation of Garhwal. The kingdom of Tehri-Garhwal came up in AD 1815 under Sudarshan Shah. Srinagar and the eastern part of the defunct kingdom of Garhwal came under direct British control. Mola Ram, then a dispirited old man of around seventy-five years of age, opted to stay at Srinagar possibly on health reason and spent rest of his life there. Probably, for his friendship with the Gurkha governor Hastidal, Mola Ram not only fell from the favour of Sudarshan Shah and the British overlords, but also lost his jagir and allowances that Jaykrit Shah had bestowed upon him. By way of pittance, the British authorities appointed one of his sons, Jwala Ram, as a clerk under the first British commissioners of Kumaon erroneously said to be Major General Sir Henry Ramsay.[3] The first British commissioner was E. Gardner.

Inheritors of Mola Ram

He had two sons, Jwala Ram (AD 1788-1848) and Shiv Ram (AD 1790-1855). Both of them adopted painting as their profession, but only Jwala Ram could make his mark as the last painter in the traditional style, which had already imbibed alien influences by that time. He painted a few pictures on the floral and faunal subjects, a few landscapes and some sketches of the mythological themes. Shiv Ram took up his ancestral profession of goldsmithery, but also casually tried his hand on painting. Mukandi Lal has published a painting from his collection. That painting, done by Shiv Ram, depicts Sulaiman Shukoh being attended by the maids. Randhawa also found some of Shiv Ram's paintings with the raja of Nurpur (M.S. Randhawa, 'Signed Paintings of Jwala Ram, Artist of Garhwal', R-L, Vol. XXXII, 2, 1961), Thompson Press, Delhi. Jwala Ram had two sons, named Atma Ram and Tej Ram. Of them, only Atma Ram painted. Shiv Ram also had two sons, Hari Ram and Tulsi Ram. Both of them painted in a much-degenerated style with the strong western influence. The name of Tulsi Ram also figures among the painters who executed wall paintings in the Guru Ram Rai Durbar at Dehradun. None of the later successors in the line ever painted, some of them adopted their ancestral profession of goldsmithery, and some became small time shopkeepers. The general reason, and that was also the main one, for the decline of painting was the absence of patronage to the artists. With the collapse of feudal system that encouraged painting as a status symbol, there was none to encourage it under the changed socio-political system. The painters were, therefore, obliged to abandon painting for more remunerative jobs.

In case of Garhwal, another curious reason is also assigned. It is said that some of the successors of Mola Ram, who use to paint, became insane. Painting was, therefore, alleged to be the cause of their malady. None, therefore, dared to learn it anymore for the fear of getting mad. Nevertheless, the successors of Mola Ram conscientiously preserved the family art treasures until his great-grand sons, Tulsi Ram (in the line of Shiv Ram) and Balak Ram, also known as Balak Ram Shah, (in the line of Jwala Ram) sold them out to connoisseurs and art-dealers. About Tulsi Ram, Mukandi Lal notes,[4] "At least one member of the family of Mola Ram (Tulsi Ram) actually worked as a goldsmith until his death in AD 1950. The writer had in his collection some fine drawings and woodcuts of sword handles, sword covers and images of gods and goddesses, which are ascribed to Mola Ram's father Mangat Ram. They were used by Mola Ram's descendants to make moulds or blocks for casting sword handles, sword covers, and metal images for sale to the pilgrims who passed Srinagar on the way to the holy mountain shrines of Kedarnath and Badrinath." Ultimately, most of them found way to private collections and museums the world over.

Finally, it is generally said that feudal patronage has certainly been responsible for the development of painting in the hills, but it may not be wholly true and certainly untrue in the case of development of painting in Garhwal. A drawing, which Mangat Ram (Mola Ram's father), made, corroborates this assumption. In that drawing, Mangat Ram is seen seated with one Hardayal Khatri, obviously an ordinary patron.[5] To corroborate this point, the collection of miniatures in the Himachal Lok Sanskriti Sansthan at Mandi in Himachal Pradesh may be cited. Although, the collection is modest, but the fact that all the painting in the collection were procured from the houses of the common people in the hills, and from the feudal houses, would establish that not only the rajas in the hills but the commoners also patronised the painters. In fact, the common people in the towns and villages were also the lovers and connoisseurs of paintings in their own humble manner.

Murals

While miniature painting has been a mobile and portable medium for the Pahari painters to cater to the religio-aesthetic and romantic feelings of the patrons since the mid-seventeenth century onwards, wall painting developed as the fixed medium to that end. Since the wall paintings in the hills have essentially been the blown-out miniatures, these hardly varied from the miniatures in style and format. The wall paintings, executed on the wall of temples, gurudwaras, shrines, houses and palaces, mostly depict mythological, cult and historical themes. The romantic or erotic themes have been very rare in this medium. More than the miniatures, the wall paintings indeed represent the Garhwal School of painting, for the fact that the Garhwali painters executed them, and if at all, the painters from other places were involved in that enterprise, their role should have been minimal. As noted earlier under 'Miniature Painting', there is a gap of about a century between Har Das (c. AD 1660) and Mola Ram (AD 1740-1833), during which period no significant painting activity is noticed at Srinagar.

Possibly, the political conditions at Srinagar were not conducive enough for the painting to flourish. The painters, therefore, opted to scatter to the *Tarai* area, where jobs for artisans were available in the temples, *akharas*, *gurudwaras*, *dharmshalas* and houses of the common people. In that context, the Guru Ram Rai *Durbar* at Dehradun and the *akharas*, *dharmshalas* and houses at Kankhal deserve notice. All these places form a compact region in the Tarai, where the artisans and painters displaced from Srinagar engaged themselves in building construction and painting activities.

Fusion of Religion and Romance

Special features of Garhwal painting were projection of beautiful and brave women of Garhwal, fusion of religion with romance, blending of poetry and passion. Some of the masterpieces of Garhwal paintings include:

- Illustration of *Ramayana* (1780 AD)
- Celebration of Balrams birthday (1780 AD)
- Series of Raginis
- Shiva and Parvati
- Ulkat Nayika

- Krishna painting—the feet of Radha
- Radha looking into a mirror
- Varsha Vihar
- Illustrations of Gita-Govinda

The rich collection of these paintings are displayed in the university Museum in Srinagar, Garhwal alongwith many sculptures and finds from Archaeological excavations. The white clouds and the blue hills also contributed towards the delicacy of 'Pahari' art. The paintings of the region have gone to various countries all over the world and some can be seen even in the British Museum in London. They are priceless relics today.

Architecture

The substructures of the standing wooden temples of Karna at Deorah and Kapil Muni at Gundiyat Gaon may be the extant evidences of the extinct stone temples that stood there in the remote past. The structural fragments and dismembered stone images of those stone temples may be found scattered around the temple sites or haphazardly fixed in the boundary walls or placed loosely in the standing wooden temples. The conscientious local people have religiously bee assembling some of such structural fragments to improvise miniature temples at many places. The Mahasu Devata Temple at Hanol and the Karna Temple at Deorah may be the good examples of that endeavour. At Hanol, even the residual part of the classical stone structure of the sanctum has been capped by the towering multi-tiered wooden structure. At Gundiyat Gaon, the people have collected some of the ancient stone images in an improvised concrete enclosure close to the standing Kapil Muni Temple.

The circumstances that led to the construction and destruction of those classical stone temples and their replacement with the wooden ones may call for thorough investigation. From the residual evidences of the ancient stone temples, it becomes evident that many of them belonged to the period between the eighth and twelfth centuries. That was the time, when the classical stone temple architecture that had flourished under the post-Gupta renaissance under the Palas, Gurjaras and Pratiharas in the Indo-Gangetic mainland was introduced in the Himalayan interiors by the local feudal lords, the *shreshthis* (nobles) and the *dhaniks* (wealthy merchants). That temple building enterprise by the non-indigenous influential class in the Himalayan interiors on the trade and pilgrimage routes had telling psychological effect of the native Khasha population. Not only they thought on domesticating and establishing their demonic gods among their midst in the villages, but also adopted many Brahminical deities, particularly Shiva, into their pantheistic fold. The reason for the destruction of the ancient classical stone temples in these areas may not be precisely known, In fact, barring a standing stone temple of Bhagawati at Lakhamandal on the west bank of Jamuna, no other standing stone temple of that period exists in the western part of Garhwal, where now wooden temples are found. Most likely, the vanished stone temples might have suffered gradual decay and disintegration under the vagaries of nature (occasional tremors in particular) and human neglect following the fall of paramount power in the Indo-Gangetic mainland in the twelfth century. After the collapse of central power in the Indian mainland, the patronage and expertise that had been vital for construction and survival of the stone temples ceased to exist. The artisans of mainland, although expert stone-workers were probably not aware of the unsuitability of the schist stone available in the Himalayan interiors for structural purpose. Obviously, the stone temples built of such a poor quality stone, without using metal clamps or mortar, started crumbling and breaking down for want of care and maintenance. The conscientious local people, therefore, might have thought of erecting wooden temples on the sites of those fallen stone temples or pulled down the precarious ones to raise the new ones in the vernacular medium. The *deodar* wood has traditionally been the most popular construction material in the Himalayan interiors. Because of its abundance in the evergreen coniferous jungles of this region, it has been used in multifarious manner for structural and artistic purposes. The wood-workers of the Himalayan interiors have developed exceptional expertise in handling it and explored possibilities of its diverse structural use. Therefore, when it came to re-creating the vanished stone temples, the local hereditary artisans—the *thawins*, *bhadhis* or *tarkhans*—who excelled in the woodwork, found wood to be the handiest and convenient structural material.

Those artisans could recreate the ancient sacred structures in timber, replicating the layout parameters of the anterior classical stone temples. It was, however, not practicable to recreate the ruined stone structures in timber in letter and spirit, adherence to 'letter' was abandoned and the element of 'spirit' of the classical mannerism fully retained. The result was the newer and indigenous version of the classical stone temple architecture rendered in wood. The *mandap* and *antaral* parts were erected with pent or composite pent-n-gable roof conforming to the roofing pattern the traditional secular buildings, but the roof over the celestial realm, the *garbh-griha*, was innovatively made loftier to replicate the stone *shikhara* by laying it independently in the multi-tiered conical form. Since, many temples were raised on' the existing stone sub-structures, the superstructures of the 'new' wooden temples were erected on the sturdy framework of the wooden beams on the existing plinth. These beams may be seen extended beyond the edges of the old substructures on the corners to secure firm lap joints, as in the Karna Temple at Deorah. In the course of time that became a standard method of erecting temples. The superstructure of the celestial realm—the *garbh-griha*—was, however, built independently in the traditional *kath-kuni* style or made totally of timber. Under the local prevailing conditions in the Tons valley, stone walls generally enclose the sanctum. A very few of the classical stone temples, which escaped serious damage to their structures, were enclosed in the wooden shell. A temple of Dundi Devi at Dhabas in neighbouring Himachal Pradesh is a good example of such improvisation. The damaged classical *shikhara* of the Mahasu Devata Temple at Hanol was replaced with an elaborate multi-tiered wooden superstructure over the *jangha*. In such temples, the standing *mulaprasada* structure of the ancient classical stone temple and the later wooden structural contraption may be found integrated together. These temples have been identified as the 'Composite Type'.

Such structure is neither of the stones nor of the wood in a strict sense, but a harmonious blend of the two. In such arrangement, the classical and the folk structural components combine to formalise an imposing structure. The Mahasu Devata Temple at Hanol and the Bhagawati Temple at Lakhamandal are the two good examples of this type. To protect the superstructures of some of the popular ancient classical stone temples against seepage of water through the fissures caused by weathering, those have been provided with the superficial canopy over the *shikhara*. Such protective wooden covers do not infringe upon the original character of the classical structure. It may, possibly, be for that safety reason that most of the standing stone temples of the early period in the mid-Himalayan belt from Jageshwar in Kumaon to Chamba in Himachal Pradesh are found fitted with the protective wooden canopy.

Mahasu (Chalda) Temple at Village Jadi is located about thirteen kilometres from Chakarata on the motorable road to Tyuni and Hanol, Jadi is a small yet beautiful Khasha (Khashia) village of Jaunsar-Bawar area. On the northern end of the village, on a terrace above the road, there stands a small but captivating temple of Mahasu. We had an interesting revelation at this temple, what is known as 'Mahasu' is invariably the 'Chalda' Mahasu. The people address the Botha Mahasu of Hanol as the 'Botha', without the 'Mahasu' suffix. The other Mahasus are also known by their respective characteristic identities only, as Basika and Pawasi, without 'Mahasu' suffix. Thus, in popular usage, only the Chalda Mahasu is addressed as only Mahasu. The temple is not very old, but of recent times. Nevertheless, its structural embellishments are significant, because these reflect the 'modernistic' trends in the folk art that combines the traditional animistic and cultic devices with the Brahminical themes.

For instance, on the panels beside the entrance on the left, Hanuman is painted and on the right is Durga on her mount, both crudely treated. Even the traditional devices are poorly and superficially carved, betraying degeneration in the folk artistry. Nevertheless, the fact that folk aesthetic sensibility is still live to the traditional values in the overall formal treatment of the temple structure is consoling. The temple is laid out on a rectangular plan measuring 4.60 × 3.60 square metres externally. The forty-five centimetres thick walls of the temple are of random stone laid dry. Wooden binders have been provided to lend stability to the structure. The roof of this temple is laid out in a typical manner by mixing the gable and pent forms together. While, its forepart is in the gable form; on the back, it is in pent form. The roofing arrangement above the altar has been made more elaborate by providing a two-tiered octagonal canopy, with a definite vertical clearing in between. The roof is covered with the galvanised iron sheets. Earlier, the temple had wooden roofing. The edges are embellished with wooden pendants, with wooden bells on the corners and in the centre of the front gable. Inside the temple on the altar, what is enshrined as Mahasu, is a small image of Shiva. It may be a subtle indication of the predominating Brahminical influence over the indigenous religio-cultural system, under which Mahasu has incessantly been loosing his original ophiological identity. He is increasingly being regarded as one of the local manifestations of Shiva. There are a few more images of the Brahminical deities on the altar, but all of them are of very recent date and bought from the market.

Pokhu Deota Temple at Naitwar

In the valley of Tons where the Rupin (from Dodra-Kwar side) and the Shupin (from Bandarpunch) meet to form the Tons, amid the thick coniferous jungle on the rugged mountain slopes is a small and remote village Naitwar, spread on both the banks. Here, on the confluence of the Rupin and the Shupin on an angle above the cremation ground is situated the wooden temple of Pokhu Devata. The people regard him and Notare of Garhwal as the twin deities of the cremation grounds.

A folk-song informs, *"notare pokhu chhora jo mareshwar mahadeo, hanol men botha mahasu jo sab deban ke deo,"* that is, Notare and Pokhu remain the great deities of the burning places; Botha Mahasu at Hanol is the God of all deities. The people regard Pokhu Devata as a fearsome demi-God. So much is the awe of this deity that even the *pujari* performs ablution and *puja* to him (which, of course, is occasional) not by facing him, but twisting his arms backwards. It is believed that confronting him would mean instantaneous death. Pokhu Devata is regarded as 'the manifestation of Karbir Dano (i.e., Karbir Danava or Karbir, the demon) after Mahasu beheaded him.

According to another tradition, drawn from the *Mahabharata*, Pokhu is said to be the local name of Bhubruvahan, who was a king of *patal-loka*. He had sympathy for the Kauravas and wanted to participate in the *Mahabharata* War on their side. Krishna, apprehensive of his expertise in archery, thought of isolating him from the Kauravas. He, therefore, impressed upon Bhubruvahan to remain neutral and watch the War from a distance, to which the latter agreed. Krishna was, however, not satisfied with the assurance of the demon. He feared that a warrior like Bhubruvahan might succumb to the temptation of trying his power of archery and join the War. Krishna, therefore, got him killed by deceit before the war could start, but he overwhelmed with the remorse for that unethical act. To expiate the guilt, Krishna granted him eternal life after the War. Bhubruvahan, however, wished at least to

air of barbaric splendour, heightened by the dark green of the casings of beetle's wings used for the emeralds worn by the lovers. These early Pahari paintings in the Basohli style, so called because of their association with a Basohli raja as well as with the Basohli durbar (places) collection, must not be mistakes for primitives from a wild environment. They have much of the ferocious elegance of the Mehta Caurapancasika paintings: like them obviously the products of a sophisticated milieu and a long tradition, they share with Rajasthani and Malwa painting, in somewhat altered form, a number of conventions, most obviously the extremely elegant two-dimensional architectural settings, topped by domes or pavilions, bands of scroll work pattern, and the use of elaborately figured rugs. Also common to the generality of sixteenth-century Rajasthani and Central Indian styles are the grey water with pink lotuses and their green pads, the inventive and varied stylization of trees, 'Chinese' clouds, and rain descending like a beaded curtain in serried lines of white dots. Slender trees with drooping flowered branches become almost an obsession. Paintings attributed to Kulu figure prominently in the early Pahari or 'Basohli' style, notably the so-called Shangri *Ramayana* with its admixture of Mughal realism and decorative motifs. The flame-coloured 'Radha and Krsna in the forest' in the Karl and Mehri Khandalavala Collection, Bombay, is tonally intensely vibrant; moreover its circular composition and the inventiveness and variety of the stylized trees, including the rare cypress, irresistibly recall the contemporary Bundi Kotah school in Rajasthan.

More naif works from Chamba, equally far into the hills, continue the early Pahari style well into the eighteenth century, as does the less idiosyncratic early painting from Nurpur. Two persistent strains of Pahari painting are already present in the Basohli style. The first is a fondness for the portraits of local rajas in plain white garments, often seated on the striped rugs of the Hill country, which are in many cases the principal evidence for the attribution of sub-styles to one state or another. In some, like the well-known portrait of Kirpal Pal of Basohli or those of Kirpal Dev (*c.* 1660-1690) [326] and Anand Dev of Bahu (Jammu), the facial idiosyncrasies of the Basohli style and the treatment of the attendant figures leave little doubt that they are contemporary. More subdued versions of these traits, as in the many likenesses of rulers of the first half of the 18th century, do not necessarily indicate later copies, for the portrait tradition of the Hills was, from its inception, Mughal-inspired, whether or not through Rajastan, for example, black smudges at the armpits, characteristic of provincial Mughal work, appear in the earliest Basohli portraits.

The second persistent subject of Pahar painting is the gods of the Hindu pantheon. There are many striking works in this genre, for the Basohli style, with its strong indigenous Indian element, is well suited of the portrayal of many-headed Sivas or many-armed Durgas. In the first decades of the eighteenth century, a horizontal format, a generally quieter tone, and the use of dark green backgrounds presage a transformation of the Pahari style around 1750 as radical as that brought about by Akbar nearly two centuries earlier and a complete rejection of the Basohli style. An illustrated Gita Govinda, for example, which can be confidently dated by inscription to 1730-5, mostly if not entirely painted by Manaku, while retaining some of the elements of the earlier style (most strikingly the lavish use of beetle's-wing casings) clearly adumbrates the second great Pahari style in its landscapes with large opaque-foliaged trees and its complex grouping of figures, particularly women. It was long thought that the exodus of painters into the Hills from the court of Muhammad Shah was provoked by political instability in the Plains after Nadir Shah's sack of Delhi in 1739 had put an end to Mughal power in all but name. The important Seu dynasty of painters, which included Manaku and his famous younger brother Nainsukh, may well have worked in the Mughal ateliers but research has shown that the family had lived in Guler for at least two generations. An undoubted result of the turmoil in the Plains was the re-routing of the trade route to Kashmir through the comparative safety of the Hills instead of through Lahore, bringing considerable prosperity, especially to Jammu and Kangra.

Jammu in particular, under two able rulers, Dhrub Dev and Ranjit Dev, was able to extend its influence over neighbouring states such as Basohli as well as to reclaim lands and privileges ceded to the Mughals. Manaku had worked in Basohli, so it is not surprising to find Nainsukh executing a whole series devoted to the activities of Balwant Singh, Ranjit Dev's younger brother, among them the first dated paintings in the fully fledged new style. A work of 1748 shows the prince listening to a party of musicians. Nainsukh's celebrated pictures of Balwant Singh, although somewhat outside the Pahari mainstream, are major achievements of Indian miniature painting. This exceptional artist produced on the one hand grandiose celebrations of the probably eccentric ruler enjoying the trappings of Mughal-style splendour (he seems to have been free for most of his life of any responsibility other than the administration of princely feudal states) and on the other irresistible and uniquely charming vignettes of his pleasurable round of daily activities, giving him, solely by this visual record, a human personality such as one glimpses only in the far great figures of Akbar and Jahangir.

Balwant Singh appears at his toilet, performing puja surveying a building site, in camp looking cold and wrapped in a huge quilt. In the master piece of them all, he is one again in camp, a paunchy, tired-looking man in undress, writing in his tent at the end of the day. Part of Nainsukh's genius was for individual portraiture, a salient feature of the later Pahari style; but his alone is the feeling for genre which led him to draw the bored and sleepy young page holding a fly-whisk behind Balwant Singh. His palette consisted of dedicated pastel shades, with daring expanses of white or grey. The second great Pahari style owes a get deal to later Mughal painting, particularly its receding planes, its fondness for quasi-realistic landscape, and its frequent enlargement of the figures on the page. But the spirit which emanates from the careful drawing and often swirling rhythms is quite different: it is by far the most poetic and lyrical of Indian styles.

Most delightful is the Guler-Kangra idealization of woman, in flowing sari, head half covered with a shawl, demure but stately, passionate and shy. The rare skill of the Kangra draughtsman can capture genuine psychological immediacy, as in the *Abhisandhita Nayika*, 'she who is estranged by a quarrel', or Radha, sulkily hunched on a low chair, resisting the entreaties of both Krsna and her confidante. At other times the artist relies on stylization of great beauty, based on line, where the harmonies of drawing enhance the poetic mood. One of the most daring of these stylizations shows a woman seated in *rajalilasana*, the drawn-up leg, bent double at the knee, a perfect upright ovoid, only wider at its base. Elsewhere the women move in pairs, emphasizing the swallow-like effect of their rounded heads and trailing veils. As a rule, no such inventiveness enlivens their male companions, the princely lovers or the semi-divine Krsna. An exception is the superb version of the Kaliya Damana, Krsna subduing the serpent Kaliya, now in the Metropolitan Museum, New York. The familiar representation of Krsna seated on a terrace with a looped wreath lying before him, with its beautifully harmonious drawing of the torso and the folds of the dhoti below, and the bold foreshortening of the left arm, is another exception. The second Pahari, style has often been equated with Kangra, which indeed seems to have been the source of more work in the late manner, including most of the great series, than any of the other Hill States. Its importance, and its ascendancy over much of the Hill country under the ambitious Sansar Chand (1765-1823), no doubt attracted painters before the evil days of Gurkha inroads followed by subjection to the rising Sikh power and, under the British, the eventual extinction of independence of all the Hill States.

Brilliant and extensive research, however, much of it on the spot, has now revealed a much more complex situation. Paintings still extant in local durbars (palace collections) or in the hands of descendants of past rulers, patrons, or painters have established that while the Guler-Kangra style became a *koine* in the Hills, much painting in organizable substyle originated in states such as Garhwal, Nurpur, Chamba, and Mandi. An all-inclusive term remains a convenience to the non-specialist nonetheless, and the most appropriate would seem to be Guler-Kangra, since the late Pahari style first appears fully fledged in Guler *c.* 1745 in works of a quality and purity never to be supposed, while Kangra, in spite of its prolific output and outstanding achievements, produced no known works earlier than *c.* 1775. Hill paintings includes *Ragamala* series, although they do not appear to have been very popular. They conform to literal specifications, leaving little scope for poetic or imaginative treatment; the Hill classification, moreover, differs from that prevalent elsewhere in India. More successful are the Brahmasa series of twelve pictures illustrating the modes of love or courtship appropriate to each month of the year. Even they lack variety, however, for the compositions consist largely of a man and a woman facing each other against a landscape of distant scenes which, though often varied and poetically evocative, would seem more suitable to mural paintings. The oval format so dear to the Guler-Kangra style, combined with monotony of composition, also recalls wall cartouches. Love is the preoccupation of most Pahari work, much of it illustrating the situations or types of the Rasikapriya of Keshav Dev (fl. 1580-1600). The elaborate classifications include the Asta Nayikas, of which the best known is perhaps the Abhisarika, she who sallies out into a stormy night to meet her lover'. Love is further divided into 'Love Separated', "Love in Union', and so on. To what height of inventiveness in design and conception the Pahari artist can nonetheless rise is demonstrated by the splendid illustrations from Kangra of *c.* 1785 to the Satsai, 'Seven Hundred [Verses]', of Bihari Lal. The 'Village Beauty' is a Guler-Kangra masterpiece. Each painting has a different focus and evokes a different mood. So pervasive was the grip upon the imagination of the adoration of Krsna that in most of the Nayaka-Nayika themes the lovers of Brindavan are either explicit or implicit. The emphasis is almost exclusively on the emotions of the woman, or on the situations in which a woman, or on the situations in which a woman in love finds herself. This, of course, parallels the emphasis which underlies all Vaisnava devotional poetry, where it is the raptures and distresses of the soul in love with God (Krsna) that are hymned, and the responses or other actions of the divinity are described, if at all, through the eyes or emotions of the devotee. The identification between Radha, the supreme Nayika, and the human soul enraptured with God is all-pervasive.

It is irrelevant that most of the love in the Nayaka-Nayika relationships was illicit. In a male-dominated and rigidly traditional society, the opportunities for amorous intrigue among well-born ladies must have been slight, in spite of the currency of romantic stories of forbidden passion. Transgressions of the imagination were legitimized by association with the love of Radha for Krsna without diminishing their passionate intensity. As Randhawa has perceptively remarked : The love norm of Hindu society is conjugal fidelity and when *parakiya* love, or love of a woman for a man other than her husband, is mentioned, it is in a spiritual sense. The sacrifice of family honour and reputation involved in adulterous love is the symbol of the soul's self-surrender to God. It is the highest sacrifice that a Hindu woman can make.

That some, probably very few, women made this sacrifice for an earthly lover is probable. Faces, very rarely in other than the preferred Indian full profile, invariably in the case of young women, follow an idealized model which varies hardly at all with time and locality. The same may be said of Krsna and the young Nayakas, although now and then, as in Rajasthan, the features of the local prince may be detected. Although the type of long predates him, the good-looking young Sansar Chand is closer to the idealized hero than the other rulers, whose large noses and heavy lidded eyes dominate their portraits. Elsewhere, the Guler-Kangra artist occasionally exercised his talent for portraiture on courtiers, duennas, and servants, although even here a certain similarity suggests that they also, after the original likeness was seized from the life, became part of the painter's stock in trade, and perhaps even passed into that of his descendants. Because the drawings upon the various themes were used over and over again, pounces even being employed as elsewhere in India, and colour schemes were repeated as well, Guler-Kangra paintings which in any case survive in vast numbers when seen *enmasse* can induce tedium and a sense of *deja vu*; there are, for example, four nearly identical series, or parts of series, of an elaborately illustrated Nala and Damayanti.

It is then that the connoisseur will begin to distinguish sub-styles by means of the squatter figures of Sirmur, or the Mandi overloading of figures and architectural ornament: then only will he appreciate the beauty and clarity of line, the chaste architectural elements, and the sheer poesy which suffuse the very best work. The more complex many-figured compositions, usually larger and horizontal in format, tend to illustrate set pieces of the Krsna legend: the cowherd god putting out the forest fire, subduing the serpent Kaliya, or bringing the kine back to the village at dusk, or the naughty child turned folk-hero uprooting the trees to which he had been tied. Of the mischievous young man stealing the clothes of the gopis, who had taken them off to bathe, and hanging them out of reach in a tree a number of quite different versions exist. The name is indisputably the finest, with its skilful handling of interrelated poses and its psychological penetration. The approach in the far distance of the fully clothed villagers and the rising sun peeping over the hill contribute a drama and urgency lacking in some of the other versions. These paintings occur in illustrated Bhagavata Puranas and with other great series like the 'first' Gita Govinda and the finest of the Nala Damayantis, constitute the supreme achievement of the later Pahari style, combining its lucid line and innate lyricism with a straightforward and skilful naturalism. The ability to handle large groups to figures is exceptional: anyone tempted to overstress the debt to Mughal painting need only compare these skilful, airy compositions with the figures ranked in rigid rows in Jahangiri durbar and battle scenes. The same gulf separates the splendid architectural drawing in the Nala Damayantis from inferior attempts in Murshidabad painting.

Modern art critics have commented on how closely the rounded hills today, the small but dense trees or clumps of trees, even the occasional great boulder, resemble the highly successful Pahari landscapes (particularly of the Beas valley in Kangra) of the Guler-Kangrà style. The exploits of Krsna and his often explicitly portrayed love making with Radha take place not in the rocky, harsh surroundings of the real Brindavan (near Mathura) but among the gently rounded hills and ample verdure of the lower Hill country. In the same way—and it has been said that Brindavan is a landscape of the mind—like Italian painters set the life of Christ among the hills and towns of Tuscany and Umbria. The later Pahari painters also share with them to an astonishing extent a fondness for landscapes with towns or clusters of houses in the distance. Curiously, the snow-capped mountains which brood over these smiling valleys practically never appear. A good deal of Guler-Kangra religious paintings base on Puranic rather than epic or later Vaisnava sources has survived, buttressing other evidence that the cults of Siva and the Devi, long established in the Hills, survived the great vogue of Krsna worship. The lyrical and realistic Guler-Kangra style was ill suited to the portrayal of Karttikeyas and Durgas with multiple heads and arms, and the results and usually embarrassing, unless a slightly more palatable derivative folk style is used. On rare occasions, as in the 'Siva and Parvati' in the Ashmolean Museum, the grace and tenderness of the style are given full rein at the same time that the anatomically bizarre is all but eliminated (Siva's son Ganesa, the elephant-headed god, is reduced to a sort of cuddly teddy-bear cradled in Paravati's lap). The result is a moving holy family.

Kashmiri Sculpture

The source of Kashmiri art is the valley of Jhelum, some seventy miles long and surrounded on all sides by mountains, and particularly the area around Srinagar and the Dal lake. As its sculpture is so similar to that of the Swat Valley to the west, they are usually considered together. Kashmir and Nepal are alike in being difficult of access and in having flourishing schools of sculpture in metal and stone and a distinct style of architecture; they differ in that historical and geographical factors peculiar to Kashmir have always given a wide-ranging cosmopolitan flavour to its highly individual art. The echoes which sound occasionally and apparently unaccountably in the art of Kashmir and particularly its architecture, can be traced only to Gandhara. The time gap is difficult to explain but not impossibly so if one takes the view that Gandhara art, on its home ground, persists through the sixth century. The earliest surviving monuments in Kashmir, mostly only at ground level, are the remains of the Buddhist establishments at Ushkur (ancient Huviskapura) and Harwan. The Ushkur stupa bases and sculpture are reflections of the late Gandhara period to the west. At Harwan around the fourth and fifth centuries, however, the quite exceptionally rough masonry of early Kashmir was clad in a novel and unique way: the caitya hall perhaps, and certainly the court around it with its raised border upon which the monks could sit, were covered with tiles, some as large as 18 by 12 in. (45 by 30 cm.), bearing moulded decoration including Indian and Sasanian themes and perhaps some Chinese motifs as well as human figures.

Probably under the influence of the great Lalitaditya Muktapida (*c.* 724-*c.* 760) of the Karkota dynasty, who controlled extensive tracts of Central Asia and India, particularly monumental cut-stone architecture appears. At Parihasapura, north-west of Srinagar, the ruins of a huge stupa and a whole complex of Buddhist buildings illustrate the new technique. The stones are often of enormous size, including a stupendous one measuring 16 by 14 by 5 ft 6 in. (4.9 by 4.3 by 1.7 m.) and weighing approximately 64 tons (65 tonnes). The blocks are evenly dressed and secured by lime mortar (a practice extremely rare in India until the arrival of the Muslims) or by metal dowels. The so-called *caitya*, a court with a central temple for the image, derives in part from Gandhara and will provide the model for the larger Hindu temples. As in Nepal, Hinduism and Buddhism continue to co-exist, at least until the Muslim conquests, and images become increasingly syncretistic. The rare Buddhas and Bodhisattvas from Parihasapura, now in the Srinagar Museum, are in a variant of the early post-Gupta style. One or two almost certainly show Chinese influence. On the top of the Takht-i-Sulaiman hill beside the Dal lake and hence seen, if only from afar, by every tourist, the Sankaracharya temple is unique. Its square plan, with recessed sides, and circular garbhagrha would seem to Indicate that it is the oldest surviving Hindu shrine in Kashmir, representing a very early stage of development.

The great temple of the Sun at Martand, beautifully sited near where the Liddar valley opens into the great Vale of Kashmir, is the largest of the Hindu temples. It shares with a number of smaller but less ruined shrines the trefoil-arched recesses, entrances, and niches beneath steeply pitched triangular pediments, as well as the fluted columns and pilasters with a capital, more reminiscent of the Greek Doric than of any Indian type. The roofs, all missing, were doubtless of the rectilinear pyramidal kind, one often capping the other. The Sun temple differs from other Kashmiri shrines, however, in that—perhaps on account of its size—the central element, which is pancayatana, includes a (detached) portico or madapa. There is also a substantial gateway to the large walled-in court with its interior peristyle surrounding the shrines a common feature of the larger temples. Some of these elements also have a distinctly Graeco-Roman flavour, both in details and in breadth and scope of execution, and it is surely not Western cultural ethnocentricity to agree with Percy Brown that 'the early mediaeval monuments of this country bring to mind, although indistinctly, recollections of some older architectural experiences, suggesting the final infiltration, towards the east, of the Graeco-Roman ideal'. Of the two temples at Avantipur, the now-vanished capital of King Avantivarman (885-83), the larger is second in size only to Martand, although little remains beyond the foundations. The other, dedicated to Visnu as Avantiswami, i.e. the Lord of Avanti (varman), is also pancayatana, and the best example of the second phase in Kashmir, although not rich in innovations. The sculpture, in niches or in the form of panels, is in a recognizable post-Gupta idiom, for all its occasional Kashmiri idiosyncrasies. The rotund, smallish figures smack faintly of folk art, like contemporary sculpture in Orissa. The earliest Hindu image in stone of any size is probably the splendid six-armed Karttikeya in the Srinagar Museum. The debt to Gandhara Bodhisattvas is obvious, but the very broad face, the powerful rounded shoulders and the realistically depicted reverse-curve bow bring Udayagiri (Vidisa) to mind. The peacock as *Vahana* is also a Gupta innovation. A late-fifth-century date seems quite possible. A Sadasiva from Fatehgarh, near Baramula, is probably a century or more later. Its iconography is explicable only by the budding syncretism between Buddhist and Hindu images. Later icons in stone tend to be smaller and carved in a highly polished black chlorite. The 'archetypal' Kashmiri Hindu image is a four-armed standing Visnu, flanked by his personified weapons, and with a minuscule bust of the earth-goddess (Bhu Devi) rising from a lotus at his feet. The god is four-faced (*caturanana*), with a boar's head and a lion's on either side, and another head in low relief on the back of the halo. Sadasivas are also common. The sculpture from Pandrenthan appears to cover several centuries. The many large and mostly unpublished sandstone images in the Srinagar Museum, including some standing Matrkas, a Sadasiva, and an amusing Kamadeva, in a lively, somewhat fruity style, are probably contemporaneous with the Sun temple (eighth century). The post-Gupta bronzes of Kashmir are well documented in literary sources of the time. Because so many are now known, their characteristics can be catalogued with some confidence. In style they broadly resemble the works in stone. Central Asian and Sasanian echoes range from 'vague reminiscences of the animal style' to textile patterns on throne cushions. Recurring items of dress, including the camail, a three-pointed little cape or bolero with an astonishingly long history, and an unexplained disc on each shoulder, point to elements of Central Asian origin—perhaps the Sahis—among the population. A short dagger is worn suspended across the thighs both by donor figures and by images of Surya—less surprisingly, for Surya's costume retains foreign elements even in twelfth-century Bengal.

The new pointed prabhamandalas almost certainly derive from T'ang custom. The pose and drapery of the few standing Buddhas reflect Gandhara versions in stone, although other features seem to point to a very late date. The first indisputably Kashmiri bronze known, the sixth-century Visnu in Berlin, is, like the stone Karttikeya at Srinagar, a Gandhara-Gupta amalgam. It must be early on account of the lion's and boar's heads sprouting from the shoulders rather than from each side of the god's face, and because there is no fourth face at the back. The drapery of the dhoti, the moustached face, the crown, and the lotus in the god's right hand all have Gandharan analogues. On the other hand the *cakrapurusa* with his huge wheel is pure Gupta.

The little torso of the earth-goddess on the pedestal, later virtually the hallmark of Visnu in stone, the vigorously muscled torso, and the slightly dropsical legs all link this statue to later Kashmiri bronzes. The greatest charm of these works lies perhaps in their variety. The inventiveness of the Kashmiri bronzecasters during the Karkota period (eighth to tenth century) seems limitless; they are constantly devising new and imaginative forms of bases and aureoles and fresh iconographical groupings, no doubt reflecting the increasingly convoluted speculations of religious thought. Saiva tantrism was to flourish in Kashmir. The quality of the work also varies, from exquisitely modelled, cast, and finished pieces to the most slapdash productions with crudely modelled faces and no attempt to finish the back of the image. Visnu is portrayed in several guises, sometimes seated on his vehicle Garuda, or in a rare androgynous form (Vasudeva Kamalaja). Buddhas too sit either in European fashion; or else in padmasana or *lalitasana* with one leg drawn up, the other hanging down, on a wicker stool above the beautiful

Kashmiri lotus with its smooth, fully rounded petals; or on a lion throne; or on cushions with textile motifs; or on base intricately carved with rocky forms in the Gupta manner and peopled with animals, devotees, and donors.

By the eighth century he has become crowned, clothed, and jewelled, sitting in an elaborate bronze in the John D. Rockefeller 3rd collection between twin stupas, a Central Asian rather than an Indian iconographical feature. The base and the lotus stalk upheld by a pair of nagas, on the other hand, are Gupta. The technique recalls the art of the jeweller rather than that of the bronzecaster or the modeller in clay. The largest of all Kashmiri bronzes so far known, 90.5 cm. high, is the standing Buddha in the Cleveland Museum of Art which once belonged to a high dignitary in Tibet. It is in fact of brass, for all its beautiful golden colour; judging by metallurgical tests, a certain amount of lead in the alloy accounts for the buttery softness of modelling of so many Kashmir metal sculptures.

The emphasis on the crinkled folds of the samghati under the lower abdomen, already noticeable in some earlier stone Buddhas and foreign both to Gandhara and to Gupta work, probably derives from T'ang China. The greatest triumph of Kahmiri metal image-making, however, is a unique *prabhamandala*, in this case a veritable metal arch, surrounded by the avatars of Visnu framed in the loops of a continuous swirling lotus tendril. At the apex stands a multi-headed Visnu, with a seated Siva below. The principal image is missing. It was obviously seated, from the inner contours of the frame, and may have been the Buddha, considered by this time one of the avatars of Visnu. The ingenuity and diversity of the Kashmiri artists, sometimes at the expense of taste, characterize the post-Gupta style elsewhere, too, as does a fondness for portraying textiles. The cult of the 'foreign' god Surya was popular in Karkota Kashmiri, as witnessed by the Sun temple, and his images abound, mostly to a strict iconographic and stylistic formula, whether in stone or bronze.

The Cleveland Surya, however, in accordance with the Kashmiri genius, resembles none of them. Instead of a single lotus, the god holds a bunch in each hand; the crown and robe are both unique, both decorated with Central Asian or Iranian textile patterns, the robe flaring out in a most extraordinary way at the bottom. Striking rather than beautiful, this statue nevertheless conveys the image of kingship in these foreign regions better than any other sculpture except of the Kaniska. Some bronzes, mostly Buddhas, with very strong Kashmiri affinities can be assigned to the Swat Valley (the ancient Uddyana), a known stronghold of Buddhism. Some were actually found there. This alone does not prove local manufacture; however, a group of Bodhisattvas sitting in latitasana on what are meant to be wicker hassocks conform closely to figures outlined in low relief on boulders in the Swat Valley, down to peculiarities in the way the *dhoti* is tied in front. The pose of these Padmapani images, the elbow of the right arm resting on the thigh and the index finger pointing back to the head, is one of pensive tenderness. They have identical predecessors, not stylistically but iconographically, in Gandhara. A number of Buddhas in padmasana, like all figures from the north-west shown seated in a yogic pose, may also perhaps be assigned to the Swat Valley. The right hand sweeps low in *varada* (conferring a boon); the left holds up the robe with the compressed end hanging down. Elbows held tight to the body with forearms and hands turned slightly outwards give an open-armed effect. Flames rise from the usnisa.

Many of the Swat Valley bronzes are very dark in colour and have noticeably narrower faces than their Kashmiri counterparts. The only Kashmiri image which can be dated with any precision is the Lokesvara dedicated during the reign of Queen Didda (*c.* 980-1003). It shows that, by the beginning of the eleventh century, changes of style had taked place, most noticeable in the more complex petals of the bases, with swollen stamens, but also in the decreased amplitude of modelling, and in the deterioration in workmanship. New murtis appear, in alidha, increasingly multi-armed, or sometimes embracing a *sakti* (the active, energetic aspect of a god, personified as his wife or consort) in sexual intercourse, such as proliferate in Tibet until modern times. Many of the later bronzes may in fact come from western Tibet, or else the western Himalayas or the Indian Hill States. Notable exceptions to a certain decline in quality are the splendid bronzes, all 3 to 4 ft. (90-120 cm.) high, from the old Chamba State, and largely *in situ.* The temples here are in a local style, with high-pitched roofs.

The shortage of stone accounts both for their wooden construction and for the fact that the principal images are in bronze. There are small more or less conventional post-Gupta temples at Jagesvar, Bajaura, Mandi, Lakhamandal, Dvarahat, and other places in the Indian Hill States. Some of the stone sculpture is very fine, in a style related to early Nepal. South of the Vale of Kashmir, Akhnur in Jammu has produced a number of small terracottas, mostly detached heads, probably of the sixth century. In finely levigated clay, they have the sensitivity of modelling and psychological penetration of the best late Gandhara stuccoes. There is little evidence in the Punjab and north-western Pakistan, the main invasion route into India, of the monuments which must once have existed in abundance after the final eclipse of Gandhara. Some statues and fragments in white marble, the finest the Ganesa in Kabul, have been attributed to the Hindu Sahis. The few temples to have survived further south, in or near the peculiar geological formation known as the Salt Range, are either much restored or—like Malot, lonely on its superb site—almost in ruins. Malot, with its gateway and fluted columns, has clear affinities with the Kashmir style, with an added elements of rococo drama. Another group in Dera Ismail Khan District forms an extension into north-west India of the architecture of post-Gupta Madhyadesa. It includes—all in very poor condition—the temples at the two Kafir Kots and the Kallar temple in Attock District, the last in brick, the others in a soft tufa which gives the same impression.

Bibliography

1. J.C. Harle, *The Art and Architecture of Indian Sub-continent*, Yale University Press, New Haven, 1944.
2. W.G. Archer, *Indian Paintings*, Oxford University Press, London, 1956.
3. S.C. French, *Himalayan Art*, Oxford University Press, London, 1931.

11

Social Culture of Kumaon Himalaya

In the Himalayan regions of Uttarakhand, castes are relatively few. Unlike the plains, in the Himalayan regions of Kumaon and Garhwal the two-fold division of castes into '*Bith*' and 'non-*Bith*' is sharp. The *Bith* category comprises the higher castes of the region who include all Brahmans and Rajputs irrespective of their being Khasiya or later immigrants from the plains. However, historically the immigrant Brahmans and Rajputs constitute the ruling aristocracy of the region and as such hold the topmost positions in the scale of hierarchy among *Bith*, who, as a rule, maintain a social distance and do not marry with the numerically predominant Khadiya. At some date of history, the Khasiyas themselves split into Brahman and Rajput divisions, yet the immigrants from plains continued to assert themselves to be the real Brahmans and Rajputs and are more rigid in their customs and practices compared to the Khasiyas. The immigrant Brahmans and Rajputs, even today do not till the land by themselves, but the Khasiya Brahman and Rajput have no such inhibition.

According to some anthropologists, the Doms, are the aboriginal non-Aryan population of these hills who are non-*Bith* or ritually impure and so untouchable (*Achhut*). They are the village artisans who are more frequently described by their occupational subdivisions, e.g., *Lohar* (black-smith), *Tamta* (Coppersmith), *Orh* (stone-worker and Mason) and so on. A sharp line of demarcation based on purity-pollution concept, has thus placed all the *Bith* groups together on one side and all the *non-Bith* low castes (untouchables) on the other side of the pollution-barrier and the caste hierarchy is basically dichotomous.

But opposed to the regional Hindu social setting are the Bhotia. It may be stated that the Bhotia valleys are not ordinary geographical entities, rather these are important structural units of the Bhotia socio-cultural framework. The Bhotia population is primarily seggregrated valleywise; each valley-based group exhibits distinct customary characteristics which, in effect, help to register these valleys as being unique social constituencies in the wider Bhotia cultural scenario. And hence, from an analytical standpoint, the valley qualifies to be the most useful unit for correctly assessing the Bhotia social affairs. However, the cultural variation is rather thin among the groups inhabiting Byans, Choudans and Darma in Kumaon and is mostly restricted to the minor areas e.g. habits, tastes, manners, courtesy rules and the like. These groups may be collectively called the 'Eastern Bhotia' who show remarkable similarity, in many major cultural fields like birth and death rites, marriage, religious and social outlook amongst them. But the Eastern Bhotia offer considerable cultural diversities with the Johari Bhotia which may be the result of the politico-historical happenings of the preceding few centuries apart from factors like isolation and lack of contact between the groups in question. The history of the Bhotia valleys reveals that the cultural similarity of Byans,

Choudans and Darma may be due to the fact that though these valleys were ruled by different powers, this did not prevent social intercourse among the people there in the past.

The chain of mountains separating these valleys was relatively less formidable. Sometimes, the Darmiya traders returned from Tibet via Byans and Choundans valleys when their own pass became blocked due to early snowfall. Moreover, during the winter months, the Darmiya and the Byansi Bhotias lived in some villages of Lower Bhot. Naturally, no major cultural difference could develop. On the other hand, people of these three valleys have marriage relations, too. But the situation was different for the Johari Bhotia. The Pachchuli chain of mountains stood as a formidable barrier separating Johar valley from the rest of Bhotia valleys of Kumaon, thereby obstructing social communication resulting in cultural isolation. The winter settlement of the Johri Bhotia, viz., Thal, Didihat and other places, are quite removed from the winter encampment areas of the Eastern Bhotia. Although the Eastern Bhotia and the Johari Bhotia met each other at Tibetan marts and also in the trade fairs of Jouljibi, Thal, Bageshwar and other places, however such trade meetings did not contribute to any intimate socio-cultural relationship.

Thus, absence of a broad-based contact between the Johari and the Eastern Bhotia groups resulted in widening cultural diversities. We may now see the phenomenon of the Bhotia's gradual march to the Hindu fold. Here it may be stated that the relative differences in the degree of Hinduisation among the Johari and the Eastern Bhotia further contributed substantially towards their cultural diversities. Of course, for this varying degree of Hinduisation of the different Bhotia groups some specific factors—historical and general—were responsible. It is difficult to ascertain when exactly the process of

Hinduisation started among the Bhotia. Absence of records relating to the event of the Bhotia social history is the biggest handicap in this regard. However, the general impression is that the phenomenon of status discrepancy among the Bhotia might have positively contributed to the Hinduisation. Besides, a few past political events also had some role in the process.

The Hindu Raja of Kumaon annexed the Johar valley in 1581 in order to effect security to pilgrims bound for Mt. Kailash and holy Mansarovar, as this valley was the passage to these holy centres. After this, the Johar was set for wider Hindu contact like the pilgrims even from the plains, apart from enjoying political patronage from the Kumaon Hindu Kingdom—all these were conducive to the initiation of Hinduisation there at a very early period. But the other three valleys of Darma, Byans and Choudans did not evoke much interest among the Hindu rulers of the region as the Johar did. In the absence of this and conversely due to content interference of diverse political and social forces, the Eastern Bhotia life of these valleys in the past remained largely outside the pale of Hinduisation which had started in the Johar valley already. This differential politico-social background, in a way, has further contributed to the growth of cultural diversity between the Johar and the Eastern Bhotia valleys even in those days. By the time the British arrived in Kumaon the Johari Bhotia became considerably Hinduised. The sketchy accounts by the early British authors profess this. We learn from these sources that the Joharis had been assiduously cultivating a distinct style of life which was a sequel of their courting some Hindu standards. The Hindu notions of social discrimination reflected in the codes of commensality had percolated into their daily life as they accepted "half-cookery *Kachi rasoi*, i.e. food cooked without clarified butter from any one except (untouchable) Dom........ (Although) they do not wear the sacred thread, but (they) adopt the uncut tuft of hair *(Sikha)* as all Hindus do...... There is no doubt that of later years the Joharis have affected more and more to intimate the scrupulous caste observance of the Hindu..........They refuse, too, to drink spirits, of which they consume large quantities, out of the same vessel with a person whom they consider to be of an inferior class, and altogether they have as much right as the Khasiyas of the less civilised parts of these districts to be considered Hindus........." wrote Atkinson.

In contradistinction the Eastern Botia style of life is enormously traditional. The Johari Bhotia continuously professed that they were "not to eat with the Tibetans, but only to drink tea with them" wrote Sherring. But unlike the Johari Bhotia, the Eastern Bhotia displayed no conscious resistance on the matter of their reported inter-dining with the Tibetans. By was of constant emphatic denial the Johari could manage to soften the local Hindu attitude to a certain degree on benefit of doubt which the Eastern Bhotia could not gain. While the Johari Bhotia made good progress in the process of Hinduisation, the Eastern Bhotia lagged far behind as evidenced in early records. Like the Johari Bhotia who "have assumed the affix 'Sinha' (Singh) to show their Rajput origin," the Eastern Bhatias styled themselves in the same fashion though "the knowledge of the Eastern Bhotias about Hinduism extends to little more than the name." According to Sherring :

But with the spread of British Administration and improvement of communication including opening of a new pilgrim route to Mt. Kailash and Manasarovar via Choudans and Byans valley, the age-old isolation of the Eastern Bhotia valleys was removed. The regular and multi-dimensional contacts that the Eastern Bhotia valleys have now, ultimately served the casue of their Hinduisation. The Bhotia society as whole was, thus, poised for an intensive involvement in the process. As border people, the Bhotia enjoyed some special privileges including heavy reduction of tax etc. Besides, the British policy encouraged the emergency of leaders and other elites to facilitate the task of administration in those remote pockets. These new Bhota leaders and elites played a very crucial role in the Hinduisation of the Bhotia. Their most important strategy was to reduce the Bhotia cultural dissimilarities with the regional Hindu cultural tradition. This was to be accomplished by either completely eliminating or modifying all such customs in Bhotia cultural inventory which offered sharp incompatibility with the Hindu cultural tradition. It is an undeniable fact that in the matter of Hinduisation, the Johari Bhotia was ahead of other Bhotia, and the former was so much transformed culturally that when the British authorities attempted to make an inquiry into the local customs of the Kumaon division, they were convinced to treat the Johari Bhotia case separately. The Johari Bhotia displayed enormous cultural dissimilarities with the Eastern Bhotia.

The Bhotias of Mana and Niti valleys of Garhwal inter-marry with the Bhotias of Pangana Johar in the Almora district. The great Hindu shrine of Badrinath and other associated temples lie in these (Mana and Niti) valleys: hence these Bhotias have come in contact with the Hindu residents, and assimilated their customs. In order to effect cultural conformity with the regional Hindu model, the Joharis modified their customs concerning the crises of life. They started celebrating the ceremonies connected with these events in a fashion similar to the high caste Hindus of Kumaon. The local Khasiya Brahmans usually officiated at the ceremonies. Stricter rules regarding marriage were enforced. Although brideprice system could not be fully eradicated instantly, an all-out effort was made to discourage its continuance. Marriage by gift (*Kanyadan*) was encourage instead. There were stray cases also where no price was charged.

It is noteworthy that when the Khasiya caste Hindus stuck to their tradition of bride price, the Johari Bhotia were endeavouring to eradicate it. By doing this the Johari were practically chiselling their cultural framework on the immigrant Rajputs' style which represented the cultural heritage of the Gangetic plains and which served as an ideal Hindu model to the local Khasiya castes as well. The orthodox Hindu attitude towards women was adopted. "*Parda* is so far practised that the elder brother never sees the face of his younger brother's wife, or does he ever speak to her, or go into the same room with her. "wrote Sherring. The traditional practice of death rite, the *Dhurung*, had been entirely abandoned by the Joharis long ago. Apart from all these, the Johari started worshipping Hindu Gods and deities and observing Hindu festivals. '*Gita* and *Ramayana* are recited on ceremonial occasions. These Bhotias, like the immigrant Rajputs, also have pictures of Rama and Krishna in their homes. All these efforts removed the cultural incompatibility substantially to ensure their Rajput status in the regional social setting.

As for the Eastern Bhotia situation of that time. Sherring reports: "These are much more backward than the others...They are looked down upon by the other Bhotias, because of their primitive ways....Although marriages are occasionally arranged through the parents...yet practically the universal custom of the three *pattis*, Darma, Byans and Choudans, is to arrange marriage at the *Ranbang*...at which men and women meet and spend the night singing lewd love songs, and drinking and smoking. The Bhotias of Johar and Niti look down upon the *Ranbang*, and will have nothing to do with it in their own country, having given it up many years ago. With the opening of another route to Mt. Kailash and

Manasarovar through Choudans and Byans valleys, the visit of the Hindu pilgrims became an annual feature. District Board Schools opened in these parts were manned with caste Hindu teachers who became a constant source of contact.

Meanwhile, Shri Narayan Swami, a Hindu ascetic from the plains, established an *ashram* and two schools in Choudans for poor Bhotias. The Swami's humanitarian works and the interest of a few local leaders created a favourable condition and expedited transformation of the Eastern Bhotia. Meanwhile an intense campaign was launched to abandon the traditional *Ranbang* institution immediately. The amoral *Ranbang* songs were banned in the society. Women were counselled to practise seclusion. A war on liquor was declared. People zealously came forward, destroyed their distilling apparatuses and vowed not to drink henceforth. After creating an ideal Hindu-type social environment, efforts were then mobilised to modify the customary *rites de passage* by Hindu parallels. The traditional *Durung* (Bhotia death rite) included ceremonial sacrifice of *yak* (considered to be a cow by the Hindu) and hence offered enormous incompatibility with Hindu values. Besides, people were discouraged to follow the traditional marriage by capture.

Consequently, many Eastern Bhotia families adopted Hindu death rite, *Shraddha*, and employed the Khasiya Brahmin to officiate at the ceremony. The Bhotias of Choudans and *Tulla* (lower) Darma took the lead in this. But the Bhotias living in the northernmost villages faced a problem. The local Khasiya Brahmans of Lower Bhot were reluctant to undertake a long arduous trek to these distant villages unless they were well paid. Sometimes it happened that in a family *Dudung* was performed for one of the deceased parent and *Shraddha* for the other. And above all, the Bhotias shortly discovered that their Brahmans mainly interested in extracing money under various pretexts, taking full advantage of their ignorance.

Disillusionment

All these factors disillusioned them as they observed that despite their sincere attempts to Hinduise their cultural outfit, the regional Hindu attitude towards them did not change. People remembered the gay life of 'the good old days' and desired a return of the same. Many argued that it was just foolish to sacrifice happiness for nothing. Because of these factors, the process of Hinduisation, while remaining operative, lost its initial momentum. The picture of Hinduisation of the Bhotia thus presente a duality. First, the Johari Bhotia's cultural achievement reached such a height that they surpassed the local Khaisya Rajput in cultural refinement and thus established cultural superiority over the latter. On the other hand, the eastern Bhotias failed to internalise the Hindu cultural traits, apart from the fact that their attempts were obviously superficial and half-hearted. They were singularly interested in "Shauka Rajput" designation which they preached readily, but did little to qualify for it. And for this reason mainly the local Kumaoni Hindus were able to repudiate their claim. In the midst of such situation, events like independence of the country and after a few years, the closure of the border with Tibet took place.

These events had far-reaching effects on the Bhotia cultural transformation. After independence the constitution of the new republic came to offer numerous privileges to the people who were officially declared as the 'Scheduled Castes/Tribes' or 'Backward Classes'. The Kumaon Bhotia, notably the Johari, had severely criticised the British policy of marking them as 'Mongolian border tribe' and had pressurised the British Government to reclassify them as Rajput. Quite unexpectedly, they changed their stand now. Instead, all the Bhotia groups joined hands to press their demand for special statutory safeguards. The leadership in this sphere came mainly from the Bhotia of Johar and Garbyang village of Byans valley. It was quite surprising. The Johari's cultural achievement and their supercilious attitude towards the Eastern Bhotia and the local Khasiya Rajputs owing to this, and the latter groups' submission to the Johari cultural superiority have, in a way, meant their victory in the struggle for Rajput status. Although the Bhotias of Garbyang had not attained that much of advancement as the Joharis did, they were nonetheless moving rapidly towards Hinduisation. Due to this they enjoyed considerable prestige among the Eastern Bhotia. Therefore, the latest move from this section of the Kumaon Bhotia community reflected a strange contradiction.

Although their constant efforts to exact special 'social economic and political' privileges did not meet with immediate success, yet this made an impact on the Eastern Bhotias who till then had not been able to make any appreciable progress in terms of Hinduisation. At this crucial time another important event occurred which directly affected the entire Bhotia people. The border with Tibet was sealed and the Bhotias' traditional trade with Tibet thus came to a halt. "The overwhelmingly trade-based traditional Bhotia economy thus suffered a temporary setback. This condition had prompted them to rearrange a new economic order to fill up the gap caused by the disruption of trade with Tibet. Under the changing conditions, the Bhotias badly felt the need for special constitutional privileges for them. The campaign for having themselves declared as 'Scheduled Tribe' by the Government was intensified. The educated Bhotia youth and others came forward to convince the authorities. A new elite group thus emerged and steadily gained hold on the common public.

The Eastern Bhotia protagonists of Hinuisation were gradually losing influence on the common Bhotia. The new elite among the Eastern Bhotia established themselves in the vanguard of their affairs which became more and more apparent with their obtaining Scheduled Tribe status in 1967. It is evident that both the Johari and the Eastern Bhotias unitedly fought for Scheduled Tribe status during the period when they were at different stages of Hinduisation. The follow-up cultural implications of their demand for tribal status were not similar. For the Johari Bhotia, the status of Scheduled Tribe was nothing more than as mechanism to acquire facilities, thereby ensuring steady progress. This had nothing to do with their cultural objectives. They refused to accept that this official status necessitated the revival of 'typically traditional culture' which they had given up long ago. In vicw of this, nothing contrary to Hinduisation could be detected there. Rather, the Johari, being comfortably placed culturally, maintained a steady progress, and of late a few influential families among them are reported to have discontinued widow remarriage in order to lead the common Johari Bhotia in this regard. But in case of the Eastern Bhotia the story is different. Being constantly frustrated in getting Hindu recognition, the Eastern Bhotia now found a convenient ground to cleverly cover up their failures.

A different trend of transformation thus crept into the Eastern Bhotia cultural life. The majority of the new elite group which had recently became very forceful, belonged to those villages where, confusion in the cultural sphere was conspicuous. Many of these new elites had a fair acquaintance with the plains areas where they stayed in connection with service, education etc. On returning to their valleys, they decided to organise the common people in order to end the chaotic atmosphere in their cultural sphere. A systematic course of action was chalked out. Dharchula, the sub-divisional headquarters, a fast-growing business centre and the most important place for all the Eastern Bhotia valleys, became the cockpit of these latest activities. Some of these elites staged dramas in some remote areas of Byans valley through which they gained popularity.

Besides, they rendered selfless service to the problem-ridden poor families. In addition to all this, their persistent efforts to attain Scheduled Tribe status were even more impressive. The new leadership, thus, outwitted the advocates of Hinduisation. After gaining a base at the grass-root level the new elite concentrated on the cultural front of the Eastern Bhotia. The "*Byans Anushuchit Janjati Byans Uththan Samiti*" was formed in 1969 under the active participation of the villagers of Nabi, Napalchu, Gunji, Kuti and Rongkang, initially with headquarters at Gunji village of Byans valley. The primary objectives of the *Samiti* are (a) to eliminate the evil practices of the traditional culture and (b) to preserve the traditional cultural identity of the Bhotia people. One important activity of the *Samiti* was to hold *Byans Mela* (fair) at Manila. The *Mela Prabandhak* committee is obviously constituted by the new elite who wanted the revival of their traditional culture. A campaign was launched to modify certain aspects of the traditional framework. Educated young people were asked to defend the traditional Bhotia culture and shun all type of complexes. The intelligent educated young men, the new political elite and others spearheaded a concerted action to establish that there was nothing in traditional Bhotia culture which was alien to the original Hindu form.

A book written for this purpose professes this, drawing numerous similes from Hindu epics and other ancient literatures. Moreover, the necessity of retaining "Socio-cultural distinctiveness" was also emphasised so that the Bhotia fit into the definition of "tribe." This was one of the significant points to the common Bhotia, anxious to derive benefit from a Scheduled Tribe status. And this contributed positively to a retreat from Hinduisation. The process of revival of traditional Bhotia culture, of course, with some reforms, was thus initiated. The practices connected with the life-cycle events were modified along traditional lines through a general consensus of village elders and others. Much importance was attached to the reintroduction of *Dudung* which had been the first casualty of Hinuisation earlier. The traditional death-rite, *Dudung*, therefore witnessed a good deal of modification. The question of *Yak* sacrifice which was obligatory by tradition, was now left to individual discretion. It was held that the poor Bhotia may complete *Dudung* by sacrificing a goat or with no sacrifice at all. But it was compulsory to make *Jo Yab Shimo* (effigy of the deceased) and *Amrhimo* during *Dudung* as was done traditionally. *Amrhimo* is a kind of traditional Bhotia lore, recited on the occasion of *Dudung*.

A part from all these, holding of *Dudung* in the months of *Sawan* and *Bhado* was banned because during these months the standing crops in the fields could be damaged as the customary *Gartimo* dance of the *Dudung* ceremony is inevitably held in the agricultural fields owing to want of spacious grounds in the residential sites of the high altitude villages. In a similar fashion, several aspects of marriage custom were modified. Marriage feasts which involved huge expenditures in the past on items like meat and *chakti* (traditional Bhotia liquor) was brought under the purview of reformation. A certain quota was fixed regarding the amount of meat and *chakti* to be consumed on this occasion. This meant considerable saving and naturally was welcomed by all. In spite of all these, the revival of the *Ranbang* tradition was strongly disfavour, fearing that the interested parties may find scapegoats in it to discredit their traditional culture. All these reforms in various aspects undoubtedly appealed to the common people. The phenomenon of traditionalisation gained support and many Bhotia families who had earlier opted for *Shraddha* and had accepted the ritual authority of Brahman, deserted both.

The *Samiti* now organises *Byans Mela* in August every year and gradually more and more villages have been participating. Leaving the recreational and other aspects, one primary objective of this three-day fair, is to generate among people a love for traditional culture. Cultural competitions are held and each village is allowed to present two songs, at least one on the theme of past glories, traditions etc. of the Bhotia people. A shield named '*Chal Jayanti Deb Singh Jasuli Rangkuli*' is awarded to the village considered most disciplined. Formal and informal discussions are held on cultural issues and emphasis is always laid on social unity in order to build up prestige of the Bhotia people. Due to these revivalistic efforts, the progress of Hinduisation among the Eastern Bhotia has suffered several setbacks. Its effect has so narrowed down that its influence is now restricted only to a few villages around Narayan Ashram and few others in Darma and Byans valleys. Therefore, the common Eastern Bhotia in general show least concern for Hinduisation, although, surprisingly they emphatically assert their "Shauka Rajput" origin.

Further, they frequently proclaim that their traditional cultural practices, in no way, contract the traditional Hindu way of life; rather, they quite wittingly point out that their traditional cultural outlook of tolerance, humanism and social freedom aptly represent the truest form of ancient Hindu ethos and tradition. A general trend in the tribal situation in India is many tribal groups' desire for acquiring a higher status in the Hindu cultural fold. This is often backed by their claims to Hindu origin initially. Such aspiring groups gradually undergo the process of cultural transformation in order to culturally qualify their claim and ensure their position in the Hindu fold. Through such process of Sanskritisation— a low Hindu Caste, or tribal, changes its customs, ritual and way of life in the direction of a, frequently, 'twice-born' caste. Generally such changes are followed by a claim to a higher position in the regional caste society than that traditionally conceded to the claimant caste (or other groups) by the local community.

The Kumaon Bhotia case of cultural transformation along the regional Hindu lines provides a suitable example in this regard. In establishing Rajput status, the Johari Bhotia met considerable success by means of their exemplary cultural modification. Their involvement in Hinduisation was a long process. But among the Eastern Bhotia this process was initiated much later and efforts of these people to establish their Rajput status was marginal in the sense that they did little to justify it culturally. But after independence some emerging realities, in a way, helped the Eastern Bhotia to register the revival of their traditional, though with certain reforms therein, which acted to preserve their *distinct* Bhotia sub-cultural identity, supposedly needed under the existing socio-political situation.

Bibliography

Atkinson, Edwint : *The Himalayan Gazatteer*, (Reprinted) Vol. III, Part I, Cosmo Publication, Delhi, 1973.

Berreman, Gerald : "Cultural Variability and Drift in the Himalayan Hills", *American Anthropologist*, Vol. 62, No. 5, 1960.

Census of India, 1961: *Village Darkot*, (Village Survey Monograph No. 9).

Das, Jagadish Chandra : "Cohesion and Conflict in a Himalayan Village: A study in the perspective of Intercaste-Relations," in 'Anthropological Researches in the Himalaya,' seminar sponsored by Anthropological Survey of India, Calcutta, 1976.

Lall, Panna : *Kumaon Local Customs.* Govt. Press, Allahabad, 1971.

Pant, S.D : *The Social Economy of the Himalayans*, George Allen & Unwin Ltd., London, 1935.

Raypa, Ratan Singh: *Sauka Simavarti Janjati* (in Hindi), RA Bros., Dharchula, 1974.

Sherring, Charles A : *Western Tibet and the British* Borderland, London, 1906.

Shrisvastava, Ramp : "Tribe Caste Mobility in India and the Case of Kumaon Bhotia; in *Caste and Kin in Nepal, India and Ceylon.* (ed. Christoph von Furer-Haimendforf.), Asia Publishing House, Bombay, 1946.

Stowell, A.V : A *Manual of the Land Tenures of the Kumaon Division*, Government Press, Allahabad, 1979.

A.K. Kapoor, and Satwanti Kapoor (ed.) *Ecology and Man in Himalayas*, M.D. Publications, New Delhi, 1994.

Christoph Von Furer Haimendrof (ed.) Asian Highland Societies— An Anthropological Perspective, Sterling Publishers, New Delhi, 1981.

12

Social Culture of Jammu and Kashmir

With an area of 84,471 square miles, Jammu and Kashmir is the homc of various races and tribes whose history goes back to thousands of years. Many strange and interesting customs and social usages are prevailing among them. It would have to take into consideration ethnic and physical factors such as the diversity of race and religion, and the influence upon the peoples' development of the vast mountain barriers and the network of rivers and hill-torrents cutting one part of the country off from another and tending to restrict mutual intercourse and confining the various population groups within limited and isolated areas.

The mountainous tract extending to the plains of the Punjab from the snowy mountains bounding the Kashmir Valley on the south is called Dugar. It is the home of the Dogras, a hardy people divided into several castes and sects, both Hindu and Musalman. Belonging to the Aryan race, they speak the Dogri language, a mixture of Sanskrit, Punjabi and Persian words, deriving its origin from the

Indo-Aryan branch of Sanskrit. There are numerous sub-castes among the Dogras of Jammu, the salient feature of all being the hardiness of the people. Their staple food is rice, wheat and pulses. The observance of common festivals like Basant, Nauroz, Sair and Dusserah testifies to an extraordinary spirit of tolerance and goodwill amongst both the Hindu and Muslim Dogras, as well as the members of other castes. They dress in a short coat or freely-flowing shirt, with pyjamas loose to the knees and tight-fitting downwards. The men generally wear a light turban and tie a *kamarband* at the waist. The women dress in a tight-fitting bodice or jumper with pyjamas similar to those of their menfolk and a shawl or a *duppata* thrown over the head.

In Jammu, the Brahmans depend upon agriculture which provides the main source of their income and the calling of religious ministers and priests is confined to a comparatively small number of families. It is strange to see Brahmans holding a position economically inferior to that of the Kshtrayas, most of them being tenants-at-will of the Rajput landlords. They are a peace-loving people and have always borne the hardships of life with a cheerful disposition. They have been greatly benefited by the Land Reforms Act of the present Government. The Dogra Rajputs are not tall men; their average height being five feet four. Of slim build, they have somewhat high shoulders and curiously bowed legs and, though not muscular, are active and untiring. The colour of their complexion is a light shade of brown, rather darker than the husk of the almond. The women because of their less exposure have a brighter tint. They possess well-formed features, composed of a slightly hooked nose, well-shaped mouth and small brown eyes.

The Dogra Rajputs are simple and child-like. They cling to their prejudices ; and the clan spirit, so common among mountain folk throughout the world, persists among them in the hard and fast rules of the *Biradari* system. They can endure long marches and stand the cold climate very well. Among the Muslim Rajputs, the Chibbalis and the Sudans are the chief sects. They also are a brave people and make the army their profession. Khatris and Mahajans form the backbone of trade and commerce in Jammu. They are less good-looking than the Rajputs and less inured to physical hardship. But they are men of judgment, and literacy has made great progress among both men and women. The working Rajputs and Thakkars follow agricultural pursuits. They are backward in education and loathe even to improve their farming methods.

There is the class of Harijans called Meghs, Chamiars and Dumbs. They form a more than fair proportion of the population of Jammu and have undergone numerous disabilities, civic and religious, at the hands of the high-caste Hindus. The levelling influence of education, which engenders tolerance and fellow-feeling, has, however, paved the way for a steady improvement of their social status. There are several interesting theories regarding the origin of the Meghs. According to one, they were originally Khatriyas but, in order to escape destruction at the hands of Paras Ram Brahman of the *Ramayana* period, they adopted the profession of weaving and called themselves Meghs. Another theory holds that their progenitors were Brahmans but a cow once died in the house of one of them and, there being nobody to remove the carcase, this odious task was undertaken by a member of the caste who was subsequently expelled from the community. Others also suffered a similar fate for one reason or another and the expelled individuals came to form the separate caste of Meghs. The Harijans are a community with clean habits and mostly follow the calling of agriculture. Only a few are cobblers or scavengers. In midst of the outer districts and the borders of the Kashmir Valley is a hilly country inhabited by a virile and active race called the Paharis. Hardy and of powerful frame, they lead a rough life, eking out a sustenance by terrace cultivation on the slopes of barren hills. Poor communications with the outside world and between the different villages (this being due to the difficulties of the terrain) have served to keep them poor. The language they speak is a mixture of Hindi, Punjabi, Dogri and Sanskrit words. They dress in grey woollen coats with *kamarband*, and wear loose pyjamas. The women are clad in long gowns tied with a *kamarband*, their attire being completed by a cap and shawl. Into this region have come the Kashmiris as settlers, inhabiting large tracts of the country and adopting the same dress. A mixture of the Pahari and the Kashmiri languages is spoken by them. Another interesting hill people are the Gujjars. The climate and pasture of certain altitudes are favourable for rearing cattle and sheep and from ancient times the Gujjars and their neighbours, the Gaddis, have been breeders. They lead semi-nomadic lives, moving in summer with their herds and flocks from the warm regions of Jammu. They are then to be found in parts of Kashmir, building their flat-topped houses on seemingly inaccessible heights and being everywhere perfectly at home with their animals. They are said to be Rajputs who migrated from Rajasthan and adopted the Muslim faith. Their language, Gujjari, is now definitely recognised to be a form of Rajasthani. Their outdoor life spent in some of the healthiest parts of the country, and their nourishing diet of bread made from corn with milk and butter as other constituents of their daily food, result in their being a long-lived people. They are a fine tall race, with a decidedly Jewish cast of features. Their good faith is proverbial and they are generously disposed. Fairly well represented in most parts of Jammu and Kashmir, they muster strong in Poonch, Riasi and Muzaffarabad districts.

Kashmir Region

The true people of Kashmir Valley are physically a fine race, the men being tall and well-built. They are an ancient race with complexions varying from olive to a ruddy and fair hue. The features of all are well-shaped and regular. Lively and intelligent, the people of the Valley are full of fun and fond of amusement. The beauty of their women has been long and much extolled.

A number of explanations, some of them verging upon the fantastic, have been advanced to account for their origin. For example, one theory puts them down as being descendants of one of the lost tribes of Israel, this perhaps being suggested by the Jewish cut of features to be found among some of the older people who look the patriarchal type. The following note by Alberuni almost clinches the matter: "They (Kashmiris) used to allow one or two foreigners to enter their country, particularly Jews, but at present they do not allow any Hindu whom they do not know personally to enter, much less other people."

According to a legend mentioned in Kalhan's *Rajatarangini* and the *Nilamatpurana*, the Valley which was a vast mountain lake was drained by Kashyapa Rishi who imported Brahmans and sages from India to live here. In those prehistoric days, it is said, tribes of Pishachas and Yakshas were living here. They used to give trouble to these Brahmans, who in order to escape their wrath followed the instructions of the author of the *Nilamatpurana* of giving presents of food etc. to them off and on to win their friendship. The festival of *Khichiamavas* is still observed by the Kashmiri Brahmans on the 15th day of the dark fortnight of Poh (Dec.-Jan.) when *Khichri* is cooked in every house and kept outside in new earthen pots as present to the Pishachas and Yakshas. A reader of *Rajatarangini* will have no hesitation to admit that before the advent of Islam in the 14th century, the population of Kashmir was not entirely Brahman. We find the names of several sects namely Nishads, Khashas, Dards, Bhuttas, Bhikshas, Damras, Tantrins, etc. who constantly gave trouble not only to the rulers of the country, but also to the Brahmans. How and wherefrom they came is a long study in itself. That the Kashmiris form a branch of the race which brought the languages of Indo-Aryan type into India, is a fact established by the evidence of their language and physical appearance. But the period of their immigration and the route they came by are still moot points among the authorities on the subject. Suffice it to say that they have till now preserved a distinct form of culture and in ancient times produced a civilisation which would have made a greater mark in the world's history, had there been a possibility of better and easier intercourse with the rest of the world. Yet during the long and chequered history of Kashmir, there have been periods when the people came into contact with the Indian, Roman, Greek and Persian civilisations resulting in a happy blending of cultures at once tolerant and sympathetic towards the ideas and beliefs of others. The Kashmiris demonstrated it practically. When for instance, Brahmanism replaced the earliest forms of Naga worship there was the least tinge of religious persecution. On the other hand the Nagas are even to this day venerated by the general populace in the various springs. Buddhism came into ascendency in the second century B.C. and in contrast to the religious feuds in the rest of India we find that Buddhist kings and ministers built *viharas* and temples dedicated to Hindu as well as to the Buddhist deities. And when Buddhism had its day, the change was marked by a conspicuous absence of force or bigotry.

Arrivals of Muslims

Similarly in the 14th century A.D. Islam entered Kashmir and as usual the broadminded Kashmiris welcomed its exponent, the great Shah Hamadan, with open arms and the synthesis of Hindu and Islamic religious thought found its greatest exponents in Lalleshwari and Sheikh Nur-ud-Din who are even to this day venerated by Hindus and Muslims alike. During the darkest periods of religious persecutions by ignorant and fanatical foreigners, the people of Kashmir lived like brothers, giving what little solace, shelter and comfort they could, to their brothers in distress. The Brahmans, popularly called Kashmiri Pandits, form a distinct class of their own and are considered to be the purest specimens of the ancient Aryan settlers in the Valley. During their numerous political vicissitudes they have suffered enormously at the hands of religious persecutors. Subsequently, during the long and peaceful reign of Sultan Zain-ul-Abidin most of them returned to their original home-land. They studied the Persian language and regained their traditional occupation, namely, government service, which was held by them throughout the later periods of Moghul, Pathan and Sikh rulers. The new-comers assumed the appelation of *Bhanmasi* in contradistinction to *Malmasi* which the indigenous inhabitants had assumed. The *Malmasis* observe the "lunar" and the *Bhanmasis* the "solar" form of astronomical calendar.

They, however, have no restriction with regard to inter-marriage, etc. The *Karkuns* or government servants having given up the study of Sanskrit in favour of Persian, employed their daughters' eldest sons as their priests who were called *Bachibhats*. In course of time, the *Karkuns* and *Bachibhats* became two sub-castes, inter-marriage between the two being restricted. The Kashmiri Pandits are divided into 133 exogamous *gotras*, each member of which claims to be a descendant of a rishi whose name the *gotra* bears. Generally, the social position is determined by the nature of occupation followed, rather than by the *gotra*.

Those who have been employed in superior state service since two or three generations hold their heads high above others. Although claiming to be the offspring of rishis and belonging to the highest branch of Brahmans, the Saraswats, Kashmiri Pandits take meat freely in strange contrast to the observance of strict vegetarianism by the Brahmans all over India.

This small community is highly advanced in education, more than 70% of their members being literate. Their chief occupation is government service. In India many well-known administrators and politicians have been Kashmiri Pandits. In the field of art, philosophy and literature, they have produced a galaxy of authors, savants and saints. They possess a knack of adapting to changed circumstances at short notice and during the present time are adopting new avenues of profession.

In Kashmir, Sikhs are another small community. Before 1947 they were chiefly concentrated in the Muzaffarabad district. But recent developments have forced them to migrate to other parts of the State. Most of them were originally Brahmans imported by Raja Sukh Jiwan and were converted to Sikhism during the reign of Maharaja Ranjit Singh. They are a hardy people and mostly agriculturists. Recently, they have taken to the military and police service of the State. An overwhelming majority of the people in the Valley professes Muslim religion. The advent of Islam during the 13th and the 14th centuries surely but slowly changed the social structure of the Kashmiris; but they maintained their traditions of love and tolerance. The influence of Islamic art from the directions of north and south is responsible, for the development of the many industries for which Kashmir is famous, e.g. shawl, carpet, papier mache, wood-carving, etc. Zain-ul-Abidin is mainly responsible for the introduction of these arts from

Samarqand and Bukhara, which were the centres of Islamic civilization then.

Numerous Muslim saints and derveshes propagated their religion through the preachings of the purest and truest doctrines of Islam. They lived the religion in their lives of complete self-abnegation and tolerance to the ideas and beliefs of others. This considerably influenced the religious and philosophic thought of the Kashmiris who adopted the new order in greater numbers. The Persian language and literature, first introduced into Kashmir by Zain-ul-Abidin, further enriched the cultural treasures of Kashmir resulting in a synthesis of the Hindu and Muslim civilizations. Kashmiris attained a great proficiency in the new language and literature and produced eminent poets and scholars like Ghani, Sarfi, Fani, etc. In the development of Kashmiri painting, architecture, music and poetry, Muslims played a prominent part. The Hari Parbat fort and the bastion wall, the Jumma and Pathar Masjids, Pari Mahal and the world-famous Moghul Gardens are living testimonies to the outstanding contribution of Islam to the art and thought of the Kashmiris.

"The Musalmans of the Valley", says Lawrence, "may have retained for some time after their conversion to Islam, some of the Hindu customs of endogamy within the caste and exogamy outside the *gotra*, but there is no trace of these customs now and the different tribal names or *krams* are names and nothing more." It is now possible for Dar to marry a girl of the *Gana kram* and vice versa, provided both are agriculturists. The intermarriage among the low caste wattals or scavengers is still a taboo. There is,' however, a sort of caste system prevalent, inasmuch as the members of one profession prefer to marry their sons and daughters among the followers of a similar profession. Thus, it is very rarely that goldsmiths (*sonars*) and blacksmiths (*khars*) contract marriages among themselves. The old *krams* or nicknames of Pandit, Bhat, Dar, etc. are, however, still retained and new ones also added by reason of the special calling of the head of the family or any of his ancestors or because of such peculiar circumstances which may have occurred to him. "For instance", says Pandit Anand Koul, "a man, named Wasdev, had a mulberry tree growing in his courtyard and, therefore, he was called Wasdev Tul (mulberry). Be, in order to get rid of this nickname, cut down the tree. But a *mund* (trunk) remained and people began to call him Wasdev Mund. He then removed the trunk of the tree but its removal resulted in a Khud (depression) and henceforth people called him Wasdev Khud. He then filled up the depression but the ground became a *teng* (mound) and he was called thereupon Wasdev Teng. Thus, exasperated he gave up any further attempt to remove the cause of his nickname and it continued to be *Teng* which is now attached to the names of his descendants."

Muslim Nicknames

The Sheikhs, Sayyids and Pirzadas are still considered to be *krams* of respectability among the Muslims. Mullahs or priests, though not numerous, are a class by themselves and every village has got a family or two to minister to the religious needs of the people and to officiate at the birth, marriage or death ceremonies. Recently they have taken to agriculture also ; but otherwise they live by the free gifts of grains bestowed on them by the villagers at harvest time. The Muslim population of the Valley is divided into the Sunni and the Shia sects, the former being in a preponderating majority. In certain Tehsils and villages there is, however, a concentration of Shias. They have monopolised the papier mache trade and during the hey-day of the shawl industry they were the proprietors of shawl factories.

Since there was an unbalanced economy between the shawl-weavers who were generally Sunnis and the capitalists, numerous Shia-Sunni riots took place then, the interested parties lending a religious tinge to these. There are some settlements of Pathans and Moghuls in certain parts of the Valley reminiscent of their rule ; but now they have been absorbed in the general population of the country, the appelation of *Khan* and *Sirdar* being only names. The Bombas and Khakhas are the inhabitants of the Jhelum Valley below Baramulla. They were a source of constant terror to the Kashmiris till Maharaja Gulab Singh subdued them. They used to carry out marauding expeditions into the Valley and even now mothers quieten their crying children by saying that *Khakhas* have come. They now follow the peaceful avocations of agriculture and trade.

The tribes like Dums and Galuans were once considered inferior to others. They have now acquired wealth and their social status has risen. Wealth alone now commands position and poverty at once degrades a family. Chaupans, the hereditary shepherds, who tend the sheep and cattle of the villagers during the summer months by taking them to green pastures on the various *margs* of high altitude, are a class of cheery, active men strictly marrying among themselves. They do not allow any outsider to usurp their hereditary calling. They have a most characteristic whistle and their healthy robust life in the high mountains makes them a lovable people except, of course, to their village clients who often have to be at their mercy with regard to the return of their sheep, etc. The Chaupans have some knowledge of simple herbs and bring them down for the poor villagers. In winter and early spring they live in the villages, where sometimes they possess a little arable land. Just like the Mullah the Chaupans get their remuneration at the time of harvesting of crops in the shape of grains and cash. The Bands or Bhagats correspond to the Mirasis in India and carry on the profession of singing and dancing and sometimes go in bands to perform short comic plays in different villages. They add piquancy and gaiety to the otherwise dull and monotonous life of the villagers and are in great demand on marriage and other festivals. The people with whom the visitors to the Valley generally come in close contact are the *hanjis* or boatmen of Kashmir. They are an ancient race and the *Rajatarangini* often mentions the *Nishads* (boatmen) and boat bridges. Some claim Noah as their ancestor but it is generally believed that they were Khashtryas before their conversion to Islam. They still disdainfully refer to a novice at boatcraft as a *Shudra*. There are many classes of boatmen known according to the boat they ply and live in. The *bahts* (barge) boatmen have recently taken to timber and grain trades and with the rise in their standard of life have acquired a respectability over other *hanjis*. The doonga and houseboat *hanji* looks cleaner and can speak English and Hindustani fairly well. He is intelligent and at a very short notice can perform the duties of an accompolished butler or an expert cook, a seasoned shikari or an experienced guide.

Most of the visitors owe their happy and trouble-free holiday in the Valley to the *hanji*, though he is more sinned against than sinning. There are other classes of *hanjis*, e.g., Dal *hanji* who carry the vegetables from the garden to the market and are considered the lowest. The *Gari hanji* are those who collect the *singhara* (waternut) from the Wular lake. The Gada *hanji* or fishermen are well-known for their close communal feelings and generally support their brothers in distress. The *hanjis* are a strong and virile race with well developed muscles. They live a hard life cramped up in one or two small rooms in their boats. Their knowledge of boatcraft is excellent and it is a pleasure to watch them punting or towing their boats up through strong and swift currents of the river.

The Kashmiri language has now been placed by Dr. Grierson in the Dardic branch of non-Sanskritic languages in his *"Linguistic Survey of India"*. This treatment of the Kashmiri language is opposed to the popular and local belief that Kashmiri was originally the language of Brahmans and has grown out of Sanskrit. There is no script of its own, but the Kashmiri language has a vast store of rich proverbs, sayings and folklore. There are some epic poems rendered into Kashmiri, as well as a good number of lyric poems. Recently the Arabic script has been adapted for its use and Kashmiri literature is growing in quantity as well as in quality.

Kashmiri Dress

The Kashmiris dress has often been criticised for being effeminate and conducive to lazy habits. It is a long loose gown buttoning at the neck and falling to the ankles. In winter it is made of wool and in summer of cotton. There is very little difference between the *phiran* worn by men and women. A pyjama of the loose type is generally worn under the *phiran* and this is all the dress of an average villager. The women wear a skull cap surrounded by a fillet of red colour in the case of Muslim and a fillet of white cloth in the case of Pandit women. A shawl or a white *chaddar* thrown gracefully over the head and shoulders, more as a protection from the sun than to hide the features, completes their headgear. Men wear a turban as a sign of respectability and affluence. It is commonly worn by the inhabitants of cities and big towns.

The ordinary peasant is content with wearing the long pointed skull cap. In winter a *kangri* is taken under the *phiran* to keep oneself warm. It consists of an earthen jar of about six inches diameter covered with a basket of wickerwork. Charcoal cinders of a special type are put in it to give a constant and a continuous heat. There is a tale current among the Kashmiris that Emperor Akbar, enraged at the dogged resistance offered by the people of the Valley to his general, Qasim Khan, forced them to wear an effeminate *phiran* in order to degrade them.

Shawl-making in Kashmir

Weaving of shawl had for long been synonymous with Kashmir. The Kashmir shawl was renowned for its fine texture, charm of colour and shade. The shawl industry of Kashmir in the opinion of some observers is as old as the Epics of *Ramayana* and *Mahabharata*. Similarly it is said, "the beautiful shawls of Kashmir.... adorned the proudest beauties at the court of Caesar when the barbarians of Britain were painted savages". Whatever be the truth about the origin of this primitive industry, the fact remains that the country was famed for its excellent shawls though they were also produced elsewhere in the world, for example in Persia and in some parts of India, but they never compared favourably with those produced by the Kashmir craftsmen.

The three staple commodities having alliteration in their names for which the country is proverbial and frequently referred to by observers are *Shawl*, *Shali* and *Shalgam*. But all this excellence in art was attained at the cost of something more precious than art itself—and that was human life. The working of the 'time-honoured' shawl system is as interesting as it is painful. The life led by these shawl weavers is in sharp contrast with the exquisite beauty of the shawls they produced. They worked for low, starvation wages in most unhealthy and unpleasant conditions of life. Their misery and abject servitude made an observer like Robert Thorp lament in 1870, saying, "Do they never picture to themselves these low-roomed, ill-ventilated abodes, where the loom-workers sit at their forced labour day after day, toiling for their miserable pittance? Those gaily coloured threads of wool are not the only ones which these looms weave to their completion; Threads of life, more costly than those of the softest poshm, whose price will be demanded by Heaven yet, are spun out there on the loom of sickness and suffering." From *Cashmere Misgovernment* by Robert Thorp.

It will be pertinent here to describe first the circumstances in which the shawls were produced, and at what cost, before the shawlmaking process itself is described. The whole shawl system was controlled by the government. A department called the Dagshawl was set up under which the two divisions of the shawl system, namely, the loom system and hand-work system worked. This department acted only as the "spectre of a godless tyranny" stamping freedom and initiative from the weavers with "machine-like efficiency". The machinery of the Dagshawl comprised elements who placed personal profits above patriotism and human feeling, and battened on the wretched weavers. The Dagshawl was placed in charge of a person called a *Darogha*. The function of this institution was to mark the shawls and affix the Government stamp on each manufactured shawl. Besides the stamp fee a tax was also levied on the shawl. No shawlmaker could escape this practice with impunity. The Government placed persons' on duty called *Shaqdars* who had to detect the smuggling cases that were likely to occur. Robert Thorp describes the process of marking the shawls manufactured by *Karkhandars* under the loom system thus : "....... Before a loom shawl can be legally made, a small piece of the intended degree of fineness must be brought to the Daghshali. The proposed size is named, and the price is thus calculated ; the piece then receives the Government stamp, and is laid up in the Daghshali. The *karkhandar* receives a paper describing the shawl and giving the date of the stamp, for which he pays at the time Rs. 18/12 per cent on the price of the shawl ; when the shawl is nearly completed, it is taken to the Daghshali and the stamped price is worked into it...."

Regarding the levy of taxes on these shawl manufacturers, he writes : "The annual tax levied on each *karkhandar* upto the 1st December 1867, was Rs. 47/8/ - (Chilkee rupees) for each shawl baf in his employ; from that date a reduction was made of 11 chilkee rupees."

The fate of the hand-workmen was sealed in a similar manner. They were directly under the Daghshawl. They could not sell any piece without the stamp being affixed on it. According to Robert Thorp the hand-made Pashmina piece was stamped twice. When it was a plain piece, the stamp was affixed on it and the tax at the rate of 10.5 chilkee rupees levied for 4.5 yards. When it was dyed and the needle-work was done on it, a second stamp was affixed. By that time the rate of tax was 18 chilkee rupees for 4.5 yards. From this it only follows that ultimately the pressure of these taxes was borne by the shawl-weaver who smarted under it. It was humanly impossible to live on the paltry sum that he got for the hard work that he had put into the shawl. This sorry state of affairs is amply clear from the following account of Moorcroft—as referred to by Lawrence in the *'Valley of Kashmir'* : "All the facts connected with this interesting and once most important industry will be found in Moorcroft's Travels Vol. II, ch. iii. Though it was a lucrative industry to the State, which took Rs. 30/- per annum from employers of shawl-weavers per head, an impost of 20 per cent on the manufactured article, an export duty of Rs. 7/15/- on a long shawl and Rs. 5/13/- on a square shawl, it was poor industry for the weavers. In 1871 one or two annas per diem was the ordinary wage for a weaver, and Moorcroft noticed that the general earnings of an industrious and expert spinner were Rs. 1/8/ per mensem and probably less." But this was not all.

These poor creatures could not get a full meal, not to speak of other amenities of life. The Government sold grain to the manufacturers of the shawls per loom at a rate higher than the market. The quantity given to them was so meagre that they could not keep body and soul together. They had to live on mulberry fruits and other coarse edibles that came their way for many months of the year. Misery was written large on the pinched faces of these sallow-complexioned, weak-framed human beings. And what was worse, they could not relinquish this profession, as that would mean a tremendous loss to the Government. Only death could relieve them from this miserable condition. The result of this strangulation was that the rate of starvation deaths gained momentum in the country.

Pandit Anand Koul has furnished detailed information regarding the system of the sale of grains to the loom-workers and the taxes on pashmina fabrics. "During the Afghan period saffron and grains, which the State got as its own share, were sold by the State at higher than the market rates to the inhabitants, of course against their wishes. The selling was called *Niliv* or *Tarah*. The loss that this system entailed on the people was ruinous. It told very severely on the shawl-weavers who then numbered 12,000. In the time of the Afghan Governor, Haji Karim Dad (1776-83 A.D.), this practice was abolished and in lieu of it the shawl-weavers were made to pay a small tax which was called *Qasuri-shali*. Subsequently, Haji Karim Dad, at the suggestion of his Peshkar, Pandit Dila Ram Quli, abolished the *Qasuri-shali*, but levied a tax on each piece of Pushmina manufactured ... Azim Khan revived the old *Niliv* system and gave ten kharwars of shali per loom. The shawl produced on the loom was taken by the State and the price of Shali together with the amount of duty leviable on the shawl, was recovered from the price of the shawl. When Kashmir passed into the hands of the Sikhs, there had remained only six thousand looms and yet the duty was further raised to three annas per rupee *ad valorem* and twelve *kharwars* of *Shali* at three rupees per kharwar of which the actual market price was only one rupee—were issued for each loom." In this way these taxes and the *Niliv* system continued from king to king till the shawl-weavers became paupers and it was in the year 1877 A.D. that this tax and the *Niliv* system were abolished, and later the remaining customs-duty also.

Like every other piece of invention there is a story behind the introduction of the words *'Shawl, Du Shawli'* and also of colour patterns. The story is referred to by Pandit Anand Koul in his book *Jammu and Kashmir State* which is the source of this piece of information. Mirza Haider of Kashgar was the Wazir of Sultan Nazuk Shah who ruled Kashmir in 1540 A.D. He had a cook named Nagz Beg who came from Khoqand (Central Asia). One day Nagz Beg presented a well-made pashmina piece to his master. Mirza, Haider was very delighted to see it and asked what it was. The cook readily replied 'a shawl' which the people of Khoqand call a blanket in their own tongue. Mirza Haider further inquired if the piece was single or double. Nagz Beg said that it was *'Du Shawl'* (a double piece). Since then it is said that the term 'Shawli, Du Shawli', became known in the country. Haider Malik rewarded his servant and asked him to prepare another such piece for him.

It may be mentioned here that the shawl industry of Kashmir witnessed many vicissitudes of fortune and it may be that in the time of Mirza Haider it was a rarity and when he was presented with a shawl it gave him delight when he saw it. But there is sufficient evidence to prove that the industry flourished in the country long before. Nagz Beg was a wonderful man. He was resourceful and inventive. The story goes that one day a weaver was slapped in the face in his presence. His nose bled and the drops fell on the pashmina piece and it looked charming with the red colour. The incident inspired Nagz Beg who was observing all this. He successfully developed a pattern of variegated colours while weaving a pashmina fabric. This was a laudable contribution indeed ! And this is the story behind the introduction of colour patterns in the shawls. The tomb of this man stands at Babribag near Zadibal, a couple of miles to the north of Srinagar.

The Kashmiri Pashmina Shawl is of two varieties: (a) *Kani* Shawl (b) Amli Shawl. *Kani Shawl* is woven on the loom. Under the loom system, various pieces are woven separately and then stitched together so neatly and skilfully that it looks all of a piece without any stitch visible. On a loom quite a number of weavers work. In the *Amli Shawl* the pashmina fabric is embroidered with needles working to a pattern. In this the *sadabaf* first weaves the fabric and then the *rafoogar* does the needle-work. The outline of the pattern is drawn by the local *naqash* and the weaver deftly uses threads with various colours working to the original pattern. The weaver has his own knack quite peculiar to him. He does not follow the original pattern. He gets the pattern translated on paper by a person who is called *khahan* wol. The translation of the original pattern is symbolical and so manipulated as to serve a key-board to the weaver who while seated on the loom uses threads and colours accordingly. So used are these weavers to this peculiar method that they work mechanically and with such agility that the beholder is amazed. This art, according to Pt. Anand Koul, was invented in the time of Azad Khan, the Afghan Governor of Kashmir (1783-1185 A.D.), by a son of the soil popularly known as Ala Baba. The innovation struck him when he observed the clawmarks left by a fowl on a plain sheet of cloth. It suggested to him a design which he worked with needles. His experiment was a success and in this way the art of Amli-shawl-making was given a good start.

Ala Baba's descendents are alive today and still pursuing their forefather's profession. Thus, with the advance of time and fashion the *Amli shawl* was developed into various designs and patterns. It sprang into favour with women who cherished it as a part of their trousseau. The impress of the country's beauty is often found in various pieces of art. In embroidered shawls the pattern of ornamentation is inspired by the flora and fauna and the splendid scenery in which the country abounds. About some elaborate patterns it is opined by a British writer thus : "The well-known cone pattern with flowing curves... and minute diaper of flowers, is elaborated in the most artistic manner and combined with floral decorations and a maze of scrolls. It has been called the Persian cone or flame pattern. The cone, I think is a purely Kashmiri idea. Some say the design was conceived from the windings of the Jhelum river and the scrolls were in imitation of the ripples of water caused by the flow near the bridges on the Jhelum. It may, therefore, be called the 'Jhelum pattern'."

Sir Walter Lawrence reproduces the opinion of an expert regarding a design of shawl developed under the patronage of the Moghuls : "According to M. Dauvergne the Kashmiri shawl dated back to the times of the Emperor Baber. The Mughal emperors wore on their turbans a jewelled ornament known as *jigha,* in shape like an almond. On the top of the *jigha* was an aigrette of feathers. An Andijani weaver imitated the design of the *jigha* in a scarf made for the Emperor, Baber, and was so successful that the *jigha* became the fashionable design in all scarves and shawls. Many Andijani weavers were brought down to India and Kashmir by the Mughal emperors, and the *jigha* design was adopted in art centres in India and also in Persia.

Many of the small carpets of Persia represent the *jigha*, and at the present time there is a class of shawls and *butadars* made in Srinagar entirely for the Persian market...

"The first shawls which reached Europe were brought by Napoleon, at the time of the campaign in Egypt, as a present to the Empress Josephine, and from that time shawls became fashionable. In those days the *jigha* varied from 1 foot in depth to 18 inches, but later on General Ventura—then in Maharaja Ranjit Singh's service sent to France shawls in which the *jigha* had attained large proportions. These shawls were known as Palms. They were 10 to 11 feet long by 4.5 a feet wide. The centre was plain, usually black in colour, the borders were covered with elongated *jighas* or palms in parallel rows..."

Notwithstanding the industry witnessed many ups and downs the shawl attained heights of perfection during various periods of Kashmir's history. For instance under the Moghuls this industry received great patronage and encouragement as mentioned above. The shawl improved in quality and fineness of texture to such an extent that when pressed, it could pass through a finger-ring. It was, therefore, known as ring-shawl and prized everywhere. Bernier visited Kashmir in the company of Aurangzeb in 1665 A.D. and he writes : "What may be considered peculiar to Kashmir and the staple commodity which particularly promotes the trade of the country and fills it with wealth, is the prodigious quantity of shawls which they manufacture and which gives occupation even to little children."

Under the Afghans rulers the industry made further progress. George Forster who visited Kashmir in 1783 A.D. wrote : "In Kashmir are seen merchants and commercial agents of most of the principal cities of Northern India, also of Tartary, Persia and Turkey who, at the same time, advance their fortunes and enjoy the pleasure of a fine climate and country over which are profusely spread the various beauties of nature".

During the Sikh period the shawl flourished. Moorcroft who visited Kashmir in 1822 A.D. wrote : "The whole value of shawl-goods manufactured in Kashmir may be estimated at about thirty-five lakhs of rupees per annum." Similarly, Lawrence says : "The best shawls ever made in Kashmir were manufactured in the time of Maháraja Ranbir Singh between the years 1865-72. They were very fine in texture, very soft in colour, and of the most elaborate and graceful patterns, of a purely Eastern style of decoration." It was after 1870 when the war between France and Germany was going on that the demand for shawls waned and the industry declined. The subsequent famine in Kashmir in 1877-79 was its ultimate doom. The present Government has taken steps to preserve the traditional arts of Kashmir by establishing 'Emporia in various parts of India which organise sales, etc., thereby saving the indigenous artisan and craftsman from the middleman and bullies who in the past sapped their very vitality.

Bibliography

1. Anonymous, *Keys to Kashmir*, Lalla Rookh Publications, Srinagar, 1957.
2. Pearce Gervice, *This is Kashmir*, Cassell & Co. Ltd., London, 1954.

13

Jagar—Spirit Possession Seance in Kumaon

Here, we will examine the structure and content of the Kumaoni ceremony known as *jagar*, perhaps the most important ceremony in the religious life of the Kumaoni Rajputs and Silpakars. A *jagar* is essentially a spirit possession seance in which a designated deity or deities (*devatas*) is induced by ritual drumming and the singing of traditional *devata* legends to possess a prearranged oracle/medium of the spirit. Fieldwork and research for this study was conducted among the Rajputs and Silpakars of the Kosi River valley about ten to fifteen miles north of Almora in the Kumaon region. The local Rajputs of this study are also known as Thakurs and formerly were called Khasa. However, this latter designation is considered derogatory and is rarely used. Likewise, the Silpakars were previously known as Dom, but the latter term has been abandoned because of its pejorative connotations. As these name changes imply, both *jatis* have been undergoing Sanskritization-like efforts over the past several decades.

Traditional patterns of marriage, including brideprice and unorthodox ceremonies are being replaced by dowry and *kanya-dan*. There is evidence that the Rajputs of Kumaon and Garhwal did not always wear the sacred thread and that Brahmanical ceremonial performance and values were not as important in the 19th century as they have become. However, the ceremonies of *jagar* have persisted despite the other areas of change. But, many people today do express ambivalence about these rituals and explain that they no longer believe in such "superstition." Despite this, belief in *jagar* remains strong and widespread, though, perhaps it is gradually declining. As modem education spreads and employment opportunities in the towns of Kumaon and cities of the plains increase, the local population realizes that *jagar* and their *gram devatas* (village gods and goddesses) are unorthodox relative to plains Hinduism. It is important that the rich folklore and ritual drama of *jagar* be recorded before these processes of change have obliterated the unique, vibrant cultural heritage of Kumaon. A *jagar* can be a public performance at a village temple for the benefit of the entire village, or, it can be a small affair performed inside the house. Although the distinction between the two is an important one to the villagers, there was a certain amount of confusion as to the precise term for each kind of performance. Many informants insisted that the public performance is called a *jaga* and that the indoor performance is a *jagar*. Others claimed that both words meant the same thing and that one distinguishes the public from the private by calling the former an "outside *jagar*" and the latter an "inside *jagar*,"

The outside *jagar* always is performed for the *gram devatas* (e.g., "Haru and his companions") and usually is held in conjunction with a cyclical festival or some major village crisis. The *jagariya* is a professional musician usually a Darji (formerly Das-Dholi *jati* cluster) and he performs on a special drum called a *dhol*. The outside *jagar* can last for several days and in the rare celebration of Baishi lasts up to twenty-two days. During Baishi a *jagar* would be held every night and sacrifices of goat and possibly buffalo would be offered. Outside *jagars* are relatively infrequent as they are expensive, difficult to organize, and time consuming. They are held only on major festival days or at times of great village crisis (e.g., epidemic or famine).

Moreover, unlike the inside *jagar*, in recent years they have been declining rapidly in popularity. In contrast to the outside *jagar*, the inside *jagar* is held in the house of an individual sponsor to meet the needs of his own family. The inside *jagar* is sung in honour of one of the household deities and is accompanied by the *haruk* drum. An inside *jagar* can be performed for any number of reasons and they are held frequently throughout the year. A *jagar* is most commonly arranged to cure disease or illness, particularly when the illness is believed to have been caused by ghost possession. Interestingly, the victims of ghost-possession illness are most frequently young married women and this probably reflects the stresses associated with patrilocal residence (wife moves into household of her husband's family) on young daughters-in-law. However many other events may precipitate a performance. A *jagar* often is held twenty-two days after a child is born, particularly if it is a boy, or after a new bride enters the house. Some people give a *jagar* annually to please their family god or in fulfilment of a vow. If a woman has been unable to conceive, she may have a *jagar* performed for her. A *jagar* may assist a person in planning a long journey, or a young man who is considering entering military service.

In other words, whenever people feel that their household deity may help them through a crisis or that the deity's blessings are needed, they may perform a *jagar*. It might seem from the above reasons that *jagar* performances are spaced relatively evenly over the year. Yet they are less frequent during the winter months when many of the men go to the plains to seek work. If possible, the performance will be postponed until the summer when they often return. Similarly, a *jagar* is supposed to be held after someone has been cured of ghost possession. But the time is fixed to meet the convenience of the family. Delay also gives time to save up the rupees to meet the financial expenditure of the performance, including often the sacrifice of a goat.

At least six functionaries necessary to perform a *jagar*. This includes the *syonkar* (the sponsor), the *jagariya* (he plays the drum, sings the legend, and leads the ceremony), the *dangariya* (the oracle/medium), a *thali* player and two *hebars* (they provide vocal accompaniment). In addition, the immediate members of the *syonkar's* family usually are present, especially the person on whose behalf the *jagar* is held. In principle, everyone from the village is welcome to come, regardless of caste. However, the size of the room limits the number of guests to about thirty or so. The closest *biradari* (lineage) agnates and friends probably often come as they may have an interest in the person(s) in whose behalf the *jagar* is held. But there are some people who are particularly fond of *jagars*, and they appeared at many of the *jagars* in the village. The music and the social aspects of the *jagar* have an obvious entertainment value and people often come "just to listen." Another reason for attendance is that, toward the end of the evening, the guests are allowed to ask questions of the deity on problems that have been troubling them. We will now examine the function and role of the essential participants in a *jagar* performance.

(i) The *syonkar* (also pronounced *sonkar*) is the sponsor or host of the *jagar*. He has called it on behalf of some member of his family (wife, son, daughter, daughter-in-law, etc.) or perhaps for the general family welfare. He is responsible for arranging the *jagar* and he will make the payments to the hired specialists.

(ii) The *jagariya* is the main officiant at the *jagar* ceremony. Neither he nor the *dangariya* is a shaman in the traditional anthropological sense of the term, but a person who has mastered spirits and who can at will introduce them into his own body.

The *Jagariya* is not possessed in the *jagar*, rather he has a skill, which when effective, induces the spirit to possess another person who is a known devotee and medium of the deity. This person, the *dangariya* is not a shaman either because he lacks the power to bring about his own possession. However, the two working together in a seance have the powers which anthropologists ordinarily associate with shamans. Since neither the *jagariya* nor the *dangariya* have the combined skills of the shaman. The *jagariya* would be an exorcist and the *dangariya* would be an oracle. While an oracle is the one... possessed by a spirit (benevolent usually) and (who) speaks while possessed; the exorcists are... specialists who expel (evil) spirits, who know the sacred sayings and steps in the ritual necessary to keep the spirits under control and to force them to leave. The *jagariya* theoretically can come from any caste; however, as the *jagar* is a non-Sanskritic ceremony, the role usually is filled by the Rajput and Silpakar *jatis*. There has been a gradual decline in the importance of the *jagar* in recent years, as the trend toward "Sanskritization" has been an accelerating process. All informants agreed that *jagars* and especially *jagariyas* were much more common a generation or two ago.

In 1986-87, Pakhura had one *jagariya* competent to perform at inside *jagars* and none who performed at the outside *jagar*. The Kosi River valley adjacent to Pakhura had about 25 villages and 6000 people but, there were only about ten *jagariyas* in the area. The *jagariya* today is a part time practitioner; that is, his performances constitute a supplementary source of income. Whether or not they ever were able to make this work a full time occupation is a moot point. Although *jagars* formerly were more popular, *jagariyas* were presumably much more common as well. The *jagariya's* fee is not fixed, and it is usually modest, a few rupees plus a meal. There was at least one Rajput *jagariya* who didn't accept any rupees. If the *jagariya* comes from another village, overnight lodging and morning tea also would be extended to him. There exists no fixed *jajmani* or *Khaukiya* relationship for *jagariyas*, people call whoever they are most comfortable with. Some caste conscious Rajput villagers prefer to only call Rajput *jagariyas*, however, most are willing to invite Silpakar *jagariyas* to perform in their homes. The job of *jagariya* requires years of preparation and must by necessity begin when one is a boy. It is not a hereditary occupation, though many *jagariyas* are the sons of *jagariyas*, nor is it acquired from a specific *guru*. A boy who is interested learns by going to as many *jagars* as he can. By hearing the stories told and retold, he gradually commits them to memory. He also must learn to play his drum, the *hurka*, an hour glass shaped double membranophone, and (or) the *dhol* (for outside *jagars*), and to become a competent singer. The success of a *jagariya* depends primarily on the quality of his skills and the number of *devata* stories that he has committed to memory. Naturally, the more legends he knows, the more *jagars* he can perform. The villagers definitely are cognizant of the abilities and reputation of a *jagariya* and this greatly effects which one they will select. One might assume that an important aspect of technical ability is knowledge of details in the legends of the *devata*. Actually most laymen are unable to judge this point, and sometimes the story is sung in an archaic mode of expression. Although the audience can follow the gist of the story, they would not be aware of changes in detail or sentence structure. Indeed, whole incidences can be left out and the audience may not notice. Skills are related more to the quality of drumming and singing and to an ability to create an exciting phrenetic atmosphere. The ultimate criterion is whether or not the *jagariya* consistently succeeds in inducing the *devata* to possess the oracle. *Jagariyas* are not understood to have the power to force the deities to possess an oracle; however, they invite the deities to come in order to dance, to hear their legends told, and to receive offerings. When the deities do come, it is believed that they enjoy the *jagariya's* music and that his offerings were satisfactory.

Thus, it is the deities who are said to judge the *jagariya's* skills. Nevertheless, some *jagariyas* enjoy a reputation for being able to bring about a better spirit possession, to keep the spirit longer and to have greater control over the spirit. A powerful *jagariya* can have several spirits enter a performance, by inducing other deities to possess some of the guests. Conversely, if a *jagariya's* skill is insufficient, he may fail to induce the desired spirit to possess the oracle or perhaps to keep him once the oracle has been possessed. However, the frequency of failure is very low.

Generally speaking, the practice of performing inside *jagar* does not adversely effect the status of the performer. Despite the necessity to sing and beat the *hurka*, there is none of the negative association that generally goes with being an entertainer as is the case with the low caste *Hurkiya*. The *Hurkiya* plays his *hurka* and sings primarily for entertainment. As the payments he receives are voluntary contributions, it gives his work the connotation of begging. On the other hand, the *jagar* is sought after and hired by the *syonkar*. While a price for his services may be arranged, the *jagariya* is not dependent on his fees for income. The *jagariya's* music may have entertainment value, but its ostensive function is spiritual. Indeed, the *jagariya* is respected for his association with the powerful beings and for his ability to exorcise ghosts.

However, performance of outside *jagars* required playing the *dhol* and this does have negative status consequences. In former days *dholi* players were called *das* "slave", but if a *jagariya* is called this offense. One *Jagariya* in Pakhura played the *dhol* with his father when his father was alive. But he refuses now, though he proudly performs inside *jagars* on the *hurka*. The role of the *jagariya* in the *jagar* is in many ways analogous to that of the Brahman priest in the Sanskritic rituals. Like the priest, the *jagariya* directs his client in the administration of the preparations and ritual details. The *jagariya* tells the *syonkar* when to sprinkle the cow urine (for purification), to light the incense, and to make the (oil lamp). He also instructs in the preparation and placement of the *dhuni* (symbolic sacrificial fire, hot charcoal) and the *dulenc* (sacred seat for the oracle). For both the Brahman priest and the *jagariya*, the success of a ceremony depends on a body of learned knowledge. Indeed, the *jagariya* regards himself as the "priest" of the ceremony.

He points out that during the performance he is addressed as the "*guru* of the *devata*", and his fee is referred to as *guru bhet* (offering to the *guru*). The latter phrase is also used by the Rajputs for the gifts they give to their priests. Although the *jagariya* is not a shaman, in some respects, his command and role in the *jagar* is greater than the power that a priest has in his role. While the priest acts as an intermediary between his client and the deity, the *jagariya* is in a position to influence and even control the deity. It is true that the *jagariya* does not force the *devata* to possess the oracle, rather he induces or persuades him by his hypnotic music and skilful narration. However, once the deity has possessed the oracle, the *jagariya* is believed to have considerable control over him. This is symbolized by the deity's addressing the *jagariya* as "my *guru*", and by his sitting at his guru's feet. Soon after the deity possessed the oracle, the *jagariya* orders the *devata* to worship the *dhuni*, the sacred symbol of Gorakhnath, who is the supposed *guru* of all the *devatas* (in the outside *jagar* the *jagariya* is understood to be functioning in place of Gorakhnath).

The *jagariya's* control is manifested in a number of ways. The *devata* must obey all his commands and answer all the questions placed before him. The *devata* often makes certain requests during the performances, but the *jagariya* can refuse them if he wants or if he feels that they are unreasonable. Often he makes the *devata* agree to compromise. When the deity has tired of dancing and answering the questions, he asks the *jagariya* for permission to go. If the *jagariya* wants more questions answered, he may refuse.

(iii) The *dangariya*, also referred to as "*devata-ka ghora*" ("horse of the deity") or nacnewala ("one who dances"), is the oracle and medium, the body through which the *devata* dances and speaks. However, when the *dangariya* is possessed, he or she is not called any of these terms, rather he/she is addressed as a *devata*, for at that time the oracle is the god.

After selecting a *jagariya*, the *Syonkar's* next responsibility is to arrange an appropriate *dangariya*. Although the sponsor may have an oracle of the deity in his family, if it is a woman, she probably will not be regarded as satisfactory. Moreover, as there are only five male *dangariyas* in the village for household deities, the *syonkar* may have to hire a *dangariya*. The fee is usually a nominal amount and is not the primary motivation for accepting an offer to be a *dangariya*. Occasionally a person is an oracle of two *devatas* and even rarely of three. However, a person is not believed to choose to become a *dangariya*; rather the god is said to select his oracle. Most women who are oracles became so after their household deity cured them of ghost possession. The men who are oracles at inside *jagars* usually began as youths, when they were possessed as peripheral mediums in *jagars* for their household deity. At outside *jagars*, *dangariyas* are selected by the *devatas* at the large *jagar* festival known as Baishi. If a person is possessed at any other time but has not been first possessed at a Baishi, then he is regarded as a "*kacca dangariya*".

Most Pakhura informants said that a Baishi had not been held for several years and that they thought it unlikely that one would be held again. The minimal requirement for becoming a *dangariya* is that the person should have reached "ritual maturity." For a girl or Silpakar this means being married and for a Rajput boy it means having gone through the *barpan* (*upanayana*, initiation) ceremony.

Aside from this, an oracle is supposed to become a devotee of his deity and to live a ritually pure life. Interestingly, many people explained their loss of faith in *jagars* by saying that the *dangariyas* were corrupt and fakes. Their reasoning was that several of the *dangariyas* were known for their bad habits (drinking, going to Almora for entertainment and failure to maintain a ritually pure life).

(iv) *Thali* player and *hebars*. The man who beats the *thali* (brass plate ordinarily used for eating) is known simply as *thali bajane wala*, "the one who beats the *thali*." He beats the plate with two thin wooden sticks in accompaniment to the *jagariya's hurka*. He follows the *jagariya's* lead in terms of the speed, tempo and volume, but the sound of *thali* is much louder than the *hurka* and adds considerably to the exciting atmosphere of the performance. Although *thali* playing is essential to the success of the *jagar* it is not considered a difficult skill. Every village has several people competent to play the *thali*. Consequently, the *thali* player is recruited from the *syonkar's* village and payment is not necessary.

Hebars are the vocal accompanists to the *jagariya*. A *hebar* is sometimes called the *heval lagane wala*, "the one who makes the *heval*." The last note of each phrase is harmonically extended for several seconds by the *hebars*, while the *jagariya* catches his breath and continues the next phrase. This extended note is the *heval*. There are usually two *hebars* accompanying the *jagariya*, though one or three are permissible. Like the *thali* player, the *hebars* are essential but unpaid performers.

Preparations

The day of the *jagar* the women thoroughly clean the house inside and out. The floor of the room in which the *jagar* will be held usually is given a fresh smooth layer of the cow-dung and mud mixture. All the people directly involved in the *jagar* are expected to bathe and to wear clean clothes (i.e., the secondary and his family, *jagariya*, *dangariya, hebars* and the *thali* player). In addition, the *syonkar* and *dangariya* are expected to fast or at least restrict their solid food intake until the evening meal. The *dangariya* is supposed to go to the temple of his *devata* to perform worship and to make offerings (i.e., he lights *diya* and incense and offers some betel and sweets). These injunctions are considered important to the success of the *jagar* and if they are not followed, the deity may not come.

Nevertheless, individuals vary considerably in the degree to which they carry out these responsibilities. The Pahari's aversion to bathing is ubiquitous, indeed it takes a pious man to bathe in the river during the fall and winter months. The person for whom the injunctions are most important is the *dangariya*. As his body is the medium through which the *devata* will enter, it is essential that he be ritually clean. Neglect on his part is considered sufficient reason for the failure of a *jagar*. In addition, it is believed that the pain of the possession will be especially harsh if he is neglectful of his duties. The *dangariya* is believed to experience some pain when the deity possesses him. The pain is believed to be greatest when the deity is trying to enter his body, and if the body is pure, the pain is believed to be acute.

Shortly after darkness has set in, the *jagariya* and *thali* player begin the *naumat*. The *naumat* consists in drumming the *hurka* and beating the *thali*, there is no singing at this time. The ostensive purpose of the *naumat* is to announce that a *jagar* is being held, and all who hear the *naumat* are welcome to come. This is, however, largely symbolic behaviour since the fact is established by word of mouth and by the villagers' observations of the preparations. Nevertheless, it also serves as a reminder and as an indication that the time has come. The length of the *naumat* is not fixed and may last anywhere from ten minutes to an hour. The *jagariya* and the *thali* player do not play their instruments continuously during this period; rather, they play for five minutes or so and rest for a few minutes. While the *naumat* is performed, villagers gradually assemble. The men all sit along the foot of the walls leaving the center area clear for the oracle's dancing. The *jagariya*, *thali* player, and *hebars* sit beside each other, often in the comer, while the *dangariya* sits across from them. The women, if it is crowded, sit in the adjoining room (there may be no door separating the rooms, just an opening); otherwise they sit in the back, at the point farthest away from the *jagariya*.

Although a division of the sexes is clearly intended, men and women sit close together at the periphery of the two groups. This is especially the case when the oracle is possessed and the women try to get close to the action. The *naumat* serves the function of giving the *jagariya* and the *thali* player a chance to warm up and get acquainted with each other's style, as they may have come from different villages. The *naumat* also provides the opportunity for the *jagariya* and the *dangariya* to become acquainted with the villagers and each other. In the meantime, the guests are arriving and everyone is exchanging greetings and gossip. The *syonkar* sees to everyone's comfort, usually by lighting a *hukah* (water pipe) or passing around some *bhang*.

The guests have arrived and the performers are ready; the *jagar* may now begin. The first portion of the *jagar* is called the *panvani* and consists primarily of recitations of names of Sanskritic gods and of invocations for their blessings. The *jagariya* recites their names and epithets while accompanying himself on the *hurka*. The gods most frequently mentioned are Siva, Krsna, Rama, and the Pandavas. Brahma, Vishnu, Parvati and Ganesa also may be mentioned as well as names of important pilgrimage places like Kedarnath, Badrinath, Hardwar, Kasi (Varanasi) and Prayag (Allahabad). At this time several last minute preparations may be completed. The *jagariya* instructs the *syonkar* to purify the room once again by sprinkling cow urine on all the people, the walls and the floor. Although the room previously has been cleansed, this is to protect against any condition of ritual pollution among the guests. The *syonkar* then is directed to light the incense and the *diya* (the wick lying on a small copper plate filled with oil). If the *dulench* (the specially purified and consecrated spot or seat where the oracle sits) has not been prepared, it will be done at this time (it should not be done ahead of time because it may get dirty). The *dulenc* consists in neatly placing a clean cloth or blanket on the floor and placing a handful of rice (called aksat), perhaps some flowers and a copper coin on it.

The *dangariya* then is directed to sit on the *dulenc*. The *dhuni* (a *thali* plate with hot ash, coals, rice grains, incense flowers and red vermilion placed on it) is prepared by the *syonkar* according to the *jagariya's* instructions and placed in front of the *dangariya*. The *dhuni* plate is actually a substitute for the large fire *dhuni* outside. Both are kept hot and burning throughout the *jagar*, as hot coals are brought in from outside to replace the dying coals on the *thali*. Gradually, the *panvani* recital gives way to the next part known as the *Mahabharat*. Whereas the *panvani* is merely a recitation of the names of the Sanskritic gods and an invocation for their blessings, the *Mahabharat* portion consists of a more extended singing of stories and legends about these gods. It is called the *Mahabharat* because the legends are popularly believed to come from the *Mahabharata*. Although in some cases the stories, but not the exact words, are loosely derived from the *Mahabharata*, portions come from other Sanskrit sources such as the Vedas, the *Ramayana* and most frequently the *Puranas*. Neither the laymen nor the specialists usually are aware of the real Sanskrit source. Although the *jagariya* fully realizes that these are not verbatim recitations from the sacred texts, many of his listeners believe they are. Indeed, one *jagariya* proudly boasted that he had made up many Mahabharat portions himself. The following are a few samples from *Mahabharat* recitations:

1. Listen *devas*, Listen Bhairu! I am telling you about the incarnation of Rama, I am telling you about the incarnation of Rama. In the Satya Yuga there were the avatars (incarnations) of those men who always told the truth. In the Dwarpa Yuga there was the avatar of Krsna. In the Treta Yuga there was the avatar of Rama. During the incarnation of Rama there was a fighting in Lanka. Listen *devas* I am telling you about the incarnation of Rama. He spent twelve years in the forest and he obeyed the words (or promise) of his father...

2. Please listen, Ganganath (a local *devata*), about the incarnation of Krsna. In the avatar of Krsna the Kas (Kans) was killed. The birth of Krsna was from Devaki and Basudev was Krsna's father. Krsna was his mother's eighth son...

3. Listen *devatas*! I am telling you of Siva. At the time when there was water all over this earth, in the *Ksir samudra*, at that time you have the reincarnation of Siva. From the navel of Visnu's stomach a lotus was born. From the lotus Brahma was born. Then Brahma saw the water all over the earth. Brahma had four heads and four hands and in each hand he held a Veda...

Listen *devatas*! Brahma thought about where the lotus came from. And then, through the stem of the lotus, Brahma went to Visnu. Brahma saw Visnu sleeping on a bed of snakes. Visnu asked Brahma to go to the Mritu Lok to perform the creation of man...

Listen *devatas*! Visnu sent Brahma back through the lotus to the waters to make the creation with Siva who was incarnated from the eyes of Visnu. Brahmaji and Sivaji then made the world into land and water and these two *bhagvans* lived on the land, Then Brahma created man on the land of Mritu Lok...

4. Listen *devatas*! I am telling you of Siva. Brahma, Visnu, and Siva met together and Vishnu and Brahma agreed that Siva was the most powerful. They said to Siva: "You are like a pipal tree to us. As the birds eat the fruit of

the pipal tree, you feed us and you are Narayana of mankind. You are senior among all the gods."

Some villagers say that the *panvani* and the *Mahabharat* are the same thing, others do not even know the terms. The distinction made here is that given by *jagariyas* and a few pakka *dangariyas*. However, one *jagariya* did agree with the popular opinion that both words meant about the same thing. He said that this section could be either a short recitation and invocation or a longer narration. He pointed out that the decision was up to the *jagariya*.

Jagar Starts

However, the majority of specialists insisted that the distinction was valid and that the *Mahabharat* portion could be omitted but the *panvani* was obligatory. All of the preceeding constitutes preliminaries to the main content of the *jagar* which is now ready to commence. The *jagariya* begins to chant the legend of the *devata* that they all have come to propitiate. Most of the *devatas* are believed to have lived on this earth, indeed, in Kumaon, and their legends are narrations of their various life exploits. Ganganath and Golu are the two most popular *gram devatas* for inside *jagars* in the Kosi valley near Pakhura. The legend invariably begins with accounts of the deity's birth and the family, caste and region where they came from. These portions of the legend usually are sung at a slow rhythmic pace. Gradually as the *jagariya* sings about the feats and exploits of the deity, the pace quickens and the volume increases.

Sometimes, during these early portions, a female guest becomes possessed as the name of her family god is mentioned in the telling of the story. These possessions are generally short and peripheral to the main performance. The main *dangariya* usually starts to exhibit the first signs of possession when the legend begins to relate incidences of the deity's childhood exploits. There was a definite pattern to Oracle's possessions and the following description will be a composite account based on several observations. For the most part possessions were typical of spirit possessions for males, although perhaps a little more acrobatic and "athletically" skilled than most. Upto the moment when Oracle first begins to exhibit signs of possession, he has been sitting silently on the *dulenc* with his legs folded in a yoga-like position. Whereas the guests and performers all are relaxed, talking to one another, smoking *bhang* or cigarettes, he has been sitting quietly in a rather fixed, rigid position. He says nothing and looks at the ground, apparently concentrating (perhaps meditating) on his *devata*. The fast sign of his possession is that his leg begins to twitch involuntarily. Gradually, as the music begins to accelerate, his twitching becomes more pronounced so that soon his whole body is affected. As his trembling increases, his face becomes taut and contorted with tightly clenched teeth and loud heavy breathing. After a while, he begins to groan and grunt through his nostrils, and his trembling, shivering body sways forward and backward. Then, while he is still in his seated cross-legged position, his whole body begins to bounce up and down off the ground.

As his breathing, grunting and snorting further intensify, he yells out loud barking sounds. Finally, when it appears as though he is at the limit of this excruciating "god-induced" pain, he leaps to his feet and lets out a long, piercing scream. The whole process has, of course, been accompanied by a gradual build-up in the volume and rhythm of the music, so that at the climax of his possession, the *hurka*, *thali* and the voices of the *jagariya* and *hebars* are all performing at the maximum possible volume and rhythmic tempo. By the time this climax has been reached, the audience has long ceased laughing, smoking and talking; all eyes are focused on the *devata*. One can hear softly whispered invocations emanating from behind the folded hands of the seated villagers.

This climatic state usually is maintained for about five or ten minutes. Although each *dangariya's* dance is innovative and individualistic, there are certain characteristic movements which tend to be repeated from one time to the next. To a certain extent, this will depend on the *devata* involved. Thus, Golu's possessions are said to be particularly violent, whereas Ganganath tends to be somewhat restrained. The Oracle's dance, like that of most male *dangariyas*, is physically exuberant and athletic. He usually dances on one leg throughout much of his possession. Sometimes, while standing on one leg, he will bend to the floor and hop in a circle; alternatively, he might jump up and down in this bent knee position. Aside from these unusual feats of agility, all *dangariyas* act out the story that the *jagariya* is narrating.

Thus, while the *jagariya* relates the deity's exploits in battling against the demons, the oracle pantomimes the thrust of a sword or the shooting of an arrow. The oracle usually performs the dance in spurts of about five or ten dance in spurts of about five or ten minutes and then falls to the floor in exhaustion. As he collapses an rests, the *jagariya* slows and softens the rhythm and volume of the music. But the narration continues and soon the momentum increases. As it does, the oracle's shaking and shivering accelerate too, so that once again he bursts to his feet and commences his pantomime dance. Again, he eventually collapses to the ground. The sequence will be repeated several times until the *jagariya* feels that the deity's thirst for the dance has been satiated. Periodically, when the oracle is resting, the "deity" may make certain requests of the *jagariya*, invariably asked to drink cow urine, and because this was expected, it already would be prepared for him. Another request, one that is common to all oracles, was to have fresh hot coals and ashes brought in to replace the coals that had cooled off on the *dhuni*. After a couple of hours business of the *jagar* can commence. The host begins by addressing the oracle with questions which are urgent to his own family.

Thus, if his daughter-in-law is not well, he will describe her symptoms and inquire as to the nature and cause of her illness. The oracle carefully inspects her by looking and smelling all around her. Assuming the cause is ghost possession (it usually is), he makes a preliminary exorcism of the ghost. There is a certain amount of variation in this, the general pattern is as follows. The oracle examines the *anuni* tray, fingers the offerings and perhaps quietly recites a personal *mantra* for a few minutes. Suddenly, he shrieks at the girl's ghost, telling him to run away and get out. He makes all kinds of threats as to what he will do to the ghost if he remains. He also may promise the ghost a sacrifice or, if it is a ghost who has possessed a young bride, a "substitute wife" may be promised to him. He usually concludes by announcing that the ghost will be completely gone within a specified period of time (about two or three months). He tells everyone, including the ghost and victim, that he will return at the end of the specified period. The final ritual is to take some warm ash from the *dhuni* and apply it to her forehead while repeating to the ghost something like the following: "Get out! Get out! I will kill you! Don't ever come back! We will bring you another bride and we will sacrifice a chicken (or a goat) for you. Leave this woman alone. Get out! Get out!"

If the *jagar* is being held to bless a new bride or a new son, then the bride or son will be brought forth to receive the *dhuni* ash and the deity's blessing. Once the host has had all the problems concerning his family dealt with, the guests have the opportunity to address the oracle. The guests ask the same kind of questions for which they too might hold a *jagar* (e.g., the health of their family, the recovery of a sick cow, or the best time to go to the plains in search of employment). The oracle's responses are usually straightforward and direct. Sometimes he indicates that a special *jagar* will be necessary, especially if it looks like ghost possession. His answers are clear and intelligible, although several *dangariyas* spoke in a short, abrupt, staccato, mono-syllabic fashion. After all the questions have been answered, the *jagariya* thanks the deity and allows him to leave the oracle. When this happens the oracle often collapses to the floor in exhaustion and then rises up as if from a deep sleep. The *jagariya* then takes the ash from the *dhuni* and applies it to the forehead of everyone present. The *jagar* is now over, and it is around midnight. Most of the guests will return to their houses, but if the *jagariya* and *dangariya* came from another village, they probably will stay overnight at the *syonkar's* house.

In sum, the *jagar* is a dramatic and important cultural performance that reflects the rich and vibrant cultural heritage of Kumaon. Folklorists, anthropologists, historians and social scientists in general need to engage in the careful collection and documentation of this heritage while it is still an integral part of a living tradition. We need to record (on tape and film, and well as in written form) as many versions and renditions of the *jagar* narratives and performances as is possible. These data will serve many functions. To the historian, it will benefit efforts to refine our history of Kumaon. To the student of Hinduism, it will help us understand the connections between orthodox Sanskritic Hinduism and the local Hinduism of Kumaon. To the sociologist, it will provide insight into the interaction of different castes men and women, and the problems in society that the *jagar* seems to both reflect and address. To the psychologists, we have case studies of trance, tension, and the curing of illness. To the political scientist, *jagars* can provide insight into conflict resolution as oracles often expose and help resolve turmoil and disputes within families or between closely related families. To the folklorist and ethnomusicologist, its value as an oral tradition will be endlessly rewarding.

In short, *jagar* is a mirror of Kumaoni culture, both its past and its present, it demands of the academic community in Kumaon a thorough multi-disciplinary exploration of its many ramifications.

Bibliography

Edwin T. Atkinson, *The Himalayan Districts of the Northwestern Provinces of India*. Vol. II. North-Western Provinces and Oudh Press, Allahabad, 1884.

Gerald D. Berreman, *Hindus of the Himalayas*. Berkeley : University of California Press, 1963.

Allen C. Fanger, *Diachronic and Synchronic Perspectives on Kumaoni Society and Culture*. Ph.D. Dissertation, Syracuse University, 1980.

——, "Brideprice, Dowry and Diverted Bridewealth among the Rajputs of Kumaon" in *The Himalayan Heritage*. M.K. Raha, ed. Delhi : Gian Publishing House, 1984.

John T. Hitchcock and L. Jones Rex, (eds.) *Spirit Possession in the Nepal Himalayas*. Warminster, England : Aris and Phillips, Ltd., 1976.

L.D. Joshi, *The Khasa Family Law in the Himalayan Districts of the United Provinces of India*. Allahabad : Superintendent, Government Press, U.P., 1929.

I.M. Lewis, *Ecstatic Religion, An Anthropological Study of Spirit Possession and Shamanism*. Penguin Books, Baltimore, 1971.

E.S. Oakley, and Tara Dutt Gairola. *Himalayan Folklore*. Allahabad : Superintendent, Printing and Stationary United Provinces, 1935.

Morris E. Opler, "Spirit Possession in a Rural Area of Northern India" in *Reader in Comparative Religion : An Anthropological Approach*. William A. Lessa and Evon Z. Gogt. eds., pp. 553-566. Evanston, Illinois : Row, Peterson and Company, 1958.

E.K. Pauw, *Report on the Tenth Settlement of the Garhwal District*. Allahabad : North-Western Provinces and Oudh Government Press, 1896.

R.D. Sanwal, *Social Stratification in Rural Kumaon*. Delhi : Oxford University Press, 1976.

Ganga Datt, Upreti, *Proverbs and Folklore of Kumaon and Garhwal*. Lodiana Mission Press, Ludhiana, 1894.

Susan Snow Wadley, "The Spirit 'Rides' or the Spirit 'Comes' : Possession in a North Indian Village" in *The Realm of the Extra-Human*. Agehananda Bharati, ed., pp. 233-251. Mouton Publishers, The Hague, 1976.

14

Nepali Art

Fusion of Hinduism and Buddhism

Nepal consists of the valley of Kathmandu, an area of less than 200 square miles (about 300 square km.) together with a few towns and sites on the valley's rim. Yet even in comparatively recent times (i.e. the sixteenth to eighteenth centuries) this astonishingly small area housed three independent city-kingdoms. At one time, c. 1100, what is now the old quarter of the present-day capital of Kathmandu actually accommodated three separate self-governing micro-states. The exiguity of the valley, its Newar population racially and culturally distinct from most of the rest of the country and with a language of its own, together with relative freedom from invasion, have all contributed to the development of Nepal's distinctive culture. Two factors have had decisive impact. The first is that here alone among the countries in which it has flourished (including, of course, India) Buddhism continues to thrive side by side with Hinduism. The second is that centuries-long isolation, allied to a very strong sense of cultural identity, have meant that in many areas time has virtually stood still for the past four hundred years or so, so that art flourishes in the living context in which it was created. Many people still inhabit or use the old rest-house, monasteries, temples, places, and most often private dwellings, all fine buildings of brick and wood often partly sheathed in splendidly worked metal.

Very different is the situation in India and Sri Lanka, where little traditional secular architecture has survived, except for a few pockets mainly in western India: elsewhere, apart from palaces, Rajput and Late Mughal echoes are all that linger. It is not surprising that the first Western students of Nepal believed that they had found a living fragment of pre-Muslim India which would provide the answers to many vexing questions about the subcontinent in ancient times, and particularly its secular architecture. However architecture in Nepal, as in most of the sub-Himalayas, was out of the main stream, and most of its buildings (though many no doubt follow pre-existing ones) date from after the fifteenth century. Neverthless, the country remains unique in its fifteen-hundred-year-old heritage, nourished at virtually a single source—India—in conditions of near-total political independence. The blurring of distinctions between Hinduism and Buddhism, accepted enthusiastically by an exceptionally tolerant people, was the result chiefly of the increasing sway over both faiths of tantric beliefs and practices. Moreover certain divinities and cults took on national singnificance, not only in terms of territorial extent but in the consciousness of the people. The king (or kings, under the three kingdoms) saw himself as closely associated with a god (the present kings of Nepal are considered avatars of Visnu), which conferred on him not divinity but legitimacy. Hence the duplication and even triplication of shrines in the three main cities and the existence, even in such a small area, of surrogate *tirthas* (holy places) and the almost unprecedented resiting of some of the most monumental images. Important finally in the religion of the valley is the cult of plain stones, often representing the Matrkas.

Sculptural Wealth

Sculptures belonging to the early Lichchavi period (300-850), generally in very poor condition, with close affinities to late Kusana work at Mathura or early Gupta remains in the western Uttar Pradesh include a pair of Haritis either in a squatting or in a pralambapada pose, and a standing Bodhisattva. These links with western rather than eastern India are confirmed by the discovery of numerous Kusana coins and the fact that the Saka era was used in the valley until the early seventh century. The affinities of the two 'royal' statues are more obscure. The earliest dated inscription at Cangu Narayana belongs to the Lichchavi king Manadeva, and the earliest dated sculpture is the famous Visnu Vikranta in a small lone tombstone-sized shrine at Tilganga (Deo Patan), disappointingly small but iconographically remarkably developed. It is difficult to believe, moreover, that the ekamukhalinga at Mrgasthali (Deo Patan), in the purest late Gupta style, is later than the mid sixth century. The greatest achievement of Nepali art, probably slightly later and already in a more distinctive style, is a small group of monumental sculptures associated with kings whose names end in Gupta, notably one Visnugupta (*c.* 640) who challenged Lichchavi rule in the area. Water, so important to the valley (witness the many public fountains), is a theme of all of them, quite literally, for they were installed (and remain) in tanks. Great serpent coils also bulk large. In the Kaliya Damana in the Hanuman Dhoka place in Kathmandu, the spent-demon's human toro and head rise from a veritable mountain of coils as he is belaboured by the little Krsna standing on his shoulder and head. The god, neither baby nor yet quite adolescent, is naturalistically rendered in full onslaught. In his small-featured, typically Nepali face signs of cruelty have been detected.

Two other sculptures, one over 21 ft. (6 m.) long at Budhanilakantha, the other at Balaju, are again totally original Nepali conceptions of the Visnu Anantasayana theme. The god lies flat, his legs crossed, bedded on the great coils of the serpent half submerged in the waters of the tank. The characteristic face has an aquiline nose, a sharply defined chin, a pouting lower lip, and rather fleshy jowls. The crown is trilobed, with kirttimukhas. A third such figure, in the Hanuman Dhoka, not yet properly examined, is probably of the same period. It has long been associated with Pratapa Malla (1641-74), who brought the Kaliya Damana to the place, and the chronicles unequivocally state that it was an old Jalasayana from a nearby site which the king installed in the Hanuman Dhoka. To this group must be added the huge standing Visnu, some 12 ft. (4 m.) tall, with his two sons as ayudhapurusas, in the Ramachandra temple at Pasupati (Deo Patan). Another great Lichchavi work, at Cangu Narayana, is the first complete example of the characteristic Nepali Garuda, on one knee, wearing his wings like a cape. Such images usually crown a pillar.

We cannot tell whether or not this one represents King Manadeva, but there can be no doubt that it is a portrait, for the sympathetic moustached face is totally different from any other in the whole of Nepali sculpture. All these images, including the fine Varaha at Dhumvarahi, are of course Vaisnava, in spite of Nepal's predominantly Saiva affiliation. Towards the end of the Lichchavi period, a number of standing Buddhas and Bodhisattvas strongly reflect the influence of Sarnath. The valley counts numerous large and important stupas, of which small stone votive versions, locally known as *Ashok caityas*, strew many of the viharas. Some with Buddhas seated back to back round a column recall caturamukha lingas, but most have high, square bases in two registers, the directional Buddhas seated on each side above, the Bodhisattvas standing below. Later the domes become more elongated, with a straight portion. The oldest supas are believed to be the four situated at the cardinal points at Patan, the most Buddhist of the three principal valley towns (the others being Kathmandu and Bhatgaon or Bharatpur). These stupas have low domes of the type associated with Asoka, although no evidence of such extreme antiquity has been found; but then Nepalese like Sri Lankan stupas remain unexcavated. A square harmika and a variety of pinnacles surmount the Patan buildings. The Swayambhu, on a hillock just west of Kathmandu, dedicated to the five *Tathagatas* (Buddhas), is the main shrine of Nepali Buddhism. The four Dhyani Buddhas stand one at each of the cardinal points, with the fifth, Vairocana, between east and south high on the hamika. Between them are five goddesses, their spiritual consorts. The pinnacle has thirteen gilded metal rings and a crowing parasol. A gilded bronze vajra five feet long stands on the top of the hill, where numerous hapels surrounding the stupa give a fore taste of the metal architectural ornament for which the valley is famous. The steps leading up to them are flanked by pairs of houses, lions, elephants, peacocks, and garudas, the vehicles of the Tathagatas.

The stupa on thc adjoining hill dedicated to the Bodhisattva Manjusri is one of the national shrines of Nepal, for Manjusri is identified with Sarasvati and consequently worshipped by Hindus as well as Buddhists. The great stupa at Bodhnath is largely a Tibetan preserve, for it lies on the trade-route which was the principal access from the Indian plains to Tibet until the easier route through Kalimpong superseded it in the nineteenth century. Instead of the four directional Buddhas, 108 little images of Amitabha are set into the base of the dome which, as in all these stupas, is low, and less than a hemisphere. The pairs of eyes painted later on the harmikas of most of the great stupas signify the 'all-seeing eyes of Buddhahood'. The thousand years from the close of the Lichchavi period, *c.* 750, to the advent of Gurkha rule in 1767-8 is usually divided into a post-Lichchavi (or Thakuri) phase, much of it still obscure, and the period of the Mallas of the three kingdoms, commencing in 1480 with Yaksa Malla, which saw the construction of almost all the valley's extant buildings. Much stone sculpture and many bronzes survive from the post-Lichchavi period, when eastern India became the principal stylistic source, except for painting. Pala influence, however, appears to be less than is usually assumed, for Nepal had firmly established its own style of sculpture. Late in the fifteenth century, the division into the three kingdoms was fomalized, consolidating to an extent the plurality of the valley's little centres of power. It was about this time, after the raid of Shams-ud-din Ilyas, that King Sthithimala instituted a brahmanization of Newar society which coincided with the final eclipse of Buddhism in India.

Until the 18th century— when Chinese influence started to permeate Tibetan, and to a certain extent Nepalese, art—Newari craftsmen and artists played a determining role in Tibet, at least in the central region around Lhasa, in the fields of painting, the decoration of monasteries, and metalwork. As long as Buddhism still flourished in eastern India, Nepal acted in part as a channel for Indian influence, but eventually it was to Newar art, often produced by resident Newari artists, that Tibet was indebted for a great deal of its artistic tradition. Except for the masterpieces of the seventh century, it would be quite wrong to class Nepalese sculpture as a original variation of Indian art; its peculiar fluency, charm, and elegance derive from a racial character that is totally distinct. In the post-Lichchavi period a favourite among Nepalese sculptors was Garudasana, that is Visnu seated on Garuda, a partially anthropomorphized bird. The first representation, in the sanctum of the Cangu Narayana temple and unseen by any art historian, it probably of *c.* 500, roughly the date of the image from eastern India in Cleveland Museum of Art. A fine ninth-century example, also at Cangu Narayana, has the four-armed Visnu seated majestically in pralambapada upon a squatting anthropomorphic Garuda whose outstretched, slightly raised arms encompass the lower part of the god. The monumental ground consists of the swirling stylized tail-feathers of the man-bird. Nowhere has a more generous setting been devised for Visnu, with its superb balance between the plain surface of the curved bowl formed by Garuda's arms and the rounded outline of the ground behind the god's torso, head, and halo. As always in Nepal, Garuda has the head of an adolescent, and Visnu holds the conch horizontally.

By the 9th century, holes in Nepal have become oval, usually, like the whole stele, with a pearl and flame border. The persistence of spiral armlets and of a fondness for rustication of the bases, together with constant repetition of ancient themes and poses and even details of costume, makes the dating of Nepalese sculpture between the eighth and the thirteenth centuries a daunting task. It is nonetheless a capacity for pastiche that has maintained almost to this day a semblance, at least, of vitality in Nepalese sculpture, rescuing it from the total degeneracy common in India. The heroic panels become more densely peopled, but psychological relationships falter, as a comparison between the latest of the known Vikranta images, from Pharping and probably of the thirteenth century with the image dated 467 makes very clear. The fine ninth-century Visvarupa Visnu at Cangu Narayana is overcrowded, even taking into account the complex iconography of this type, and the organization of the multifarious elements is somewhere simplistic. After the Lichchavi period, Visnu appears most commonly standing in samapada, flanked on one side by Laksmi, on the other by Garuda, who occasionally appears in this position in western India but never in the east. It has been proposed that this icon represents the *para*, or highest, aspect of Visnu. A version exists from as late as 1695. Stone Suryas are very frequent, and caturmukha lingas recur throughout the valley. The oldest for which there are any references, installed in the Pasupatinatha temple at Deo Patan, or its immediate predecessor, was destroyed by the Muslim invaders, but its fourteenth-century replacement is said to be based on the original.

As in Kashmir, the torso of the god, or at least two hands, is represented on all four sides of the lingas, as well as the head. The predominance of this *niskala* (abstract) form of Siva and the paucity of other Saivite icons may be due to the dominance of the Pasupatas in the formation of Nepali Saivism. The only anthropomorphic (*sakala*, literally 'having parts') Saiva icons of any currency is Uma-Mahesvara, Uma sitting on the lap of Siva or cuddling up to him, a Kalachuri creation endlessly reproduced in Nepal until modern times. Nepali sculpture at times recalls and even foreshadows Pala sculpture, although there are no pierced grounds. As a rule, however, forms are smoother and more lissom, and muscles are unknown. Nepali sculpture retains its individuality in part through a subtly different placing of sashes and ornaments. Until the twelfth century, bhangas are relatively restrained. Thereafter, in metal sculpture, jewellery and ornament are less adornments of the flesh than important subjects in their own right. After the twelfth century vitality and originality are rare in stone but not—inexplicably—in metal, perhaps in part due to the introduction of tantric themes, which were largely confined to bronzes. In 1278 Aneko and sixty Nepalese craftsmen were sent to Tibet and thence to China to the court of Kublai Khan, witness to the high esteem in which Nepalese metalwork was held. The earliest surviving securely datable bronze of importance was donated by a nun from Lalitpur (Patan) in 591. Nearly indistinguishable in style from the rare contemporary bronze Buddhas from Uttar Pradesh and Bihar, it may indeed have been an Indian import. The robust plasticity of the fine tenth- and eleventh-century Visvarupa Visnu now in the Boston Museum of Fine Arts and the Tara in the British Museum also parallels contemporary Indian sculpture. Nepali bronzes, like Tibetan ones, often lack surrounds (*prabhavallis*), either by design or by accident of loss. From now on, the images are often gilded. The superb seated Avalokitesvara from the Golden vihara in Patan, probably of the fourteenth century, is an example of Nepalese sculpture pursuing its own development.

The infinite suavity of modelling, the gentleness and calm of the seated pose, associated with yoga, and the beauty of the face are far remote from anything Indian, whether contemporary or later. This image is one of the high points of bronze sculpture in Nepal, to be rivalled only by a few pieces of the fourteenth and fifteenth centuries, among them some of the many Indras wearing mitre-shaped crowns and seated in rajalilasana, often without base. Nepal has always had a penchant for repousse. A sheath for a Garudasana Visnu was made in 607, and a fine gilt bronze plaque of a standing Visnu with a richly worked background, now in the Los Angeles County Museum, is dated 983. In the seventeenth and eighteenth centuries, if not earlier, repousse images in the round appear, some as large as the eighteenth-century Tara in San Francisco. Edges are sharper, angles more pronounced, and there is a certain stylization, of the breasts, for example. Here, as in the many architectural applications of repousse work, the Nepalese craftsman makes metal and to a much lesser extent wood—appear, in Percy Brown's phrase, more tensile than it really is. In the later bronzes, jewellery is picked out with small cabochon semi-precious stones (paste in modern examples). Closely allied in style to the large gilt-metal seated portraits of later Malla kings set on top of pillars in front of temples or the entrances to palaces are the countless votive or donor couples, often inscribed and dated.

Architecture

The architecture of the Kathmandu valley—whether private dwellings, special communal buildings (*sattals*), palaces, monasteries, or the several kinds of shrines—is of brick and timber, with sloping the roofs. The more elaborate buildings may use metal, usually copper, for finials, to cover roofs, as repousse cladding for wooden reliefs, or—particularly beautifully—on the spouts of public fountains. Silver is exceptional, a particularly munificent offering to the god. Wooden pillars, intricately carved door and window surrounds, and elaborately patterned lattices for windows and balconies are plentiful. Ground plans are usually square, the buildings, once entered from the street, grouped around a courtyard. *Caityas* (stupas) and 'pagoda' temples occupy similar courtyards or stand detached in the streets or on the great durbar squares upon which the places face. The typical Newar scene is urban, the houses joined together, with paved streets and courtyards. Abundant wood-carving, together with the Newar fondness for raising building on wooden pillars, for screened balconies, and for building to two and three storeys, all contribute to the picturesqueness of the valley towns, unexplained elsewhere on the subcontinent. Newar architecture uses not only the same materials but the same methods of construction for all types of building. Here there is a striking and instructive parallel with the entirely wooden structures of early Indian architecture, otherwise known only from the reliefs and rock-cut caves. The forms and methods of construction may be very different, although verandas and wood lattice-work are common to both, and there is the same homogeneity between secular and sacred architecture.

Even the decoration of Newar buildings, closely associated with or determined by structural features, is essentially the same throughout, varying only according to the building's importance and, secondarily, with religious or iconographic demands. The most common feature of Nepalese buildings after the tiled pitched roof is the wooden door or window lintel, and sometimes the sill as well, set into a brick wall and projecting far beyond the jambs. In its most exaggerated form it is responsible for the extraordinary wing-like appearance of the doorways of major temples. The struts (*tunalas*) carved with standing figures and their vehicles or supporters extending from the cornices to the ends of the overhanging eaves, so arresting in Newar temples, were originally intended to support the overhang of the heavy tile roof, often lined with clay. A fascinating thing about Nepalese architecture is that it is possible to identify ancient themes of Indian doorways and gateways in buildings no more than two or three hundred years old. The projecting lintel can be traced back to Kusana times, and it is standard in Gupta temples. The side panels, however disguised by oblique stylized outlines, plainly originate in the positions occupied by the river goddesses in the Gupta period, and frequently bear female figures today. Some motifs on the lintels and jambs of doorways, like the beam ends in the form of lions' heads, can be traced back Gandhara or to Gupta temples in India proper. The zigzag round the innermost part of the door-frame, observed on a number of Gupta temples as well as at Ajanta but surviving only briefly thereafter in eastern India, is plainly recognizable on the doorways of many 'pagoda' temples. The difference is that the form is never anything but trapezoidal. The 'alternating triangle' motif of the Gupta and post-Gupta period can be identified on at least one temple doorway. The brackets or struts carved as human figures (at first yaksis) go back to Sanci. Except for the last, all these motifs had vanished in India by *c.* 1000.

Of all the wood-carved forms of Nepal, the finest are unquestionably the early tunalas, probably of the thirteenth or fourteenth century, in the form of yaksis. With the exception of a carved wooden figure found at Dhaka in Bangladesh, they are without peer in the wood-carving of the subcontinent. Later tunala figures are usually many-armed tantric divinities, the arms added separately. The most common public buildings in the valley are the dharmasalas, called *sattals* in Nepal, from Sanskrit *sattra* (almshouse). They range from simple wayside shelters to the three-storeyed Kashthamandapa, the largest and (though much restored) the oldest building in Nepal in traditional style, probably dating from *c.* 1100. It has given its name to Kathmandu. The simplest type, in Nepal *pati* (Newari *phale or phalaca*), is nearly always rectangular and consists of a platform and a two or four-sided pitched tiled roof raised on pillars. There is usually a back wall, except when the patri is built into a house. The mandapa is a particular kind of sattal, always completely unwalled and almost always square. Mandapas usually have only one storey and belong to the village or town, not the wayside. The sattal proper, usually of more than one storey, 'caters to a more permanent occupation', although still the preserve of the wandered; fixed communities preferred the monastery, Buddhist (*vihara*) or Hindu (*matha*). Sattals may have as many as four storeys, the upper ones plentifully supplied with pillars.

The ground floor usually incorporates a shrine, and sometimes even shops. This elasticity of use, and its importance in determining what the building is considered to be, is well exemplified by the Dattatreya, built by Yaksa Malla (1428-82) in Bhatgaon, his capital, as a sattal but later converted into a temple. Viharas (Newari *baha* or *bahi*) are of two storeys, sometimes higher over the shrine. Centred on a courtyard, unlike Newari houses they have few windows on the outside walls. Entrance is usually by an ornamental doorway opposite the main shrine, of Sakyamuni for example, or Avalokitesvara, guarded by Sariputra and Mudgalyana, with another above it for a tantric Vajrayana deity. The tunalas are generally carved with the Dhyani Buddhas, many-armed, crowned, and identified by their vahanas. There is always at least one caitya (stupa) in the courtyard (sometimes a pagoda-type shrine), a pit for the sacred fire, and a mandala with

Vairocana at the centre and the Tathagatas at the cardinal points. Few vihara buildings are as old as the fourteenth century, and most date from the seventeenth and eighteenth. In Nepal the gods of Hinduism and Buddhism are sheltered in many a different fashion or not at all. Besides temple, they are worshipped at *pithas* (open-air shrines), in sattals and monasteries, and occasionally in private houses. The type of building depends largely on the nature of the deity and of the worship conducted there. It is usually a matter of adapting domestic types: the *agama-che*, the private temple of clans or associations, are very much like private houses and so are the temples of the Matrkas (sometimes worshipped in the form of unshaped stones), which are almost always rectangular. In the sattal at Bhatgaon the Matrka shrines are at the cardinal and intercardinal points, with Tripurasundri at the centre, according to a mandala which determines the religious geography of the town and even the names of its various quarters.

A mark of sacredness is the tympanum (somewhat misleadingly called a *torana*), a large panel of wood or wood sheathed in metal, usually with tantric deities in relief between addorsed makaras. Above is a garuda or a kirttimukha, and then a ringed, horn-like projection, a stylized form of the parasols above the caityas. Most impressive, highly specialized, and intriguing are the so-called 'pagoda' temples (Newari *dya-ga* or *dega*). As their popular name implies, they have analogues elsewhere, the closest the pitched-roof temples of Himachal Pradesh. The earliest surviving dega are the shrine of Pasupatinatha, the supreme deity of the valley, at Deo Patan (second half of the fourteenth century), and perhaps the Indresvara at Panauti, just beyond the valley (1294?). They spring up fully evolved, and modifications in later versions, some as late as the nineteenth century, can easily be recognized as developments from the earliest type. The dega, on low platforms at first, are square *sarvatobhadrika* temples (i.e. with entrances on all four sides), of brick and timber, like all Newari buildings, with an internal circumambulatory passage and an inner shrine-room or garbhagrha also open on all four sides. Above is an empty shrine-room. The brick walls of the dega are structurally essential. The silhouette of sloping overhanging roofs, receding in size, is common in other sorts of buildings, too. The earliest of the dega appear to have had only two roofs; a third was sometimes added later. As is the case with all the more elaborate Newari buildings, the roofs have metal horn-like or bird-like elements at the bottom corners, giving them an additional 'Chinese' upturned look. The building is always crowned by a gilt metal finial which is shaped like a stupa. Tunalas extending from cornice to roof-end at an angle of 45 degrees are indispensable. There are six to a side on the lowest art of the Indresvara, with griffins or sardulas at the corners, to a total of twenty-eight. They include a couple of Matrkas, a number of yaksas and yaksis and, oddly enough, the Pandavas and members of their entourage.

The numbers of tunalas decrease as the building rises. Entry is usually through three doorways close together, the central one with a torana above, within an extremely intricately carved surround with a cornice and separating pillars. On the sides, tying the doorways into the brickwork, is an upper bracket with river goddesses, and lower projection with a stylized all highly stylish oblique line to its upper edge, all carved in relief with deities and other figures. The results is the most intricate, and artistic, bonding of wood to brick ever devised. The elaboration of the doorways is in marked contrast to the completely plain-not to say mean—aspect of the circumambulatory passage and sanctum. Mandapas are completely foreign to the dega—one result of their multi-directional orientation, for, in spite of their external decoration, they are in essence simple mandalas. The two earliest surviving dega are Saiva and enshrine caturmukhalingas. The early Narayan temples at Patan (1564), the Jagannatha at Kathmandu, and the Dvarkanatha at Bhatgaon have the same plan, with sarvatobhadrika images. The *caturvyuhas* (emanatory forms of Visnu according to the Pancaratra doctrine) are represented on the four sides, the Narayana invisible in the centre of the image. The famous Cangu Narayana temple is a foundation of the fifth century or earlier, but no surviving building dates from before the eighteenth century. If the original temple enshrined a Garudasana Visnu, as appears probable, it could not have been multi-directionally oriented. Some of the later dega are not, and on occasion the circumambulatory passage is divided into shrine-rooms. The platforms acquire more steps, sometimes as many as seven, as at Taleju in Kathmandu, the largest of the dega, constructed in 1576. Roofs are added, or dega are built with as many as five receding roofs, like the Kumbhesvara in northern Patan, or the better known if less impressive Nyatapola at Bhatgaon on its artificial mound. In spite of much speculation, we still do not know the origin of the dega, or what kind of a temple it is. The best we can do is to note, for example, that superimposed sloping roofs occur in regions of high snow- or rainfall in many parts of the world, from Kerala to Norway; that Gupta temples have no mandapas, and some have inner circumambulatory passages and upper shrine-rooms, and that multidirectional shrines accord with ancient Indian traditions and persist until the sixteenth century, notably in Rajasthan and Kerala. Masonry temples in a Nepali version of contemporary North Indian styles appear occasionally from the seventeenth century onwards. They bow to the national predilection for pillared halls, in the form of peristyles.

Sikharas tend to culminate in stupa-like features. Secular building was resumed in the mid nineteenth century, at first in Late Mughal or Rajput styles, but turning later to European models. Nepal has also produced a cornucopia of painting, from murals (the least important) and palm-leaf and paper manuscripts and their wooden covers [287-288] to paintings on paper and, most important of all, on cotton scrolls (*patas;* Newari *paubhas*). The earliest dated illustrated manuscripts, of the first half of the eleventh century, closely resemble eastern Indian ones (both ultimately derive from Ajanta), but differences in style and particularly in colour already distinguish the Nepali work, which includes Hindu as well as Buddhist manuscripts. In this it differs from the Indian tradition which, moreover, ceased abruptly after the thirteenth century, whereas in Nepal manuscripts continued to be illustrated for hundreds of years, changing over to paper without basic alteration in format. 'Illustration' is perhaps a misnomer, for these hieratic little paintings of gods and goddesses, and occasionally vignettes of holy sites or Buddhist canonical events, usually bear little if any relationship to the texts: they are primarily objects for worship, and were decorated as such with holy symbols. It is no exaggeration to say that the patas, until the eighteenth century almost all of the highest quality, include many of the finest paintings produced in the subcontinent over a period of several hundred years. They continue the ancient tradition of Indian scroll painting with almost no admixture of foreign styles and a negligible folk element, in contrast to the Mughal-Rajput schools. The connection between Nepalese patas and Tibetan *thankas*, many of them equally fine, is a close but complex one, and it is often difficult to distinguish between them, particularly when they portray tantric divinities in sexual congress with their saktis, never a subject for Indian images.

However the waves of Chinese influence which washed from time to time over Tibetan painting barely affected Nepal. Most important, the tradition of hanging-scroll painting was transmitted to Tibet principally by Newars, who continued to paint many of the thankas. It is natural, then, in a highly Indianized society that the patas (and many of them are Hindu) should continue more of the ancient Indian traditions. Nepali patas occasionally illustrate scenes from real life, and lay donors figure largely, some of them commemorating a particular religious observance that they have undertaken. Many are votives. All this is either unknown in Tibet or cloaked in the anonymity of monastic communities. The finest patas were produced between the twelfth and the sixteenth centuries. The earliest to survive is a mandala dated 1367, the first of several. Characteristically Nepali features include a black background and the use of a fine brick red, a 'brocaded' background of tight vegetal scrolls in red or green, the introduction of architectural motifs, and the picking out in white of tiny delicate lamps and vessels, often overhung with equally delicate festoons, all with a curious air of the European late Renaissance. Individual figures or scenes in little square panels line the sides, and parts of the consecration scene appear at the bottom along with the donors. The beautiful 'Green' Tara in the Cleveland Museum is a supreme example of another type of pata in which a divinity either stands or is enthroned beneath a prabha composed of the same elements as the 'toranas' of Nepal shrines. The classical Indian style and pose here contrast most successfully with the typical Nepali *millefleurs* on the black ground and the beautifully painted little trees. Another superb example of this type, the mid-fifteenth century Agastyavrata pata, commemorating the performance of a Hindu rite, is notable for the bold and imaginative use of brightly coloured rock forms, a Nepali favourite, for the prabha.

In order patas close to similar Tibetan thankas a tantric deity, either in angry mood or in sexual union with his sakti, backed by a large flame-edged aureole, occupies most of the painting. Splendidly detailed patas illustrating, or associated with, the performance of rites for the donors are also unique to Nepali painting. The best known is the picture of the Bhimaratha rite with outsize portraits of the couple who commissioned it. Also remarkable for its prominent donors listening to a preaching Budha in three-quarters view, which adds a note of realism, is a pata dated 1649, also in Cleveland. Tibetan influence is responsible for the perfunctory clouds squeezed in at the top of the painting. In the typical Nepali boxes at sides and bottom are aptly chosen jakata stories told in comic-strip style. The figure of King Pratapa Malla, one of the more important Malla kings, in the first dated appearance of the Rajput dress which will gradually come to prevail is of great art historical importance, and so are many other Mughal-Rajput features introduced here. Another example, unquestionably the finest so far, of the arrival of these new elements is the painting of 1664 of the same Pratapa Malla offering the *tuladana* (a gift of specie equivalent to the weight of some person balanced on a scale) before the Taleju temple in Kathmnadu, with such constituent of a Mughal durbar scene as formal assemblies of courtiers and gaily caparisoned elephants. A tradition of narrative scrolls illustrating stories from the epics, the Puranas, and popular folk tales from the Hitopadesa and the Pancatantra, either rolled or joined together in accordion pleats (*kalapustakas*), culminates floridly in the sixteenth century.

Lively as the figures are, their repertoire of poses is always somewhat limited, and it is the decorative impulse that takes over. By the end of the seventeenth century what we have is a hybrid of Nepalese elements and the imported Mughal-Rajput-Pahari style.

Bibliography

1. J.C. Harle, *The Art and Architecture of Indian Sub-continent*, Yale University Press, New Haven, 1994.

15

Ladakhi Popular Culture

Surrounded by lofty barren mountains and beset by difficult climatic conditions.

Ladakh, the northernmost region in the Indian Himalaya has a special position in the cultural and literary history of the country. Though influenced by other parts of India and Tibet, the people of Ladakh have succeeded in developing their own distinctive culture. Ladakhis are simple and more or less traditional in their religious practices and they stick to the old cultural values. The distinctive Ladakhi way of life is upheld not only in the far-flung villages of the region but also in the comparatively modernized city of Leh. In his book Magic Ladakh, Major M. L. A. Gompertz wrote 'Ladakh is very much a self-supporting country, and produces everything, or nearly everything it wants except tea, which is the staple drink of the country'.

Similarly, an interesting Kashmiri proverb says that 'Ladakhis eat *sattu* (roasted barley flour)', wear *pattu* (woollen clothing) and ride *tattu* (ponies)'. This saying indicates some of the principal themes in Ladakhi life. Buddhism penetrated Ladakh during Emperor Ashoka's time in 204 B. C. However, the Buddhist practice in Ladakh was not the same then as it is today. The form of Buddhism which is popularly called Mahayana Buddhism came to Ladakh with the blessing of the land by the great Buddhist saint Padmasambhava in the eighth century A.D. It was Padmasambhava who, along with the great Bhikshu Santaraksita, firmly established Buddhism during the reign of the most powerful Tibetan emperor Trisong Detsen. Ever since the people of Tibet have followed the religion of the Buddha. The Tibetans and others who follow what we now call Tibetan Buddhism, including many Ladakhis, regard these three great pioneers with a sense of deep gratitude and admiration. Collectively they are called 'The Abbot, the Teacher and the Dharmaraja' (*mkhan-slob-chos-gsum*). Since Buddhist thought and ideas dominate the life and culture of the people, certain scholars have described Ladakhi culture as being a Mahayana Buddhist culture. In Mahayana Buddhism, in addition to Gautama, the historical Buddha (who attained enlightenment under the Bodhi tree at Gaya more than 2530 years ago), we find many other buddhas and bodhisattvas in various forms such as compassionate, forceful, and wise manifestations. They are worshipped to bring happiness, prosperity, and peace. In contrast to Hinayana Buddhism this system also includes incarnate lamas representing various buddhas and bodhisattvas in human form, popularly known as 'trulkus' (Tib. *sprul-sku*). The trulkus are believed to have taken birth in this disturbed world to guide all suffering beings to teach the Buddha's doctrines and to reinforce his message. They not only sit and meditate in their respective monasteries or hermitages, but pay frequent visits to the villages in order to secure the health, happiness, and prosperity of the people.

The Ladakh region may be divided into seven parts, namely Sham (Lower), To (Upper), Zhung (Centre), Nubra, Changthang, Purig, and Zanskar. All these seven parts of

Ladakh have distinctive cultural and literary identities. For example, Zanskar, the southern part of Ladakh, has been called 'Chosyul' (Chos-yul), the 'Country of Religion', because it has the highest literacy rate of all Ladakh. Similarly, the northern part is called Nubra (lDum-ra), the 'Garden of Flowers'. 'Buddhism is practised by the people there and Nubra boasts some of the finest monasteries of Ladakh. Various types of flowers blossom there and a celebration called the 'Festival of Flowers' (*Me-tog ldad-mo*) is held in spring. On this occasion, people perform various types of dances, presenting flowers in their hands as a gesture in the form of an offering to the Buddha. As with Zanskar and Nubra there are certain peculiarities in the culture of every region of Ladakh.

For instance the people of Changthang wear a distinctive dress which really suits the harsh climate of the area. Language and literature are said to be the main constituents of an indigenous culture. Ladakhis are very fortunate in having their own written language, the history of which goes back to the seventh century A.D. It was Thonmi Sambhota, the learned minister of King Songtsen Gampo of Tibet, who developed an alphabet of thirty consonants and four vowels. On this point the specialist could say that this is the history of Tibetan language and literature and not of Ladakhi. While this is technically correct, the Ladakhis would reply that they never treated or thought of Tibet as an alien country with respect to language and literature. If one studies the history of Tibetan language and literature one finds an equal participation of both Ladakhi scholars and Tibetans. Moreover there exists a popular folk story according to which Rigpachen, the learned minister of King Songtsen Gampo, was a Shargola-born Ladakhi.

Image-making, Painting and Metal-Casting

In addition we find various Ladakhi 'lotsawa' (*lo-tswa-ba*), translators whose writings are equally acknowledged in the Tibetan canons. Tibetan and Ladakhi have the same grammar, but there is some difference in vocabulary and literary style and the Ladakhi style has been praised by many scholars. It is said that abounded wherever the law of the Buddha flourished and in Ladakh the art of making images, whether it is engraving, metal casting, painting, or carpentry, received great attention from early times. The dignified wall-paintings and wood-carvings still existing at Alchi, the nine-storey lion palace of Leh and various giant statues of the buddhas and bodhisattvas of the region are among the finest examples of Ladakhi art and crafts. It was Lotsawa Rinchen Zangpo from Guge who first introduced the use of an artistic style which is still practised in Ladakh. It is said that Rinchen Zangpo came with thirty artisans from Kashmir to Ngari, and built 108 temples, including three religious enclaves (*chos-'khor*). He also introduced the art of image-making, wood-carving, and fresco art throughout Ladakh, Spiti, and certain regions of western Tibet.

According to S. S. Gergan, prior to Rinchen Zangpo's appearance on the cultural and religious scene of Ladakh and Tibet, the art of making images did not exist in Tibet and Ngari, which includes Ladakh. The Mon people were to introduce work in iron, copper, and wood as arts and crafts in Ladakh. It is said that the Mon race who settled in Ladakh originated from the Lahul and Spiti district of modern Himachal Pradesh. These people are also credited with the introduction of the popular Ladakhi musical instruments known as *daman* and *surna*. King Deden Namgyal (r. 1620-1640) of Ladakh is said to have brought eight artisans from Nepal to build the two-storey copper statue of the Buddha at Shay and the statue of Maitreya at Basgo. After accomplishing these works they remained and settled in different villages of Ladakh, including Chemde, Leh, Gya, and Chiling. At present the descendants of these artisans pray to the god Mahadeva, reflecting their Nepali origin, and abstain from eating beef.

Handicrafts also received due attention in traditional Ladakhi society. Among the popular handicrafts were spinning, weaving, wood-carving and painting. According to popular Ladakhi tradition the earliest two industries of Ladakh were cloth weaving and watermilling. Likewise, embroidery received due recognition. Among the well-known embroidery products of Ladakh is the world famous thangka of Padmasambhava, which was made by the great artist Sopa Palai at the request of Gyalse Rimpoche of Hemis monastery in the eighteenth century.

Ladakhi Songs and Dances

Ladakhis are very fond of song and dance and they have not forgotten the songs sung by their ancestors, having adopted and preserved them as part of their heritage. In Ladakh every social and cultural event begins and ends with singing. Among the popular types of song are religious, congregational, heroic, and love songs; plays on words and satires; songs for marriage, drinking, and work; and the 'trashipa' (*bkrashis-pa*) songs which participants in any cultural event sing while performing a dance. Each song has its own distinctive tune (*dbyangs*). As with the songs, Ladakh has a rich heritage of dances. These have been so common and popular that they passed as an oral and practical tradition from one generation to another. Ladakhi dances are so simple in their step movements that to learn them does not require a rigorous or long training. But by careful observation, the movement of the dance, although not fast, appears to express the personality of the male or female dancer. The movements show the confidence or lack of confidence, the shyness or stage fright of the dancer. Whether they have an artistic temperament or a sense of humour is also expressed in the dance. And above all, the performance of a dance or a song provides the participants with an opportunity for meditation. Each dance opens with homage to the Triple Gem (the Buddha, the Dharma and the Sangha) and each has three parts. The first is slow.

With a further expression of homage the dance develops into the second stage when the music and movement become faster. The third stage is reached without homage and it develops with the music. In the field of music, the Ladakhi musicians claim to have 360 tunes, called 'music for the gods' (*lha-rna*). This type of music would be played by the Mon or Beda, wandering minstrels who were musicians at functions attended by incarnate lamas and ministers. The *lha-rna* tunes are subdivided into two categories, popularly known as music for lamas, and music for kings or ministers or the members of noble families. Among the popular Ladakhi musical instruments are the *daman*, a pair of kettledrums, and the *surna* of *harip*), a flageolet; also the *sgra-snyan*, a string instrument like a banjo; the *gling-bu* (flute), and the *daff*, a large wooden-frame drum having only one side covered with leather. Of the origins of these musical instruments it is said that the *daman* or *tam-tam* came from Kashmir, while the *surna* (which resembles the shawm, a religious musical instrument popularly called *rgya-gling* and used by the monks for ceremonies) originates from India, where a similar type of instrument is known as *shehnai*. Lastly, the *daff* is said to have its origin in Iran, and in Farsi this instrument is also called *daff*.

Drama

Theatre and drama (*zlos-gar*) are also a part of the Ladakhi heritage without which the culture of Ladakh would be incomplete. Since the people of Ladakh have been practising Buddhism from early times it is not surprising to find that the history of the past lives of the Buddha is the main theme or plot of Ladakhi traditional dramas. These dramas were most kindly told by the Enlightened One, the

Buddha, relating stories his numerous previous lives when he was living as a compassionate bodhisattva, always helping living beings in his various forms. Among the many tales is the legend of the noble prince Norzang and his beloved wife Yitrok, a most beautiful and enchanting woman. It is so popular in Ladakh that in certain villages the stories are narrated for several nights on end. This is just one instance of the pervasiveness of Buddhist culture and philosophy in every sphere of Ladakhi life and action. This is the case not only with the Buddhist houses and monasteries, but equally with the Muslim mosque.

Ladakhi Medicine

In Leh town, the most precious relics preserved in the mosque are the staff and boots of Lama Stagtsan Respa Ngawang Gyatso, the first hierarch of Hemis monastery. A similar situation exists with traditional medicine. The type of medical system which flourishes in Ladakh is called the *'emchi' (am-chi)* system, which was taught by the enlightened Buddha more than 2530 years ago. The word *emchi* refers to the medical practitioner or doctor. The *emchis* do not have advanced equipment like X-ray machines, yet they can diagnose a sick person by examining their pulse, urine, stool, etc. In this form of medicine the individual's faith is of equal importance and so there are prayer books devoted to Bhaishajayaguru, the Buddha of Medicine. According to the Ladakhi historian Tashi Rabgias, the first religious service text of the Tibetan Buddhist was the *Sman-lha bde-chog* (1984:66). In places where Tibetan Buddhism is practised, such as Tibet, Bhutan, Sikkim, Nepal, and Ladakh, we find oracles who act as healers. The oracles obtain their power from a god and with it treat both human beings and animals. In the Buddhist medical system, the words of the Buddha, the medical practitioners, and the power of the gods all play equal roles, and each of these aspects needs careful research before an adequate understanding of this form of medicine can be attained. The New Year celebration is an important part of the great Ladakhi culture. Unlike the Tibetans, or any other neighbouring Himalayan people, Ladakhis celebrate their New Year (*lo-gsar*) on the first day of the eleventh month of the Tibetan calendar. The popular account says that the Ladakhi king Jamyang Namgyal (1560-1590) wanted to lead a military expedition to neighbouring Baltistan and so he decided to celebrate the New Year on the first day of the eleventh month. In fact the New Year celebration begins on the twenty-fifth day of the tenth month, which is the birthday of Tsongkhapa, the founder of the Gelugpa sect of Tibetan Buddhism. On this day people illuminate their houses with butter lamps, and they light up the temples by organizing special religious ceremonies including illuminations. This day is also called the Big Day of Leh (*Gle-pa'i zhag-bzang*), and from then onwards the youths of Leh assemble at a particular spot and make a procession with fire on every night until the thirtieth. As in many other cultures, the New Year celebration has a special place in Ladakhi society. It marks a time of transition. The smiths and carpenters, mainly the Mon, stop working with their tools and instead light butter lamps beside them. The illumination, the banking or burning of seven ibex made of wheat flour and the tying of a branch of evergreen juniper to the pillar of the kitchen are some of the important features of the New Year celebration. We can certainly say that some of these features owe their origin to the ancient Dard culture. The ibexes and juniper branch are needed to please the family god or the village god (*Voice of the Himalaya* 1976). Ladakhis do believe in such gods and follow simple rules to live in harmony with them.

On the occasion of New Year, traders refrain from business for three days, and presents of tea, alcohol, and bread are exchanged. In the good old days there was a tradition of the king organizing a feast in the banquet hall of Leh palace. On this occasion the king would invite a number of people belonging to the noble families of Leh and nearby villages. The official beer-maker (*chang-ma*) would serve alcohol to the guests and the court dancers (*drag-shos-ma*) would entertain them. On the third day of the new year, the king himself would appear before the public wearing a crown, and riding a beautifully decorated horse for the horse-race. Similar festivals were organized by the residents of different villages to mark the occasion. Among the popular village festivals organized in conjunction with New Year are Lama-Zugi, A-ki Meme and Skinkar *(sKin-dkar)* and Skin-nak, *(sKin-nag)*, and the Black and White Ibexes. Besides all these, Buddhist families would carry food and drink to the family cemetery and offer food to their ancestors.

According to the existing material written on these subjects, still other faiths flourished in Ladakh and the western Himalaya before the introduction of Buddhism. These beliefs were Babaswami which advocated animal sacrifice, and the Bon religion. In past, the Muslim population of Ladakh, particularly the Shias, would join in the New Year celebrations. On this occasion, they too would perform dances and take an active part in the functions held in Leh and the villages. According to Mohammad Ali Khan of Turtuk, it is said that until the year 1984 there was a tradition of organizing festivals to mark the celebration of New Year. During these festivals, which were held on 21 December, the shortest day of the year, inhabitants of Turtuk would hold a fire procession through the village by discarding the procession.

Other Festivals

Beside the New Year celebration one can see various other religious and cultural festivals. Among them, the *dus-mchod* (monastic ceremonies involving offerings of religious services), which are usually organized in the courtyards of the respective monasteries, are worth noting. In these festivals the monks play the role of actors and perform religious dances wearing masks representing various gods and goddesses. Every religious dance festival includes a distinctive dance *(cham)* of the protective deity *(srung-ma)* These religious festivals are conducted every year according to the local calendar and last for three days. Popular among them are Leh Domoche, Hemis, Thiksay, Pethup, and Fyang in Central Ladakh; Likir and Lamayuru in Sham; Karsha in Zanskar; Diskit in Nubra, and Mahe and Anlay monasteries in Changthang. According to a popular saying, these religious festivals are performed for the health, happiness, are prosperity of all human beings. Among the many social and cultural festivals of Ladakh are marriage ceremonies, birth ceremonies, village archery competitions, and harvest festivals. The historical and social backgrounds of the Ladakh religious and social festivals are so varied that it would be necessary to write separate chapter for each festival. It is recorded in the many historical writings of European travellers that Ladakhis were honest, kind, and hospitable people. Theft and cheating were unknown. Even the killing of small insects was considered sinful. Thus, the people of traditional Ladakhi society were faithful in the observance of religious teachings.

They would not do anything unless they first went through the appropriate religious rites. For instance before starting a business, engaging in trade, making a journey, or holding a marriage they would consult astrologers, lamas and oracles. This is also the case with agricultural tasks. Oral histories reveal that in the past certain villages had to invite a butcher belonging to another faith to slaughter animals. In the field of trade, Ladakh hid very close and cordial links with the neighbouring states of Baltistan, Tibet, Kazakhstan, and Turkestan as well as Kashmir and Punjab. Above all, trade relations with the highlands of Ngari, Guge, and Purang had a very significant role in Ladakh's economy due to geographical, cultural, and climatic similarities. Although the trade with these regions of western Tibet was limited to a very few items, such things satisfied Ladakh's immediate requirements. Among the essential goods were livestock, especially yaks and horses, and also salt and wool.

Ravine Dwellers

The Tibetans called the Ladakhis *Rong-pa*, the ravine-dwellers. As a matter of fact that Ladakhis, unlike the nomadic people of Ngari, were a settled race engaging in agriculture and keeping domestic animals such as horses, yaks, dzos and dzomos (hybrids of yaks and cattle), mules, and chickens. Thus, the Ladakhis were able to meet the demands of the Ngari people for such items as barley, grain, fruit, spices, and cotton fabrics as these were available in Ladakh in large quantities as a result of its trade connections with Punjab and Kashmir. Thus, the life of the Ladakhis in the past was very relaxed and free of the sort of strain that exists now.

The modern world measures the standard of living by the amount of annual consumption per head of population, assuming all the time that a man who consumes more is better off than a man who consumes less. This way of thinking is quite contrary to Buddhist ideals, for the Buddhist objective of life is not just to earn money, become rich, and lead a luxurious life, but rather to attain liberation from this sorrowful world by performing good and exemplary tasks in one's life. Jawaharlal Nehru's view of culture as 'restraint over oneself and consideration for others' has a very close connection with Mahayana Buddhism and its view of society. In Buddhist thinking the Self is placed very low and work for betterment of all sentient beings, including animals and insects, is placed very high. But Ladakh today is no longer the same as witnessed several years ago by both natives and outsiders. The culture of its people and their social structure has changed a great deal. While in principle there exists no conflict between religious values and economic progress, every Ladakhi should nevertheless question the nature of change which Ladakh is currently undergoing. The recent opening of Ladakh to foreign tourists after its long closure accounts for much of the change in its people and culture. At the same time, it has opened up many new avenues for enterprising young Ladakhis. Other important influences include government development and education programmes, and the large military garrisons which owe their presence to Ladakh's role as a sensitive border district.

It is a good thing for every Ladakhi to make progress. At the same time, the younger generation should carry forward old cultural values and adhere to the traditional inner harmony inherent to Ladakhi culture in order to make the region a perfect place to live. Bearing in mind the remarks regarding the preservation and continuation of a flourishing Ladakhi culture, all Ladakhis must consider the good things of past Ladakh. Only that awareness can save the culture of Ladakh from the onslaught of modern civilization.

Bibliography

Maj. M.L.A. Gompertz, *Magic Ladakh.* London, 1928.

J. Nehru, *Glimpses of World History.* London, 1982.

D.L. Snellgrove, *Buddhist Himalaya*, Oxford University Press, London, 1957.

N.K. Rustomji and Charles Ramble, Himalayan Environment and Culture, Indian Institute of Advanced Studies, Indus Publishing Co., New Delhi, 1990.

Index

C

D

N

S